CRITICAL THINKING AND COMPOSITION

CRITICAL THINKING AND COMPOSITION

First Edition

ARACELI NEUNER, PH.D.
San Diego State University

SAN DIEGO

Bassim Hamadeh, CEO and Publisher
Mieka Portier, Senior Acquisitions Editor
Michelle Piehl, Senior Project Editor
Susana Christie, Senior Developmental Editor
Jeanine Rees, Production Editor
Emely Villavicencio, Senior Graphic Designer
Laura Duncan, Licensing Coordinator
Stephanie Adams, Senior Marketing Program Manager
Natalie Piccotti, Director of Marketing
Kassie Graves, Senior Vice President, Editorial
Jamie Giganti, Director of Academic Publishing

Copyright © 2024 by Cognella, Inc. All rights reserved. No part of this publication may be reprinted, reproduced, transmitted, or utilized in any form or by any electronic, mechanical, or other means, now known or hereafter invented, including photocopying, microfilming, and recording, or in any information retrieval system without the written permission of Cognella, Inc. For inquiries regarding permissions, translations, foreign rights, audio rights, and any other forms of reproduction, please contact the Cognella Licensing Department at rights@cognella.com.

Trademark Notice: Product or corporate names may be trademarks or registered trademarks and are used only for identification and explanation without intent to infringe.

Cover image copyright © 2022 iStockphoto LP/JuSun.

Printed in the United States of America.

Brief Contents

CHAPTER 1	Arguments	1
CHAPTER 2	Inductive Reasoning	19
CHAPTER 3	Writing with Clarity	35
CHAPTER 4	Emotional Appeals	51
CHAPTER 5	Deductive Reasoning	71
CHAPTER 6	Sentence Logic	89
CHAPTER 7	Ethical Reasoning	109
CHAPTER 8	Other Ethical Theories	141
CHAPTER 9	Writing Philosophy	163

Bibliography   185

Detailed Contents

CHAPTER 1   **Arguments** 1
    Exercise 1-A: Premises and Conclusion   3
    Deductive versus Inductive Arguments   5
    Exercise 1-B: Deductive versus Inductive   7
    Plato and the Trial of Socrates   8
    Exercise 1-C: Reading Questions on Plato's *Apology*   12
    Descartes and the Cogito Argument   13
    Exercise 1-D: Reading Questions on Descartes's *Meditations*   17

CHAPTER 2   **Inductive Reasoning** 19
    Strength and Cogency   20
    Exercise 2-A: Inductive Strength and Cogency   22
    Exercise 2-B: Types of Inductive Arguments   23
    Exercise 2-C: True or False Questions   23
    Fallacies of Weak Induction   24
    Exercise 2-D: Fallacies of Weak Induction   27
    Paley and the Teleological Argument   30
    Exercise 2-E: Reading Questions on Paley's *Natural Theology*   32
    Hume and the Problem of Induction   32
    Exercise 2-F: Reading Questions on Hume's *Enquiry*   34

CHAPTER 3   **Writing with Clarity** 35
    Exercise 3-A: Fallacies of Ambiguity   37
    Definitions   38
    Exercise 3-B: Kinds of Definition   40
    Exercise 3-C: Broad and Narrow Definitions   41
    Hume and the Problem of Evil   41
    David Hume: *Dialogues* (The Problem of Evil)   42
    Exercise 3-D: Reading Questions on Hume's *Dialogues*,
      The Problem of Evil   44
    Rhetoric and Loaded Language   44
    Exercise 3-E: Rhetorical Devices   46
    Hume and Objections to the Teleological Argument   47
    Exercise 3-F: Reading Questions on Hume's *Dialogues*,
      Objections   49

CHAPTER 4   **Emotional Appeals** 51
    Exercise 4-A: Emotional Appeals   53
    Exercise 4-B: Fallacy Letter   55
    Fallacies of Presumption   56

Exercise 4-C: Fallacies of Presumption 58
Exercise 4-D: Fallacy Letters 59
Pascal and the Wager 60
Exercise 4-E: Reading Questions on Pascal's *Pensées* 61
Russell and the Teapot 62
Exercise 4-F: Reading Questions on Russell 62
Plato and Piety 62
Exercise 4-G: Reading Questions on Plato's *Euthyphro* 70

CHAPTER 5 **Deductive Reasoning** 71
Valid Argument Forms and Formal Fallacies 73
Exercise 5-A: Deductive Validity and Soundness 77
Exercise 5-B: Types of Deductive Arguments 79
Exercise 5-C: True or False Questions 79
Exercise 5-D: Valid Argument Forms 79
Exercise 5-E: Valid Inferences 80
Exercise 5-F: Complex Arguments 81
Anselm and the Ontological Argument 83
Exercise 5-G: Reductio Ad Absurdum 85
Exercise 5-H: Reading Questions on Anselm's *Proslogion* 87
Epicurus and Death 87
Exercise 5-I: Reading Questions on Epicurus's *Letters* 88

CHAPTER 6 **Sentence Logic** 89
Conjunctions, Disjunctions, and Negations 89
Exercise 6-A: Propositional Translation with ~, &, ∨ 95
Conditional Statements 95
Exercise 6-B: Propositional Translation with ⊃ 97
Exercise 6-C: Complex Propositional Translation 99
Sentence Logic and Passage Analysis 100
Exercise 6-D: Translation and Validity of Arguments 103
Necessary versus Sufficient Conditions 103
Exercise 6-E: Necessary versus Sufficient Condition 105
Equivalent Expressions in Propositional Logic 106
Exercise 6-F: Equivalent Statements 107
Exercise 6-G: Equivalent Pairs of Sentences 108

CHAPTER 7 **Ethical Reasoning** 109
Objective Moral Theories 110
Ethical Egoism 110
Exercise 7-A: Reading Questions on Plato's "Myth of Gyges" 114
Utilitarianism 114
Exercise 7-B: Reading Questions on Bentham and
  Mill's *Utilitarianism* 118

Divine Command Theory   118
  Kant and Duty Ethics   119
  Exercise 7-C: Reading Questions on Kant's *Metaphysics of Morals*   124
  Rawls and Justice   125
  Exercise 7-D: Reading Questions on Rawls's *Theory of Justice*   128
  Aristotle and Virtue Ethics   129
  Exercise 7-E: Reading Questions on Aristotle   134
  Fallacies in Ethical Discourse   134
  Exercise 7-F: Moral Fallacies   138
  Exercise 7-G: Fallacy Letter   140

CHAPTER 8 **Other Ethical Theories** **141**
  Existentialism   141
  Kierkegaard and Christian Existentialism   142
  Exercise 8-A: Reading Questions on Kierkegaard's *Fear and Trembling*   148
  Nietzsche and Atheistic Existentialism   148
  Exercise 8-B: Reading Questions on Nietzsche   154
  Sartre and Existentialism   155
  Exercise 8-C: Reading Questions on Sartre's "Existentialism is a Humanism"   156
  Eastern Philosophy—Buddhism   156
  Buddhism and the Four Noble Truths   156
  Exercise 8-D: Reading Questions on Buddhism   162

CHAPTER 9 **Writing Philosophy** **163**
  Exercise 9-A: Sentence Revisions   164
  Writing an Expository Essay   165
  Writing an Argumentative Essay   165
  The Writing Process—How to Begin?   169
  Exercise 9-B: Thesis or Main Claim   170
  Exercise 9-C: Main Claim and Subclaims   171
  Objections—How to Respond?   172
  Exercise 9-D: Reply to Objections   175
  Fallacious Counterarguments   175
  More Fallacies in Writing   177
  Exercise 9-E: Fallacious Counterarguments   178
  Writing a Compare-and-Contrast Essay   181
  Exercise 9-F: Venn Diagrams   182
  Exercise 9-G: Thesis for Compare-and-Contrast Essay   183

  Bibliography   185

x

CHAPTER 1

Arguments

> In Chapter 1, we will introduce the components of an argument, types of inductive arguments, and types of deductive arguments. After completing the chapter, readers will be able to
> - define an argument and identify its parts (premise vs. conclusion),
> - identify premise and conclusion indicator words,
> - differentiate between deductive and inductive arguments,
> - distinguish the different types of inductive and deductive arguments, and
> - analyze logical reasoning in passages of Plato's *Apology* and Descartes's *Meditations*.

We are all equally entitled to hold our opinions, but not all opinions are equally reasonable. Some are more sophisticated, more robust, and well-founded than others. Since our beliefs can have a lasting and profound impact on how we make decisions and conduct our lives, we must take care to choose them wisely. Opinions based on lucky guesses, superstitions, wishful thinking, or faulty logic can lead to a multitude of problems and negative consequences. Critical thinking is vital in teaching us how to distinguish truth from error. It does this by offering us the logical tools for understanding and evaluating human reasoning whether that be our own or someone else's.

Our reasoning is often communicated through our arguments. An argument is an attempt to support a statement by giving reasons for believing it. A single **argument** consists of a set of statements, one of which is the conclusion and the rest are the premises. The **conclusion** is that statement someone is trying to convince others to believe, whereas the **premises** are the reasons offered in support of the conclusion.

For many arguments, key words are contained in the passages that can help to distinguish the premises from the conclusion. Sometimes there are conclusion indicator words that are placed near the conclusion of an argument to emphasize that it is the main point of the argument. **Conclusion indicators** such as the words "so" or "consequently" point out that the conclusion of the argument is nearby. In this passage by Arthur Schopenhauer, the conclusion is made clear by the word "therefore":

> **Conclusion Indicators**
> therefore, thus, it follows that, consequently, in short, whence, we may infer, hence, so, accordingly, wherefore, entails that, implies that, as a result, we may conclude
>
> **Premise Indicators**
> since, because, for, as, due to, given that, seeing that, in view of, for the reason that, after all, inasmuch, owing to, as evidenced by, in that, after all

No error is harmless: sooner or later it will bring misfortune to him who harbors it. Therefore, deceive no one, but rather confess ignorance of what you do not know and leave each man to devise his own articles of faith for himself.

Premise indicator words can also alert us to the reasons offered in an argument. Words such as "since" or "because" often precede a premise. Premise indicator words may help to identify which statements are intended to serve as the reasons in support of the conclusion. Niccolò Machiavelli offers this argument:

> Men ought either to be indulged or utterly destroyed, for if you merely offend them, they take vengeance, but if you injure them greatly, they are unable to retaliate.

The word "for" acts as a premise indicator word. It informs us that the conclusion precedes "for", and the premise follows it.

Not all arguments contain indicator words. In these cases, in order to identify the conclusion, we must then ask the following questions: What is the main point of the passage? What is the arguer trying to prove? To further complicate things, an argument's conclusion or one or more of the reasons may not be directly stated as an **explicit premise**. The same holds true of the conclusion that is not clearly stated. We then must interpret what the arguer is trying to say and determine what the **implicit** statements are. What is being said between the lines? What has the arguer implied but failed to explicitly state? Consider this quote from Mark Twain. What are the implicit premises? What is the conclusion Twain wants us to infer?

> If you pick up a starving dog and make him prosperous, he will not bite you. This is the principal difference between a dog and man.

On the other hand, the presence of words such as "thus" or "because" does not automatically mean that a certain passage contains an argument. For example, the following passage is best interpreted as illustrating rather than arguing a point.

> Treat those who are good with goodness, and also treat those who are not good with goodness. Thus, goodness is attained. Be honest to those who are honest and be also honest to those who are not honest. Thus, honesty is attained. (Lao Tzu)

In this context, the word "thus" does not act as a conclusion indicator word because the passage is not an argument. It is illustrating how something is done rather than supporting the truth of a statement based on reasons. The Daoist sage, Lao Tzu, elucidates how goodness and honesty are attained and uses the word "thus" to mean "in this way" or "in this manner," rather than as a conclusion indicator word synonymous to "therefore" or "consequently."

Likewise, in the next passage, the word "because" does not act as a premise indicator word in an argument. This passage contains an explanation. People may confuse arguments with explanations. An argument aims to prove that a certain claim is true based on reasons, while an explanation tries to show why something happens. An explanation is meant to shed light on a certain event. In the following passage, Joseph Campbell is explaining how fear and desire prevent one from having certain experiences; he is not offering proof that this sort of experience is real.

> The experience of mystery comes not from expecting it but through yielding all your programs, because your programs are based on fear and desire. Drop them and the radiance comes. (Joseph Campbell, *Thou Art That: Transforming Religious Metaphor*)

Moreover, an argument is an attempt to prove the truth of a statement by providing reasons and evidence. The person giving an argument draws an inference from purported facts or reasons to a certain conclusion. In making an argument, a person is making two claims. The first is a **factual claim**. The premises of an argument present the support or evidence. Second, an **inferential claim** is being made that the truth of another statement, the conclusion, follows from the premises. That is, the arguer contends that the premises imply or entail the truth of the conclusion. Whether or not the premises indeed provide adequate support for the conclusion is another matter that we may later judge when we evaluate an argument for its strength or validity.

Exercise 1-A: Premises and Conclusion

All of these passages contain an argument. Underline the conclusion of each argument and circle any premise or conclusion indicator words.

1. My neighbor must be taking care of his lawn. For when people don't take care of their lawns, weeds grow with the grass and the grass turns brown. However, my neighbor's lawn has no weeds, and its color remains a vibrant green.
2. The coffee I had this morning did not taste the same as it normally does. This implies that the milk has spoiled. For I have been using the same coffee beans as usual.
3. Dogs with long hair tend to shed all over the house. I have heard they also have a lot of fleas. You should not get a long-haired dog.
4. Jack is a horrible driver despite never receiving a ticket. He weaves in and out of traffic on the freeway, cuts cars off, and talks on his cell phone while driving. The worst part is that he thinks he is such a great driver.
5. Las Vegas is about 350 miles away and I'm driving 70 miles an hour. Consequently, I should arrive home in approximately five hours.

6. In order for a democracy to function properly, it is necessary that the people have their voices heard. Given that the best way for the people's voices to be heard is through the process of voting, everyone should participate in the voting procedures.
7. It will rain today. The weatherman reported that there is a storm heading this way and the clouds are starting to accumulate in the area.
8. Death is the mother of beauty; hence from her, alone, shall come fulfilment to our dreams and our desires ... (Wallace Stevens)
9. The *Walking Dead* is a show with flesh-eating, walking zombies. You really should not watch the *Walking Dead* before bedtime because zombies are scary and can cause bad dreams.
10. Wild coyotes are responsible for 15 percent of domestic pet illnesses and death in San Diego County. Furthermore, coyotes cause illness by spreading disease through bites and by contaminating outdoor spaces with feces. Since it is more expensive to treat all wild coyotes in San Diego than to treat illnesses, the wild coyotes should all be killed.
11. Research has found that learning a musical instrument corresponds to an increased ability to think abstractly. Thinking abstractly increases one's ability to draw connections between dissimilar matters, which is necessary to navigate in this world. Accordingly, students should learn a musical instrument as part of their education. After all, isn't the goal of education to enable students to navigate this world?
12. If we have no knowledge of cause and effect, then we could not make predictions. Since it is obvious that we are capable of making predictions, it follows that we have some knowledge of cause and effect.
13. There is suffering in life; this suffering has a cause; suffering must be caused to cease; suffering can cease if one knows the right way. The suffering inseparably connected with existence is mainly due to desire. Therefore, the extinction of desire will lead to the cessation of existence by rebirth and of consequent suffering. (Buddha, Four Noble Truths)
14. Shingles are experienced by people who have had chicken pox in the past. Since my dad had shingles last week, he must have had chicken pox in the past.
15. Just as the body bears the traces of its phylogenetic development, so also does the human mind. Hence there is nothing surprising about the possibility that the figurative language of dreams is a survival from an archaic mode of thought. (CG Jung, CW 8: *The Structure and Dynamics of the Psyche*; "General Aspects of Dream Psychology")
16. Most pugs have breathing problems from birth, and collars can restrict their airway. This shows that if you own a pug, you should get a harness instead of a collar.
17. Neither a borrower nor a lender be, for loan oft loses both itself and friend. (Shakespeare)
18. You have enemies? Good. That means you've stood up for something, sometime in your life. (Winston Churchill)

Deductive versus Inductive Arguments

Rhetorical devices and fallacious reasoning can be effective tools of persuasion, but they do not make for good arguments. As previously stated, an **argument** is an attempt to support a statement by giving reasons for believing it. A single argument consists of a set of statements, one of which is the conclusion and one or more of the statements are the premises. The statement being argued for is the argument's conclusion. The premises are the statements that provide the data, evidence, or principles offered in support of the conclusion. The premises and the conclusion of an argument are special kinds of sentences called **statements**. A statement is a sentence that has a **truth-value:** either the statement is true or false. Your English teacher will refer to these as declarative sentences because they make assertions or claims. Unlike other sentences such as questions or commands, a statement is a sentence with a truth-value; it is either true or false and cannot be both. Questions such as "What time is it?" or commands such as "Stand up" have no truth-values, for they are neither true nor false.

Arguments may be divided into two broad groups, **inductive** and **deductive**. One way to differentiate deductive from inductive arguments is to point out the kind of reasoning involved in these two types of arguments. Inductive arguments contain or claim to contain probabilistic reasoning, whereas deductive arguments contain or claim to contain necessary reasoning. So, to decide whether an argument is best treated as an inductive or a deductive argument, we should first consider how good the argument is. If the premises of the argument provide the necessary support for the conclusion, then the argument is deductive. If the argument is good but its premises provide only probable support for the conclusion, then the argument is inductive. This works for arguments that are good to the extent that the conclusion is either necessarily or probably true given the premises. However, some arguments provide neither necessary nor probable support for the conclusion.

In these cases, we may still be able to distinguish inductive from deductive arguments by considering two factors: the presence of other indicator words or the argument type. First, indicator words such as *probably, likely, certainly,* and *necessarily* inform us whether the conclusion is purported to be probably true or necessarily true. Second, the reasoning may fit a certain argument type. Five argument types often categorized as inductive include predictions, arguments from authority, causal inferences, inductive generalizations, and analogies. For no matter how good the prediction, how qualified the authority, how linked two events, how large one's sample, or how fitting the analogy, arguments of this type can never guarantee with absolute certainty that the conclusion will be true.

TYPES OF INDUCTIVE ARGUMENTS

Prediction: argument about future event based on past or present events

Authority: argument based on the testimony of others, typically experts

Causal Inference: argument based on a cause-effect relationship

Inductive Generalization: argument about larger group from smaller sample

Analogy: argument based on a similarity between two different objects

> **TYPES OF DEDUCTIVE ARGUMENTS**
>
> **Arguments from Definition**: arguments based on a definition of a word or phrase
>
> **Arguments from Math**: arguments based on a mathematical principle
>
> **Categorical Syllogism**: arguments with two premises and a conclusion and each sentence begins with the word "all" "no" or "some"
>
> **Disjunctive Syllogism**: arguments with two premises and a conclusion and one of the premises is a disjunctive statement (Either A or B)
>
> **Hypothetical Syllogism**: arguments with two premises and a conclusion and at least one of the premises is a conditional statement (If A, then B)

In contrast, some argument forms are best categorized as deductive arguments because they have the potential of generating necessarily true conclusions. These argument forms include arguments from math, arguments from definition, categorical syllogisms, disjunctive syllogisms, and hypothetical syllogisms. If the math is done well, or the definition is accurate, or the syllogism is valid, the conclusion would be necessarily true given the premises.

The three different kinds of syllogisms will have a few things in common. Syllogisms are deductive arguments that contain two premises and one conclusion. The three syllogisms are easy to distinguish from one another by the special words they contain. Each of the three statements in a standard **categorical syllogism** begins with a word that quantifies the sentence, a word such as "all," "no," or "some." These words quantify the subject of the sentence. Here are a few examples:

> "Some fortunate events are surprises. Some surprises are not nightmares. Thus, no nightmares are fortunate events."
>
> "All psychics are fortune tellers. Some gypsies are fortune tellers. Accordingly, some gypsies are psychics."

A **disjunctive syllogism** contains a disjunctive sentence of the form "Either X or Y." For a disjunctive statement "X or Y" to be true only one of the component simple statements need be true. The disjunct X can be true, disjunct Y can be true, or both X and Y can be true. For example, "Jane is happy or excited" is a true disjunction when one or both of its component statements "Jane is happy" or "Jane is excited" is true. An example of a disjunctive statement:

> "Either Jane is happy or excited. Jane is not happy. So, Jane must be excited."

The third syllogism is called a **hypothetical syllogism** and it contains a conditional statement that is typically expressed "If X, then Y." A conditional statement consists of two parts: the statement following "if" is known as the antecedent, while the other statement which follows "then" is the consequent. A conditional is true except for the case when its antecedent X is true and its consequent Y is false. Consider the sentence "If it is January, then it is winter." This conditional is false when the antecedent "it is January" is true while the consequent "it is winter" is false. A hypothetical syllogism contains at least one conditional statement as a premise, but all three of the statements can be conditionals. The following are examples of hypothetical syllogisms:

"If it is January, then it is winter. It is not winter. Thus, it is not January."

"If it is raining, then it is January. If it is January, then it is summer. Hence, if it is raining, then it is summer."

Both of these examples are hypothetical syllogisms and should be categorized as deductive arguments, although the second argument clearly has a problem. So, it seems that classifying an argument as deductive does not guarantee that the conclusion will in fact be true. The attempt to do deductive reasoning may not be successful. In relation to mathematical arguments, some calculations may be erroneous due to faulty measurement, wrong formulas, or misapplied mathematics. In these cases, instead of saying that such arguments are not deductive arguments from math, we will simply say that they are arguments from math, and they are deductive arguments, but they are bad ones.

Exercise 1-B: Deductive versus Inductive

The following arguments are all valid deductive arguments or good (strong) inductive arguments. Identify which arguments are deductive and which are inductive arguments. Also, identify any argument forms. In later chapters, we will learn how to categorize invalid/bad arguments as deductive or inductive.

1. All violinists are musicians. Jack is a violinist. So, Jack is a musician.
2. Either tomatoes are fruits or vegetables. Tomatoes are not vegetables. Consequently, tomatoes are fruits.
3. The neighbors' dog Rex must be in a dog kennel this weekend. For whenever our neighbors, Dave and Carol, go out of town, they put their dog Rex in a dog kennel. Dave and Carol did go out of town this weekend.
4. It will rain today. The weather forecaster reported that there is a storm heading this way, and the clouds are starting to accumulate in the area.
5. All squares are rectangles. This figure is a square. So, this figure is a rectangle.
6. Sue must have gone to the beach because her swimsuit is wet, and her shoes are full of sand.
7. A horse is a warm-blooded animal. Seabiscuit is a horse. It follows that Seabiscuit is a warm-blooded animal.
8. Two nickels have the same value as one dime. A dime is worth ten cents. Since I have two nickels, then I must have at least ten cents.
9. No one would blame a bartender for having a few drinks on the job. But an airline pilot is no less a human being than a bartender. Therefore, no one should blame an airline pilot for having a few drinks on the job.
10. All of the dogs in the kennel can bark. Hence, it follows that most dogs can bark.
11. The specimen in the jar is a crustacean. After all, my uncle Bert, who is a respected marine biologist told me so.
12. No felines are canines. Hence, since all tigers are felines, no tigers are canines.

Plato and the Trial of Socrates

By Brandon Walton

In the *Apology*, Plato gives an account of the trial of Socrates. Socrates has been brought to court on charges of practicing philosophy—namely, of corrupting the youth and of not believing in the gods of Athens. Really, all this amounted to was that he was going around town and questioning the self-proclaimed wise men and finding out, one by one, that they were not really as wise as they thought they were—he was the "gadfly" that stirred the pot. It is important to note that Socrates is not *apologizing* for his conduct in the same sense as we would usually employ the term "apology" as saying "sorry." Instead, Socrates is simply giving a speech to the jurors in his own defense. His defense, however, as he is fully aware, is futile—the slanders against Socrates were already too deeply set into the minds of the jury members. Nonetheless, as Socrates is compelled by the gods and his love and respect for truth, he proceeds anyway.

Socrates led a unique lifestyle, and it was this unique lifestyle that often got him into trouble. The god at Delphi, when asked by a friend of Socrates, said that there was no one wiser than Socrates. Socrates did not think of himself wise at all, but he didn't think that the oracle at Delphi would lie. As part refutation, part confirmation, Socrates set out to question all of Athens' most esteemed citizens—to prove that he was not the wisest man, and in the process, learning from wiser men than himself. He talked to politicians, orators, poets, and craftsmen. At each meeting, Socrates came to the same conclusion: the men who think they are the wisest were often the ones who knew the least. And this was what made Socrates different: that he did not know and did not claim to know. Unfortunately, this style of questioning made Socrates very unpopular and not well-liked in the city. The first round of accusations came shortly after.

As Socrates explains to the jury, it was his constant pursuit of the truth and obedience to the gods that led him on this unpopular path. Socrates never claimed to be a teacher, yet many privileged youths in the city chose to follow him during his travels, watching him question anybody who claimed knowledge. As a result, many of these youths came to do their own abrasive questioning, much to the dismay of others. But those who came into contact with these "pupils" did not direct their anger at them; they directed it toward Socrates. This was the charge of corrupting the youth.

The most important point prevailing throughout Socrates's entire apology is the idea that truth is important. Moreover, it is the idea that we may arrive at the truth by constantly questioning and seeking after it. Not even death ought to lead a person to deviate from this goal: "the unexamined life is not worth living." In fact, death is nothing to be feared. For all we know, Socrates said, death is the simple cessation of all perception, or else it could be the soul's relocation to another place. In either case, Socrates insisted that if the jury sentenced him to death, it would be of no harm to him—for he did not believe that a good person could ever be harmed, in life or in death. The ones who would suffer Socrates's death, however, were the people of Athens: for Socrates was a divine gift of sorts whose purpose was to provoke discussion and question people's basic beliefs and claims; although Socrates's incessant inquiry was frustrating for the people being taken to task, its aim was to achieve excellence and health of the soul. He was practicing philosophy.

The Apology

By Plato; trans. Benjamin Jowett

How you, O Athenians, have been affected by my accusers, I cannot tell; but I know that they almost made me forget who I was—so persuasively did they speak; and yet they have hardly uttered a word of truth. But of the many falsehoods told by them, there was one which quite amazed me;—I mean when they said that you should be upon your guard and not allow yourselves to be deceived by the force of my eloquence. To say this, when they were certain to be detected as soon as I opened my lips and proved myself to be anything but a great speaker, did indeed appear to me most shameless—unless by the force of eloquence they mean the force of truth; for it such is their meaning, I admit that I am eloquent. But in how different a way from theirs! Well, as I was saying, they have scarcely spoken the truth at all; but from me you shall hear the whole truth: not, however, delivered after their manner in a set oration duly ornamented with words and phrases. No, by heaven! but I shall use the words and arguments which occur to me at the moment; for I am confident in the justice of my cause (Or I am certain that I am right in taking this course.): at my time of life I ought not to be appearing before you, O men of Athens, in the character of a juvenile orator—let no one expect it of me. And I must beg of you to grant me a favor:—If I defend myself in my accustomed manner, and you hear me using the words which I have been in the habit of using in the agora, at the tables of the money-changers, or anywhere else, I would ask you not to be surprised, and not to interrupt me on this account. For I am more than seventy years of age, and appearing now for the first time in a court of law, I am quite a stranger to the language of the place; and therefore I would have you regard me as if I were really a stranger, whom you would excuse if he spoke in his native tongue, and after the fashion of his country:—Am I making an unfair request of you? Never mind the manner, which may or may not be good; but think only of the truth of my words and give heed to that: let the speaker speak truly and the judge decide justly.

I dare say, Athenians, that someone among you will reply, 'Yes, Socrates, but what is the origin of these accusations which are brought against you; there must have been something strange which you have been doing? All these rumors and this talk about you would never have arisen if you had been like other men: tell us, then, what is the cause of them, for we should be sorry to judge hastily of you.' Now I regard this as a fair challenge, and I will endeavor to explain to you the reason why I am called wise and have such an evil fame. Please attend then. And although some of you may think that I am joking, I declare that I will tell you the entire truth. Men of Athens, this reputation of mine has come of a certain sort of wisdom which I possess … I will refer you to a witness who is worthy of credit; that witness shall be the God of

Plato, *The Apology: Phaedo and Crito of Plato*, trans. Benjamin Jowett, P. F. Collier & Son, 1909.

Delphi—he will tell you about my wisdom, if I have any, and of what sort it is. You must have known Chaerephon; he was early a friend of mine, and also a friend of yours, for he shared in the recent exile of the people and returned with you. Well, Chaerephon, as you know, was very impetuous in all his doings, and he went to Delphi and boldly asked the oracle to tell him whether—as I was saying, I must beg you not to interrupt—he asked the oracle to tell him whether anyone was wiser than I was, and the Pythian prophetess answered, that there was no man wiser. Chaerephon is dead himself; but his brother, who is in court, will confirm the truth of what I am saying.

Why do I mention this? Because I am going to explain to you why I have such an evil name. When I heard the answer, I said to myself, What can the god mean? and what is the interpretation of his riddle? for I know that I have no wisdom, small or great. What then can he mean when he says that I am the wisest of men? And yet he is a god and cannot lie; that would be against his nature. After long consideration, I thought of a method of trying the question. I reflected that if I could only find a man wiser than myself, then I might go to the god with a refutation in my hand. I should say to him, 'Here is a man who is wiser than I am; but you said that I was the wisest.' Accordingly I went to one who had the reputation of wisdom, and observed him—his name I need not mention; he was a politician whom I selected for examination—and the result was as follows: When I began to talk with him, I could not help thinking that he was not really wise, although he was thought wise by many, and still wiser by himself; and thereupon I tried to explain to him that he thought himself wise, but was not really wise; and the consequence was that he hated me, and his enmity was shared by several who were present and heard me. So, I left him, saying to myself, as I went away: Well, although I do not suppose that either of us knows anything really beautiful and good, I am better off than he is —for he knows nothing, and thinks that he knows; I neither know nor think that I know. In this latter particular, then, I seem to have slightly the advantage of him. Then I went to another who had still higher pretensions to wisdom, and my conclusion was exactly the same. Whereupon I made another enemy of him, and of many others besides him.

Then I went to one man after another, being not unconscious of the enmity which I provoked, and I lamented and feared this: but necessity was laid upon me—the word of God, I thought, ought to be considered first. And I said to myself, "Go I must to all who appear to know, and find out the meaning of the oracle." And I swear to you, Athenians, by the dog I swear! For I must tell you the truth—the result of my mission was just this: I found that the men most in repute were all but the most foolish; and that others less esteemed were really wiser and better. I will tell you the tale of my wanderings and of the 'Herculean' labors, as I may call them, which I endured only to find at last the oracle irrefutable. After the politicians, I went to the poets ... The poets appeared to me to be much in the same case; and I further observed that upon the strength of their poetry they believed themselves to be the wisest of men in other things in which they were not wise. So, I departed, conceiving myself to be superior to them for the same reason that I was superior to the politicians.

At last, I went to the artisans. I was conscious that I knew nothing at all, as I may say, and I was sure that they knew many fine things; and here I was not mistaken, for they did know many things of which I was ignorant, and in this they certainly were wiser than I was. But I observed that even the good artisans fell into the same error as the poets;—because they were good workmen they thought that they also knew all sorts of high matters, and this defect in them overshadowed their wisdom; and therefore I asked myself on behalf of the oracle, whether I would like to be as I was, neither having their knowledge nor their ignorance, or like them in both; and I made answer to myself and to the oracle that I was better off as I was.

This inquisition has led to my having many enemies of the worst and most dangerous kind and has given occasion also to many calumnies. And I am called wise, for my hearers always imagine that I myself possess the wisdom which I find wanting in others: but the truth is, O men of Athens, that God only is wise; and by his answer he intends to show that the wisdom of men is worth little or nothing; he is not speaking of Socrates, he is only using my name by way of illustration, as if he said, He, O men, is the wisest, who, like Socrates, knows that his wisdom is in truth worth nothing. And so I go about the world, obedient to the god, and search and make enquiry into the wisdom of any one, whether citizen or stranger, who appears to be wise; and if he is not wise, then in vindication of the oracle I show him that he is not wise; and my occupation quite absorbs me, and I have no time to give either to any public matter of interest or to any concern of my own, but I am in utter poverty by reason of my devotion to the god.

There is another thing:—young men of the richer classes, who have not much to do, come about me of their own accord; they like to hear the pretenders examined, and they often imitate me, and proceed to examine others; there are plenty of persons, as they quickly discover, who think that they know something, but really know little or nothing; and then those who are examined by them instead of being angry with themselves are angry with me: This confounded Socrates, they say; this villainous misleader of youth!

Someone will say: And are you not ashamed, Socrates, of a course of life which is likely to bring you to an untimely end? To him I may fairly answer: There you are mistaken: a man who is good for anything ought not to calculate the chance of living or dying; he ought only to consider whether in doing anything he is doing right or wrong—acting the part of a good man or of a bad ... For the fear of death is indeed the pretense of wisdom, and not real wisdom, being a pretense of knowing the unknown; and no one knows whether death, which men in their fear apprehend to be the greatest evil, may not be the greatest good.

And now, Athenians, I am not going to argue for my own sake, as you may think, but for yours, that you may not sin against the God by condemning me, who am his gift to you. For if you kill me you will not easily find a successor to me, who, if I may use such a ludicrous figure of speech, am a sort of gadfly, given to the state by God; and the state is a great and noble steed who is tardy in his motions owing to his very size, and requires to be stirred into life. I am that gadfly which God has attached to the state, and all day long and in all places am always fastening upon you, arousing and persuading and reproaching you. You will not easily find another like me, and therefore I would advise you to spare me.

Let us reflect in another way, and we shall see that there is great reason to hope that death is a good; for one of two things—either death is a state of nothingness and utter unconsciousness, or, as men say, there is a change and migration of the soul from this world to another. Now if you suppose that there is no consciousness, but a sleep like the sleep of him who is undisturbed even by dreams, death will be an unspeakable gain. For if a person were to select the night in which his sleep was undisturbed even by dreams, and were to compare with this the other days and nights of his life, and then were to tell us how many days and nights he had passed in the course of his life better and more pleasantly than this one, I think that any man, I will not say a private man, but even the great king will not find many such days or nights, when compared with the others. Now if death be of such a nature, I say that to die is gain; for eternity is then only a single night. But if death is the journey to another place, and there, as men say, all the dead abide, what good, O my friends and judges, can be greater than this? What would not a man give if he might converse with Orpheus and Musaeus and Hesiod and Homer? Nay, if this be true, let me die again and again. I myself, too, shall have a wonderful interest in there meeting and conversing with Palamedes, and Ajax the son of Telamon, and any other ancient hero who has suffered death through an unjust judgment; and there will be no small pleasure, as I think, in comparing my own sufferings with theirs. Above all, I shall then be able to continue my search into true and false knowledge; as in this world, so also in the next; and I shall find out who is wise, and who pretends to be wise, and is not. What would not a man give, O judges, to be able to examine the leader of the great Trojan expedition; or Odysseus or Sisyphus, or numberless others, men and women too! What infinite delight would there be in conversing with them and asking them questions.

Exercise 1-C: Reading Questions on Plato's *Apology*

1. How does Socrates compare his arguments to his accusers' methods of persuasion?
2. What question does Socrates's friend, Chaerephon, ask the oracle of Delphi? What was the oracle's answer to Chaerephon's question?
3. Why does Socrates seek out and examine various politicians? What does he discover about the politicians he encounters?
4. After the politicians, whom else does Socrates question? What does he discover about these two groups?
5. How does Socrates finally interpret the oracle's message? Can anyone else be as wise as Socrates?
6. How has Socrates's association with young men angered his accusers?
7. According to Socrates, should a good person fear death? Why or why not?
8. Socrates argues that for the sake of Athens, his life should be spared. What analogy does he use to compare his relationship with Athens?
9. Socrates claims that death is one of two things. What are these two possibilities?
10. According to Socrates, is death a bad thing? What argument does he give?

Descartes and the Cogito Argument

By Michael Lin

In the seventeenth century, French philosopher, Rene Descartes, undertook a major project of reexamining his beliefs. His goal was to find truths that were indubitably true beyond any possible doubt. Descartes insisted that he could not be satisfied with beliefs based on superstition, folklore, or tradition. Even highly probable truths could not pass Descartes's high standard. In his *Meditations*, Descartes scrutinized his beliefs, hoping to uncover necessary truths that could not possibly be doubted.

In the *First Meditation*, Descartes asks the question, What can he be sure of? Can he be sure of his sensations or that he even has a physical body? Can he be certain that he is awake and not just dreaming? He may just be imagining that he sees lights, hears noises, or feels heat when, in reality, he is only dreaming. Can he even be sure of his own existence? Descartes states that, for all he knows, it can be the case that there is an evil higher power who is controlling or toying with his mind.

One activity stands out to Descartes, and that is thinking. Try as he might, he cannot doubt the proposition, "I think." To do so would generate a self-contradiction. This would amount to someone saying, "I think that I am not thinking," which is impossible. This leads Descartes to conclude that other beliefs may possibly be false, but the statement "I think" must be true necessarily. In Latin, "I think" is translated as "cogito." Thinking may involve a number of mental acts such as doubting, understanding, conceiving, affirming, denying, willing, refusing, etc.

From the premise "I think," Descartes concludes "I exist." While he is not yet convinced that he has a physical body, he is assured that he exists at least as "a thing that thinks" for as long as he thinks. By the end of the *Second Meditation*, Descartes delivers his famous deductive Cogito Argument: "Cogito; ergo sum." This may be translated as "I think; therefore, I am."

The Meditations of First Philosophy

By Rene Descartes; trans. John Veitch

MEDITATION I: Of the Things on Which We May Doubt

Several years have now elapsed since I first became aware that I had accepted, even from my youth, many false opinions for true, and that consequently what I afterward based on such principles was highly doubtful; and from that time I was convinced of the necessity of undertaking once in my life to rid myself of all the opinions I had adopted, and of commencing anew the work of building from the foundation, if I desired to establish a firm and abiding superstructure in the sciences. But as this enterprise appeared to me to be one of great magnitude, I waited until I had attained an age so mature as to leave me no hope that at any stage of life more advanced I should be better able to execute my design. On this account, I have delayed so long that I should henceforth consider I was doing wrong were I still to consume in deliberation

Rene Descartes, *The Method, Meditations and Philosophy of Descartes*, trans. John Veitch, 1901.

any of the time that now remains for action. To-day, then, since I have opportunely freed my mind from all cares [and am happily disturbed by no passions], and since I am in the secure possession of leisure in a peaceable retirement, I will at length apply myself earnestly and freely to the general overthrow of all my former opinions. But, to this end, it will not be necessary for me to show that the whole of these are false—a point, perhaps, which I shall never reach; but as even now my reason convinces me that I ought not the less carefully to withhold belief from what is not entirely certain and indubitable, than from what is manifestly false, it will be sufficient to justify the rejection of the whole if I shall find in each some ground for doubt. Nor for this purpose will it be necessary even to deal with each belief individually, which would be truly an endless labor; but, as the removal from below of the foundation necessarily involves the downfall of the whole edifice, I will at once approach the criticism of the principles on which all my former beliefs rested.

All that I have, up to this moment, accepted as possessed of the highest truth and certainty, I received either from or through the senses. I observed, however, that these sometimes misled us; and it is the part of prudence not to place absolute confidence in that by which we have even once been deceived.

But it may be said, perhaps, that, although the senses occasionally mislead us respecting minute objects, and such as are so far removed from us as to be beyond the reach of close observation, there are yet many other of their informations (presentations), of the truth of which it is manifestly impossible to doubt; as for example, that I am in this place, seated by the fire, clothed in a winter dressing gown, that I hold in my hands this piece of paper, with other intimations of the same nature. But how could I deny that I possess these hands and this body, and withal escape being classed with persons in a state of insanity, whose brains are so disordered and clouded by dark bilious vapors as to cause them pertinaciously to assert that they are monarchs when they are in the greatest poverty; or clothed [in gold] and purple when destitute of any covering; or that their head is made of clay, their body of glass, or that they are gourds? I should certainly be not less insane than they, were I to regulate my procedure according to examples so extravagant.

Though this be true, I must nevertheless here consider that I am a man, and that, consequently, I am in the habit of sleeping, and representing to myself in dreams those same things, or even sometimes others less probable, which the insane think are presented to them in their waking moments. How often have I dreamt that I was in these familiar circumstances, that I was dressed, and occupied this place by the fire, when I was lying undressed in bed? At the present moment, however, I certainly look upon this paper with eyes wide awake; the head which I now move is not asleep; I extend this hand consciously and with express purpose, and I perceive it; the occurrences in sleep are not so distinct as all this. But I cannot forget that, at other times I have been deceived in sleep by similar illusions; and, attentively considering those cases, I perceive so clearly that there exist no certain marks by which the state of waking can ever be distinguished from sleep, that I feel greatly astonished; and in amazement I almost persuade myself that I am now dreaming.

Let us suppose, then, that we are dreaming, and that all these particulars — namely, the opening of the eyes, the motion of the head, the forth-putting of the hands — are merely illusions; and even that we really possess neither an entire body nor hands such as we see. Nevertheless it must be admitted at least that the objects which appear to us in sleep are, as it were, painted representations which could not have been formed unless in the likeness of realities; and, therefore, that those general objects, at all events, namely, eyes, a head, hands, and an entire body, are not simply imaginary, but really existent. For, in truth, painters themselves, even when they study to represent sirens and satyrs by forms the most fantastic and extraordinary, cannot bestow upon them natures absolutely new, but can only make a certain medley of the members of different animals; or if they chance to imagine something so novel that nothing at all similar has ever been seen before, and such as is, therefore, purely fictitious and absolutely false, it is at least certain that the colors of which this is composed are real.

And on the same principle, although these general objects, viz, [a body], eyes, a head, hands, and the like, be imaginary, we are nevertheless absolutely necessitated to admit the reality at least of some other objects still more simple and universal than these, of which, just as of certain real colors, all those images of things, whether true and real, or false and fantastic, that are found in our consciousness (*cogitatio*), are formed.

To this class of objects seem to belong corporeal nature in general and its extension; the figure of extended things, their quantity or magnitude, and their number, as also the place in, and the time during, which they exist, and other things of the same sort. We will not, therefore, perhaps reason illegitimately if we conclude from this that Physics, Astronomy, Medicine, and all the other sciences that have for their end the consideration of composite objects, are indeed of a doubtful character; but that Arithmetic, Geometry, and the other sciences of the same class, which regard merely the simplest and most general objects, and scarcely inquire whether or not these are really existent, contain somewhat that is certain and indubitable: for whether I am awake or dreaming, it remains true that two and three make five, and that a square has but four sides; nor does it seem possible that truths so apparent can ever fall under a suspicion of falsity [or incertitude].

Nevertheless, the belief that there is a God who is all powerful, and who created me, such as I am, has, for a long time, obtained steady possession of my mind... [Then Descartes questions whether God exists and entertains the possibility of a deceiving demon that exists instead.]

...I will suppose, then, not that Deity, who is sovereignly good and the fountain of truth, but that some malignant demon, who is at once exceedingly potent and deceitful, has employed all his artifice to deceive me; I will suppose that the sky, the air, the earth, colors, figures, sounds, and all external things, are nothing better than the illusions of dreams, by means of which this being has laid snares for my credulity; I will consider myself as without hands, eyes, flesh, blood, or any of the senses, and as falsely believing that I am possessed of these; I will continue resolutely fixed in this belief, and if indeed by this means it be not in my power to arrive at the knowledge of truth, I shall at least do what is in my power, viz [suspend my judgment], and guard with settled purpose against giving my assent to what is false, and being imposed upon by this deceiver, whatever be his power and artifice...

MEDITATION II: Of the Nature of the Human Mind; And That It Is More Easily Known Than the Body

The Meditation of yesterday has filled my mind with so many doubts, that it is no longer in my power to forget them. Nor do I see, meanwhile, any principle on which they can be resolved; and, just as if I had fallen all of a sudden into very deep water, I am so greatly disconcerted as to be unable either to plant my feet firmly on the bottom or sustain myself by swimming on the surface. I will, nevertheless, make an effort, and try anew the same path on which I had entered yesterday, that is, proceed by casting aside all that admits of the slightest doubt, not less than if I had discovered it to be absolutely false; and I will continue always in this track until I shall find something that is certain, or at least, if I can do nothing more, until I shall know with certainty that there is nothing certain...

I suppose, accordingly, that all the things which I see are false (fictitious); I believe that none of those objects which my fallacious memory represents ever existed; I suppose that I possess no senses; I believe that body, figure, extension, motion, and place are merely fictions of my mind. What is there, then, that can be esteemed true? Perhaps this only, that there is absolutely nothing certain.

But how do I know that there is not something different altogether from the objects I have now enumerated, of which it is impossible to entertain the slightest doubt? Is there not a God, or some being, by whatever name I may designate him, who causes these thoughts, to arise in my mind? But why suppose such a being, for it may be I myself am capable of producing them? Am I, then, at least not something? But I before denied that I possessed senses or a body; I hesitate, however, for what follows from that? Am I so dependent on the body and the senses that without these I cannot exist? But I had the persuasion that there was absolutely nothing in the world, that there was no sky and no earth, neither minds nor bodies; was I not, therefore, at the same time, persuaded that I did not exist? Far from it; I assuredly existed, since I was persuaded. But there is I know not what being, who is possessed at once of the highest power and the deepest cunning, who is constantly employing all his ingenuity in deceiving me. Doubtless, then, I exist, since I am deceived; and, let him deceive me as he may, he can never bring it about that I am nothing, so long as I shall be conscious that I am something. So that it most, in fine, be maintained, all things being maturely and carefully considered, that this proposition (*pronunciatum*) I am, I exist, is necessarily true each time it is expressed by me, or conceived in my mind...

And here I discover what properly belongs to myself. This alone is inseparable from me. I am — I exist: this is certain; but how often? As often as I think; for perhaps it would even happen, if I should wholly cease to think, that I should at the same time altogether cease to be. I now admit nothing that is not necessarily true. I am therefore, precisely speaking, only a thinking thing, that is, a mind (*mens sive animus*), understanding, or reason, terms whose signification was before unknown to me. I am, however, a real thing, and really existent; but what thing? The answer was, a thinking thing... But what, then, am I? A thinking thing, it has been said. But what is a thinking thing? It is a thing that doubts, understands, [conceives], affirms, denies, wills, refuses; that imagines also, and perceives.

Exercise 1-D: Reading Questions on Descartes's *Meditations*

1. At the beginning of his *First Meditation*, what did Descartes realize about his beliefs, and what did this inspire him to do?
2. In Descartes's view, when should one reject a belief?
3. What does Descartes observe about his senses? Can sense perception be trusted?
4. What doubts does Descartes claim that only insane people would have?
5. Where is Descartes as he is examining his beliefs in the "First Meditation"?
6. What is the second reason that Descartes considers for doubting his beliefs?
7. Although the body, hands, limbs, etc., may not be real, Descartes points out that the basic elements such as color must be real. What other qualities does he claim to be real?
8. Which scientific fields does Descartes believe to be doubtful? In contrast, which subjects do Descartes claim are certain and indubitable?
9. For years, what did Descartes believe about the creator of the world? What new possibility does Descartes entertain about the creator?
10. At the beginning of the *Second Meditation*, what does Descartes call into doubt?
11. In comparison to the deceiving demon, how does Descartes describe God?
12. Can the existence of God or aspects of myself be doubted according to Descartes?
13. Even if an evil genius or deceiving demon existed, what belief remains true and cannot be doubted?
14. In answer to the question, what am I, what does Descartes answer?
15. What does the phrase "Cogito; ergo sum" mean? What are the premise and the conclusion?

CHAPTER 2
Inductive Reasoning

> In Chapter 2, we will focus on inductive reasoning and learn how to evaluate inductive arguments. We will compare strong inductive arguments from informal fallacies involving weak induction. After completing the chapter, readers will be able to
> - identify types of inductive arguments;
> - evaluate arguments as strong, weak, cogent, or uncogent;
> - identify fallacies of weak induction; and
> - analyze logical reasoning passages of Paley's *Natural Teleology* and Hume's *Enquiry into Human Understanding*.

As previously stated in the first chapter, a person who offers an **argument** attempts to support a statement by giving reasons for believing it. Thus, an argument is a set of statements, one of which is the conclusion and the rest are the premises. The premises are claimed to provide the data, evidence, or principles in support of the truth of the conclusion. On the other hand, the conclusion may be said to follow from or be the consequence of the premises. Thus, an argument often expresses the reasoning behind the belief in certain assertions (conclusions) based on other claims (premises). The premises and the conclusion of an argument are special kinds of sentences called "**statements**." Statements are sentences that have **truth-values**. The possible truth-value of a statement is either true or false, one or the other and not both. An English teacher would refer to these as declarative sentences because they make assertions or claims. Unlike statements, questions and commands do not have truth-values. Questions such as "What time is it?" or commands such as "Stand up" have no truth-values for they are neither true nor false.

Arguments may be divided into two broad groups, **deductive** and **inductive**. One way to differentiate deductive from inductive arguments is to point out the kind of reasoning involved in these two types of arguments. Inductive arguments contain or claim to contain probabilistic reasoning, whereas deductive arguments contain or claim to contain necessary reasoning. For inductive arguments, the premise(s) is intended to provide probable support for the conclusion.

> **TYPES OF INDUCTIVE ARGUMENTS**
>
> **Prediction:** conclusion about future event based on past or present events
>
> **Authority:** conclusion based on the testimony of others, typically experts
>
> **Causal Inference:** conclusion based on a cause-effect relationship
>
> **Inductive Generalization:** conclusion about larger group from smaller sample
>
> **Analogy:** conclusion based on a similarity between two different objects

If the inductive argument is a good one, then based on the information given in the premises, one would reasonably believe that the conclusion is true.

There are certain argument forms typically categorized as inductive arguments because they have the potential of giving, at best, probable support for the conclusion. Among these inductive argument forms are predictions, arguments from authority, causal inferences, inductive generalizations, and analogies.

Strength and Cogency

We will evaluate inductive arguments using the terms strong or weak, and cogent or uncogent. At the most general level, we call an argument good if it provides support for a particular claim. Instead of calling inductive arguments "good" and "bad," we will rate arguments by more specific evaluative terms. The evaluative terms reserved for inductive arguments will be parallel to the terms we will use in subsequent chapters for deductive arguments.

One way an inductive argument can be good is by being considered "strong." An inductive argument is said to be **strong** just in case the conclusion is probably true given the premises. In other words, an argument is strong if, whenever all its premises are assumed to be true, the conclusion is unlikely to be false. Because we are using inductive reasoning, the truth of the premises can only make the truth of the conclusion highly probable or likely, but not certain. In other words, the conclusion of a strong argument must follow with probability from its premises.

The strength of an argument concerns the relationship between the premises and the conclusion, and not the actual truth-values of the component statements. The premises do not all have to be true for an argument to be strong. If an argument is strong, this fact does not guarantee that all the premises are true nor that the conclusion is true. This strong inductive argument illustrates this point:

> Most dogs are cold-blooded animals (F).
> Therefore, Lassie is a cold-blooded animal (F).

Even though all the statements in the above argument are false (indicated by the F at the end of the statement), the argument nonetheless is strong. What we can maintain is this: if an inductive argument is strong, then the conclusion is probably true given that all the premises are true. Furthermore, it is important to note that the terms "strong" and "weak" refer to arguments, not to statements. An argument that is intended to be strong, but is not, is considered "weak." Inductive arguments, unlike deductive arguments, will vary in levels of strength and weakness; however, we will learn that deductive arguments are either valid or invalid and have no in-betweens. We say that an inductive argument is strong when the premises provide enough support for us to believe that the conclusion is probably true.

Finally, we call an argument **cogent** if it is strong and all its premises are actually true. Thus, a cogent argument must meet two conditions: (1) the conclusion probably follows from the premises, and (2) all the premises are true. This means that an argument is uncogent if any of its premises are false or if it is weak. From the definition of cogency, it follows that the conclusion of a cogent argument is probably true, and in most instances, the conclusion of a cogent argument will indeed be true.

> Most birds can fly (T). Sparrows are birds (T). Therefore, sparrows can fly.

However, since the conclusion of a cogent argument is only probably true, it is sometimes the case that the conclusion ends up being false. Consider this example of a similar inductive argument; this time the conclusion is false, and yet the argument remains strong and cogent:

> Most birds can fly (T). Ostriches are birds (T). Therefore, ostriches can fly.

This example illustrates an interesting thing about inductive reasoning. Even if all the facts or observations are correct, induction does not guarantee the truth of the conclusion. Inductive reasoning does not deliver certainty, for there is always the possibility that a counterexample can be found. Some philosophers such as David Hume claim that induction ultimately has no rational justification despite its apparent usefulness. Hume is an extreme skeptic, of course, with stringent standards for knowledge. For science, inductive reasoning is a very powerful and useful method employed by researchers who strive for the best hypothesis based on the available evidence. Furthermore, many people of various professions, including scientists, detectives, lawyers, doctors, drivers, and cooks, rely on inductive reasoning in their investigations and everyday decision-making.

There are then three possibilities for inductive arguments: (1) strong, cogent; (2) strong, uncogent; and (3) weak, uncogent. Here are a few more examples to help illustrate the strength and cogency of arguments.

Strong
If all the premises are assumed true, then the conclusion is PROBABLY true.

Cogent
(1) it is a strong argument, and (2) all the premises are true.

Example One (strong, cogent)	**Example Two** (weak, uncogent)
Most Americans speak English. <u>George Clooney is an American.</u> George Clooney speaks English.	Most Americans speak English. <u>Jennifer Lopez is an American.</u> Jennifer Lopez speaks Spanish.
Example Three (strong, uncogent)	**Example Four** (weak, uncogent)
Most Americans speak French. <u>George Clooney is an American.</u> George Clooney speaks French.	Most Americans speak Spanish. <u>Jennifer Lopez speaks Spanish.</u> Jennifer Lopez is an American.

When evaluating an argument as strong or weak, begin by assuming or pretending that all the premises are true. Then ask whether the conclusion would probably be true based on that assumption. A strong argument is one in which the conclusion would probably be true if one pretended that the premises were true. After that, label all weak arguments uncogent. Strong arguments with true premises are cogent, while strong arguments with at least one false premise are uncogent.

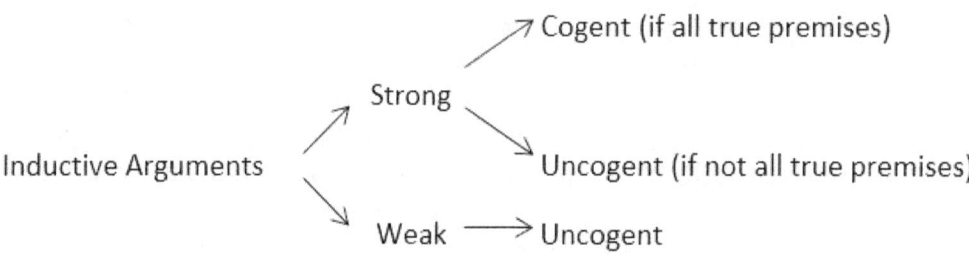

IMG 2.1

Exercise 2-A: Inductive Strength and Cogency

Determine whether the inductive argument is strong or weak, and cogent or uncogent. The truth-values of the premises are indicated in parentheses.

1. Ray Charles and Stevie Wonder are musicians (T). They are both blind (T). This entails that the majority of musicians are blind.
2. The parking enforcement officer told me that the parking meter was out of order (T). So, the meter is probably not working.
3. Sue must have gone to the beach since her swimsuit is wet (T), and her shoes are full of sand (T).
4. The fortune teller looked into her crystal ball and said that I would have a long and happy life (T). Accordingly, a long and happy life is ahead of me.

5. No one would blame a bartender for having a few drinks on the job (T). But an airline pilot is no less a human being than a bartender (T). Therefore, no one should blame an airline pilot for having a few drinks on the job.
6. Lassie, Benji, and Rin Tin Tin are all dogs who have been in the movies (T). Hence, it follows that most dogs are movie stars.
7. My math teacher said that octagons have eight sides (T). Thus, octagons must have eight sides.
8. There are mushrooms growing on my front lawn (F). They look like the kind of mushrooms I buy from the grocery store (T). Therefore, they are probably healthy and delicious to eat.
9. Some dogs have rabies and bite little children (T). Hence, most dogs are dangerous and vicious.
10. The cookies Jan baked are burnt to a crisp (F). She must have left them in the oven too long.
11. Most Europeans are South Americans (F). Jean is European (T). So, Jean is South American.
12. Larry is Joe's friend (F). Joe is Tina's friend (F). It follows that Tina is probably Larry's friend.
13. Kevin is taller than most guys on his basketball team (T). George is on Kevin's basketball team (T). Consequently, Kevin is probably taller than George.
14. Rita is looking at Fred (T). Fred is looking at Jody (T). So, it is likely that Rita is looking at Jody.
15. Ninety-five percent of the people born in Arizona are Native American (F). Joe was born in Arizona (F). So, it is likely that Joe is a Native American.
16. Ninety percent of farm animals are pigs (F). Oliver is a pig (T). So, Oliver is probably a farm animal.
17. Most fish can swim (T). Porcupines are fish (F). So, porcupines can probably swim.
18. Most birds can fly (T). Penguins are birds (T). So, penguins can fly.
19. Most birds can fly (T). Emus can fly (F). So, emus are birds.
20. Most journalists are good writers (T). Bart is a journalist (T). Thus, Bart is likely a good writer.

Exercise 2-B: Types of Inductive Arguments

For the first ten problems of Exercise 2-A, identify the inductive argument form: prediction, argument from authority, causal inference, inductive generalization, or analogy.

Exercise 2-C: True or False Questions

Answer "true" or "false" to the following statements:

1. The question "What time is it?" is a statement.
2. "Five is an even number" is a statement with a truth-value.

3. All statements have a truth-value.
4. An inductive argument must have two premises and one conclusion.
5. A causal inference draws a conclusion about a whole group from a smaller sample.
6. An analogy is a type of inductive argument.
7. All inductive generalizations are strong arguments.
8. Some arguments from authority can be weak.
9. All cogent inductive arguments are strong.
10. All strong arguments have a true conclusion.
11. A cogent argument may have a false conclusion.
12. A strong argument may be uncogent.
13. A weak argument must be uncogent.
14. A statement may legitimately be spoken of as "strong" or "weak."
15. A statement may legitimately be spoken of as "true" or "false."
16. An argument may legitimately be spoken of as "true" or "false."
17. An inductive argument with false premises must be uncogent.
18. A strong argument must have true premises.
19. A cogent argument must have true premises.
20. An inductive argument with true premises and a true conclusion must be strong.
21. An inductive argument with false premises and a false conclusion must be weak.
22. Even the best inductive argument cannot guarantee the truth of its conclusion.
23. All causal inferences are weak inductive arguments.
24. Some predictions are strong inductive arguments.
25. All uncogent arguments are weak arguments.

Fallacies of Weak Induction

While inductive arguments can be strong, some are weak. There are weak arguments from authority, causal inferences, generalizations, and analogies. These weak arguments are so prevalent that they are labeled by a certain fallacy name. A fallacy is a defect or error in reasoning. In the following section, we will identify fallacies of weak induction.

Appeal to Unqualified Authority justifies a claim by pointing to an alleged expert in the subject matter at hand. An appeal to authority can make for a strong argument if the person, book, or group named as the authority is a credible source. Sometimes, it is reasonable to believe someone's claim if that person is a legitimate and reliable expert on the issue who appears to have no ulterior motives. We might also disbelieve a claim because we suspect that the person saying it is unreliable. The credibility of sources is usually a matter of their expertise on the one hand, and their truthfulness and objectivity on the other.

Even eyewitness testimony is subject to scrutiny. Before accepting the reports of eyewitnesses, you must judge the accuracy of the observations, how good their memory is, and the trustworthiness of the witnesses. Judging the expertise of one's sources also involves factoring in her level of education, training, expertise, reputation, and experience. Of course, all sources lose credibility when there is reason to suspect them of bias. Bias can arise when the source has something to gain personally or financially or has special interests to protect. It is also important to consider whether the subject matter is one with which the experts in the field disagree, or perhaps it is a subject for which there is no one expert, as may occur in fields such as political science or religion. In this case, citing one particular source or many sources may not be sufficient.

> My workout trainer urges me to drink kombucha, for he says it will give me energy. So, it has to be true.

Closely associated with unqualified authority is the problem of misplacing the burden of proof (**Shifting the Burden of Proof**). This fallacy occurs when one places the burden of proof on the wrong party or places the burden of proof more heavily on one side than it should be. Generally, the burden of proof rests with the person who is making a controversial or implausible claim. For example, if you claim that a ghost lives in your attic or that you levitate when you do yoga, the burden would be on you to provide support or evidence for these extremely dubious claims. Thus, you would commit shifting the burden of proof:

> Of course, I levitate whenever I do the Sleeping Swan yoga pose. Can you prove I don't?

A special type of burden of proof fallacy is called an **Appeal to Ignorance**. This is the view that an absence of evidence *against* a claim counts as evidence *for* that claim. This fallacy attributes truth to a claim that has not been proven to be false. Conversely, such an argument may assume that a claim is false because it has not yet been proven true. Nonetheless, lack of proof does not establish either the truth or falsity of a claim. The critical thinker in the absence of proof should suspend judgment.

> Since there is no proof that life exists in the Andromeda galaxy, we should conclude there is no life in that galaxy.

False Cause occurs when an unlikely causal connection is drawn between events or circumstances. We will distinguish several subvarieties of the false cause fallacy:

Post Hoc Ergo Propter Hoc (also called Coincidental Correlation). This fallacy's name in Latin means "after this; therefore, because of this." Post hoc fallacies occur when the arguer arbitrarily attributes a cause-and-effect relationship between two events, simply because one event happened after the other. Yet, just because one thing follows another does not mean that the one is the cause of the other.

> I see that the right headlight of my car has burned out. I had lent my car to my friend, Rudy, and he was the last person to drive the car. So, he must have done something to burn out my headlight!

Wrong Direction (Reversing Cause and Effect). In this type of false cause fallacy, the relation between cause and effect is reversed. For example, someone might argue that having lung cancer causes a person to smoke heavily when in fact it is the reverse. In this quote by Bertrand Russell, he suggests a wrong direction fallacy has occurred.

> The man who is unhappy will, as a rule, adopt an unhappy creed, while the man who is happy will adopt a happy creed; each may attribute his happiness or unhappiness to his beliefs, while the real causation is the other way round.

Oversimplified Cause (Complex Cause) identifies only one of a number of causes that together bring about an effect. The fallacy of oversimplified cause ignores other causal factors and the complexity of the situation. For example, a student might do well on an exam and attribute the cause to buying a new laptop. This oversimplifies the situation by leaving out the influence of attending class, going to office hours, reading the text, studying with friends, etc.

Slippery Slope (or Wedge Argument) fallacies suppose a chain of events that starts off with a seemingly innocent step and snowballs into some disastrous end. You can think of a slippery slope as a sequence of causal inferences, with event A leading to B, B to C, C to D, etc., until, eventually, some undesirable event occurs. The structure of the slippery slope fallacy is deductively valid. For if A implies B, B implies C, and C is undesirable, then you have produced an argument against A. What makes slippery slope fallacious is that the chain of events is an unlikely one in which one or more causal connections are weak. Benjamin Franklin commits a slippery slope in the following famous passage:

> For want of a nail the shoe was lost; for want of a shoe the horse was lost; for want of a horse the rider was lost; for want of a rider the battle was lost; for want of a battle the kingdom was lost; and all for want of a horseshoe nail.

The **Gambler's Fallacy** is also a weak causal inference. This fallacious reasoning is based on the belief that past random occurrences influence the next occurrence. It is believed that, in order to reach predicted ratios, the next events have to "catch up." The gambler's fallacy occurs often in nongambling contexts. You might think, "We've had four boys in a row. The next child is more likely to be a girl." Although large samples do tend to produce the numbers one expects, those numbers do not influence any particular event. Each time is a new flip of the coin, a new toss of the dice. Previous tosses have no causal effect on future ones.

Hasty Generalization draws a conclusion based on a biased or insufficient sample. The size of the sample may be too small to support the conclusion, not representative of the population as a whole, or is an exception to the rule. In a hasty generalization, the premise states that some subset X has a known property p. The conclusion drawn is that a larger set Y (which contains X) must also have the property p. Some generalizations can be strong arguments when we are extrapolating from a large and randomly selected sample. However, when we draw inferences from just a few cases, we run the danger of presenting merely anecdotal evidence that does not accurately reflect the larger population. Hasty generalizations can also be the source of unwarranted and harmful stereotypes against whole groups based on the behavior of some of their members. The following are examples of hasty generalization

Fred, the Australian, stole my wallet. Thus, all Australians are thieves.

I asked a few of my friends whether they liked the new T-shirts I designed. They all thought that the pink aardvark logo was really cool. So, it will be a huge hit at the swap meet!

A **Weak Analogy** is a fallacy based on the comparison of two objects that are shown to be similar. Then it is argued that since X has property p, Y also must have property p. An argument from analogy follows this pattern: We know that X has certain properties (a, b, c, etc.). We also know that Y has some of the same properties as X, and thus X and Y are similar in certain respects. Additionally, X is not a subset of Y. Furthermore, we happen to know that X has some additional property p. Because of these three premises, the argument concludes that Y also has the additional property p. The inference rests on the idea that if X and Y are similar in some ways, they must be similar in other ways as well. An analogy fails when X and Y are different in a way that affects whether they both have property p.

> Ben and Harry are death-defying tightrope walkers who work for the circus. Ben joined the army when he was 21. So, Harry must have joined the army when he was 21 too.
> Tigers and horses have four legs and a tail. They both can run faster than a human. Horses like to eat carrots. Consequently, tigers are carrot-loving animals.

To recognize a weak analogy, consider the set of properties the two objects or events have in common. Then show how the properties they share do not affect whether they have the property in question. Another strategy is to show how the two things have relevant differences. Arguments from analogy can be very useful when discussing a complex issue, including those involved in ethical discussion. Strong analogies may help open new ways of seeing things or coming to an agreement on a new and confusing situation. Yet, weak analogies abound, and the critical thinker must use caution when attributing unknown properties to a thing based on its alleged similarities to other things we happen to be more familiar with.

Exercise 2-D: Fallacies of Weak Induction

Identify the fallacy committed in each argument. In a few cases, more than one fallacy may apply. Fallacy list: appeal to unqualified authority, shifting the burden of proof, appeal to ignorance, false cause, slippery slope, gambler's fallacy, weak analogy, and hasty generalization.

1. Logic should be banned from college courses. For when people study logic, they begin to think logically about things. After a while, they are less swayed by emotions and feelings and more by "cool" reason. Soon they will eliminate emotions and feelings from their lives. Before you know it, they are cold and uncaring, and are incapable of sympathy, caring, and love.
2. Sure, babysitting is nothing to worry about. It's just like taking care of a puppy. If you have plenty of snacks and don't mind cleaning up after it, then it's a breeze!

3. You can't prove definitely that violence in the media has a direct effect on people's actual behavior. Therefore, we should conclude that people's actions are not affected at all by the violence they watch on television and in the movies.
4. Buying car insurance is like throwing money in the trash. I work too hard for my money to throw it away in the trash. So, I'd be crazy to buy car insurance!
5. Last week, a philosophy student told me that she did not believe in truth. So, this leads me to believe that anyone who studies philosophy does not believe in truth.
6. Senator Rudman has a "pizza theory" of how to resolve a deadlock in a debate. He observed that in his committee, budget negotiators were stalled for five hours. However, after Rep. Aspin had pizza delivered, they reached an agreement in 20 minutes. Accordingly, Senator Rudman has concluded that bringing in a pizza will resolve a deadlock.
7. Joe's therapist put Joe on Prozac, and it made him happy and improved his self-image. Shortly after Lisa began taking it, her depression disappeared, and she could return to work. Also, Prozac gave Karen a new lease on life. Clearly, Prozac can work wonders for everyone.
8. Ms. Peters, who owns a baby blanket factory, claims that her largest competitor, Fuzzywuzzy, manufactures flammable blankets that pose a hazard to their users. Given Ms. Peter's knowledge of blankets, we must conclude that Fuzzywuzzy manufactures a dangerous product, and we should shut the factory down immediately.
9. After John returned from work the other day, he switched on his air conditioner, and a few seconds later, a power failure struck the city. Therefore, to prevent power failures, John should keep his air conditioner shut off.
10. Eating steak is like eating a dead animal carcass. Therefore, no one should ever eat steak.
11. My brother, who is a huge Pistons fan, said that the Detroit Pistons are going to win the NBA championship this year. So, the Detroit Pistons are going to win the NBA championship this year.
12. The women factory workers have asked that we adopt a policy of maternity leave. But if we grant this request, the men will then ask for spousal leave. The next thing you know, they will want time off for golf and fishing, and then the women will want the same thing for shopping, cooking, and social hours. In the end, no one will be working at all, and the factory will shut down. Clearly, this request must be denied.
13. Wendi taught herself to read when she was only three, and Connie and Mark did the same at age four. Obviously, everyone can teach themselves to read. Let's eliminate grade schools!
14. If you join the US Army, then you'll start smoking cigarettes. If you start smoking cigarettes, then you will want a drink with your cigarettes. If you start drinking, then you will start doing meth. So, if you join the US Army, you'll end up doing meth. So, it's not a good idea to join the US Army.
15. A few minutes after Governor Harrison finished his speech on television, a devastating earthquake struck southern Alaska. For the safety of the people up there, it is imperative that Governor Harrison makes no more speeches.

16. I'm sure to hit the jackpot with this slot machine; no one has won with it in the last 500 tries.
17. The first frat guy I met was a jerk who partied constantly and was completely apathetic toward his grades. I will never choose to hang out with another frat boy, as they are only concerned with partying and don't try in school.
18. A cocker spaniel is a friendly little dog, and no one should be afraid to pet one. But a pit bull terrier is no less of a dog than a cocker spaniel. So, no one should be afraid to pet a pit bull terrier.
19. Terry Olds testified at trial that she clearly recognized the defendant as the person who struck her on the head with a pickax. On this evidence, we must conclude that the defendant is guilty, even though Terry has had total amnesia ever since her injury.
20. We don't have proof that taking vitamins actually improves a person's health. So, we can conclude that vitamins are simply a waste of money.
21. I really am the best candidate for the job. Unless you prove otherwise, you'll have to hire me.
22. After Florida relaxed its concealed weapons law, the crime rate dropped. Clearly, allowing people to carry concealed weapons results in a reduction in crime.
23. Same-sex marriages should never be licensed by the state. If these arrangements are licensed, they will become an attractive alternative to heterosexual marriage. Married couples will start abandoning their spouses and link up with same-sex partners. Before long, everyone will adopt this lifestyle, and no one will have any more kids. The extinction of the human race will follow soon thereafter.
24. McGuire is bound to hit a home run today because he's not had a single hit in a whole month.
25. What is taught on this campus should depend entirely on what students are interested in. After all, consuming knowledge is like consuming anything in our society. The teacher is the seller; the student is the buyer. Buyers determine what they want to buy, so students should determine what they want to learn.
26. Congressman Jenkins violated campaign regulations; Senator Meadows bends to special interest; Governor Stanton has accepted bribes. It should be clear to everyone that politicians these days are totally rotten.
27. If Mrs. Worthington, ukulele enthusiast and three-time winner of the Louisiana gumbo taste test, says that celery juice will make you look younger, well that's enough for me! I'll be drinking celery juice by the gallon!
28. Of course, leprechauns own pots of gold. Can you show me they don't?
29. That man over there is wearing baggy clothing and has tattoos all over his arms and neck. I bet he is a violent gang member!
30. Joining the military is just like joining a big fraternity. Both groups consist of guys who have common goals and share similar interests. Military guys, just like frat brothers, want to hang out, tell stories, and drink beer. Since you had great fun in your college fraternity, you probably will enjoy being in the military.

Paley and the Teleological Argument

The following excerpt is an example of an inductive argument written by the eighteenth-century British philosopher William Paley. Paley offers one famous version of the Teleological Argument, which argues for the existence of God. The term "teleological" derives from the Greek word "telos" meaning phenomena exhibiting design, order, or purpose. This argument is also commonly referred to as the "Watchmaker Argument" or "Argument by Design."

1. The universe is like a watch (e.g., design, complexity, order, purpose).
2. A watch is created by an intelligent designer.
3. The universe is more complex and gigantic than a watch.
4. Therefore, the universe was probably created by an even more powerful and vastly intelligent nonhuman designer, i.e., God.

The Teleological Argument is categorized as *a posteriori* because some of its premises depend on empirical data gathered from our knowledge of the world. The reasoning Paley employs is inductive as he attempts to prove the probable existence of God by means of analogy and causal inference. Paley argued that we can know with probability that God exists from our experience of the world and how things work. We have observed complex things such as watches and know that these are made by intelligent designers—namely, watchmakers. According to Paley, if one looks at the universe, one finds an even greater order and complexity, which suggests the existence of a powerful, intelligent creator, God. Paley concludes that God is most likely the cause of the order and design of the universe. This excerpt is taken from his book written in 1800 called *Natural Theology*.

Natural Theology

By William Paley

In crossing a heath, suppose I hit my foot against a *stone*. Suppose I were asked how the stone came to be there. I might possibly answer that, for anything I knew to the contrary, it had lain there forever. It would be difficult to show that this answer is absurd.

But suppose I had found a *watch* upon the ground, and it should be asked how the *watch* happened to be in that place. I should hardly think of the answer which I had before given—that for anything I knew the watch might have *always* been there—would be an acceptable answer.

Yet why should not this answer serve for the watch as well as for the stone? Why is it not as admissible in the second case as in the first? For this reason, and for no other: namely, that when we come to inspect the watch, we perceive—what we could not discover in the stone—that its several parts are framed and put together for a *purpose*. The parts are so formed and adjusted as to produce motion, and that motion so regulated as to point out the hour of the day. If the different parts had been differently shaped from what they are, of a different size from

William Paley, *Natural Theology; Or, Evidences of the Existence and Attributes of the Deity*, 1809.

what they are, or placed after any other manner or in any other order than that in which they are placed, either no motion at all would have been carried on in the machine, or none which would have answered the use that is now served by it.

To reckon up a few of the plainest of these parts and of their offices, all tending to one result, we see a cylindrical box containing a coiled elastic spring, which, by its endeavor to relax itself, turns round the box. We next observe a flexible chain—artificially wrought for the sake of flexure—communicating the action of the spring from the box to the fuse. We then find a series of wheels, the teeth of which catch in and apply to each other, conducting the motion from the fuse to the balance and from the balance to the pointer, and at the same time, by the size and shape of those wheels, so regulating that motion as to terminate in causing an index, by an equable and measured progression, to pass over a given space in a given time. We take notice that the wheels are made of brass, in order to keep them from rust; the springs of steel, no other metal being so elastic; that over the face of the watch there is placed a glass, a material employed in no other part of the work, but in the room of which, if there had been any other than a transparent substance, the hour could not be seen without opening the case. This mechanism being observed—it requires indeed an examination of the instrument, and perhaps some previous knowledge of the subject, to perceive and understand it; but being once, as we have said, observed and understood—the *inference we think is inevitable, that the watch must have had a maker-that there must have existed, at some time and at some place or other, an artificer or artificers who formed it for the purpose which we find it actually to answer, who comprehended its construction and designed its use.*

I

It wouldn't, I think, weaken the conclusion *that the watch had a maker* if we had never seen a watch made, if we had never known an artist capable of making one, if we were altogether incapable of executing such a piece of workmanship ourselves, or if we did not understanding the details of how watches are made (suppose watchmaking was a lost ancient art, or that it was, to most of humanity, one of the more curious productions of modern manufacture). Does one man in a million know how oval frames are turned? Ignorance of this kind exalts our opinion of the unseen and unknown artist's skiff, if he be unseen and unknown, but raises no doubt in our minds of the existence and agency of such an artist, at some former time and in some place or other. Nor can I perceive that it varies at all the inference *that the watch has a maker*, whether the question arise concerning a human agent or concerning an agent of a different species, or an agent possessing in some respects a different nature.

II

Neither, secondly, would it invalidate our conclusion, that the watch sometimes went wrong or that it seldom went exactly right. The purpose of the machinery, the design, and the designer might be evident, and in the case supposed, would be evident, in whatever way we accounted for the irregularity of the movement, or whether we could account for it or not. It is not necessary that a machine be perfect in order to show with what design it was made: still less necessary, where the only question is whether it were made with any design at all ...

Exercise 2-E: Reading Questions on Paley's *Natural Theology*

1. In your own words, what are the premises and conclusion of Paley's Teleological Argument?
2. Why is Paley's argument classified as inductive?
3. Is Paley's argument a posteriori? Why or why not?
4. Why has Paley's argument been named "teleological"?
5. What two things did Paley imagine finding on the ground?
6. What do you think of the strength and cogency of Paley's argument?
7. According to Paley, would it weaken his conclusion that a person may have never seen a watchmaker or never known anyone capable of making a watch? Why or why not?
8. What factors, claims Paley, would not invalidate his conclusion or bring uncertainty to his argument?

Hume and the Problem of Induction

By Dustin Gray

David Hume is an eighteenth-century Scottish philosopher (1711–1776) who is known especially for his philosophical theories of empiricism and skepticism. As an empiricist, Hume claimed that all our beliefs are ultimately derived from experience. According to Hume, we experience two kinds of perceptions. The first are *impressions* which include desires, emotions, and sensations such as the sensation of cold, red, bitter, sharp, wet, etc. The second category of perceptions is *ideas*, which are copies of impressions experienced upon reflection. Ideas are less lively, less vivid, and less reliable than the original impressions which they reflect. For example, the memory of a broken arm is an idea that is less vivid and less forceful than the impression, the sharp pain you felt the moment you broke your arm.

As a skeptic, Hume claimed that we can never know anything about the world with certainty. We cannot prove that any of our beliefs are necessarily true, and even inductive reasoning is problematic for Hume. This is because inductive reasoning makes predictions or draws inferences about unobserved things based on what we have observed. However, Hume argues that induction assumes, without justification, that the future will resemble the past or that the nature of the world is uniform. We engage in inductive reasoning every day. Even in attempting to start your car, you might think, "My car will start when I turn the key." After all, that is what has happened nearly every time you attempted to start the car in the past. Yet, Hume cautions that we cannot predict that the car will start again when you turn the key regardless of how many times the car has done so in the past.

Hume is skeptical that we can arrive at probable truths by means of inductive generalizations, predictions, or causal arguments. With respect to causation, we might observe two events A and B such that whenever A occurs B follows. Observing this correlation between events A and B, we might think that A is the cause of B. We might draw the causal inference that there is a necessary connection between A and B, that event A will *always* precede event B. This belief in causation comes from habit or custom. Hume maintains that we can offer no reasonable grounds for such causal inferences.

Despite his extreme skepticism, Hume advises that we proceed with our daily lives as if it's business as usual. To maintain a "normal" productive life, Hume recommends that we continue to reason inductively. In fact, our minds and the force of habit won't allow us to do otherwise. We cannot help but make predictions, draw cause-effect relationships, believe in the existence of the external world, and posit the unity of the self. Nevertheless, we should realize that we have no rational justification for our inductive reasoning.

An Enquiry Concerning Human Understanding

By David Hume

1. All the colors of poetry, however splendid, can never paint natural objects in such a manner as to make the description be taken for a real landscape. The most lively thought is still inferior to the dullest sensation.
2. We may divide all the perceptions of the mind into two classes or species ... The less forcible and lively are commonly denominated *Thoughts* or *Ideas*. The other species ... let us ... call them *Impressions* ... I mean all our more lively perceptions when we hear, or see, or feel, or love, or hate, or desire, or will.
3. After the constant conjunction of two objects—heat and flame, for instance, weight and solidity—we are determined by custom to expect the one from the appearance of the other.
4. All inferences from experience ... are effects of custom, not of reasoning.
5. Custom ... is the great guide of human life. It is that principle alone which renders our experience useful to us, and makes us expect, for the future, a similar train of events with those which have appeared in the past.
6. There appears not, throughout all nature, any one instance of connection which is conceivable by us. All events seem entirely loose and separate. One event follows another, but we never can observe any tie between them. They seem *conjoined*, but never *connected*. And as we can have no idea of anything which never appeared to our sense or inward sentiment, the necessary conclusion seems to be that we have no idea of connection or power at all, and that these words are absolutely without any meaning, when employed either in philosophical reasonings or common life.

David Hume, *An Enquiry Concerning Human Understanding*, Clarendon Press, 1902.

7. Our idea ... of necessity and causation arises entirely from the uniformity observable in the operations of nature, where similar objects are constantly conjoined together, and the mind is determined by custom to infer the one from the appearance of the other.
8. Beyond the constant *conjunction* of similar objects, and the consequent *inference* from one to the other, we have no notion of necessity or connection.
9. Tis evident that all reasonings concerning matter of fact are founded on the relation of cause and effect, and that we can never infer the existence of one object from another, unless they be connected together, either mediately or immediately ... Here is a billiard ball lying on the table, and another ball moving toward it with rapidity. They strike; and the ball which was formerly at rest now acquires a motion. This is as perfect an instance of the relation of cause and effect as any which we know, either by sensation or reflection (*An Abstract on A Thesis on Human Nature*).
10. It is universally allowed that nothing exists without a cause of its existence ... But it is pretended that some causes are necessary, some not necessary. Here then is the advantage of definitions. Let anyone define a cause, without comprehending, as a part of the definition, a necessary connection with its effect; and let him show distinctly the origin of the idea, expressed by the definition; and I shall readily give up the whole controversy. But if the foregoing explication of the matter be received, this must be absolutely impracticable. Had not objects a regular conjunction with each other, we should never have entertained any notion of cause and effect; and this regular conjunction produces that inference of the understanding, which is the only connection, that we can have any comprehension of. Whoever attempts a definition of cause, exclusive of these circumstances, will be obliged either to employ unintelligible terms or such as are synonymous to the term which he endeavors to define.

Exercise 2-F: Reading Questions on Hume's *Enquiry*

1. How does Hume distinguish impressions from ideas? What examples does he give to explain the difference?
2. What causes us to draw inferences from our experience and expect that the future will be just like the past?
3. Between two events, can we know if there is a necessary causal connection? Explain.
4. What objects does Hume mention to be "as perfect an instance of the relation of cause and effect" as we have experienced?
5. What do the terms "skepticism" and "empiricism" mean?
6. Given the problem of induction, does Hume recommend that people hold beliefs based on causal inferences or predictions? Why or why not?

CHAPTER 3

Writing with Clarity

> In Chapter 3, we will focus on avoiding vagueness and ambiguity when communicating arguments. Toward this end, we will learn how to recognize common fallacies of ambiguity and how to define our terms in clear and precise ways. After completing the chapter, readers will be able to
>
> - identify fallacies of ambiguity,
> - differentiate specific types of denotative and connotative definitions,
> - compare broad versus narrow definitions,
> - understand rhetorical devices and loaded language, and
> - analyze logical reasoning in passages of Hume's *Dialogues*.

To clearly communicate arguments, we should take the time to define our key terms and concepts. We also should carefully choose our words to avoid ambiguity and vagueness. Whereas a **vague** claim is one that lacks precision, a claim is **ambiguous** if it can have more than one meaning without having to depend on the context. A claim is said to be semantically ambiguous if its multiple meanings are due to the ambiguity of a word or phrase.

Because of semantic ambiguities, people can fall prey to the informal fallacy of **equivocation**. An informal fallacy is a defect or error in reasoning that can be found by analyzing the content of the argument or the meaning of the words. Equivocations occur when parts of a claim, such as a specific word or phrase, can have multiple possible meanings. For example, the claim that "the burrito is really hot" can be ambiguous because the word "hot" can be interpreted as describing either the temperature or the spice level of the burrito. To avoid equivocations, we should stay clear of ambiguous terms or define our terms precisely. Also, in our writing, we ought to be consistent with our use of terms so that we do not shift from one meaning to another.

Another kind of semantic ambiguity is a grouping ambiguity. A **grouping ambiguity** occurs when it is unclear whether a word refers to the individuals in a group or to the group as a whole. Consider the statement: "The middle class pays more taxes than the upper class in this country." Should we interpret the terms "middle class" and "upper class" as referring to individuals?

That is, each individual from the middle class pays more taxes than an individual from the upper class. Alternatively, we could interpret the terms as referring to the groups collectively. More likely, the statement intends to say that the middle class collectively pays more taxes than the upper class because the middle class is so much larger than the upper class. As a group, the middle class has more members paying taxes, so collectively the sum total of middle-class taxes is greater than the total paid by the few upper-class citizens.

In contrast to semantic ambiguities, there are syntactic ambiguities. A syntactic ambiguity is due to faulty sentence structure or syntax. A syntactic ambiguity can lead to the informal fallacy of **amphiboly** because the interpreter cannot decide the meaning of a claim although the meaning of each individual word is clear. Groucho Marx once joked,

> One morning I shot an elephant in my pajamas. How he got into my pajamas I'll never know.

This is an example of an amphiboly because the faulty sentence structure causes the ambiguity, yet we are not confused about the meaning of every single word. The dangling modifier is "in my pajamas." This phrase should be placed next to the pronoun "I," which it modifies instead of next to "elephant." Amphibolies may result from problematic word order, lack of punctuation, ambiguous modifiers, or ambiguous pronouns. The following is an amphiboly due to an ambiguous pronoun:

> Before leaving for college, Sam said farewell to his mother and girlfriend. Sam promised that he would visit his hometown as often as he could and would write to *her* every day.

"Her" is the ambiguous pronoun, as it is unclear whether it refers to his mother or his girlfriend. To remedy most syntactic ambiguities, we need to rewrite the whole sentence to allow for the one intended interpretation.

Closely related to grouping ambiguity is the informal fallacy of **composition.** In a composition, we have the mistaken belief that what holds true of things individually must hold true of them collectively. This occurs if we were to conclude that a dress sewn from the finest cloth must be the finest dress. With the fallacy of composition, because the parts have a certain property, it is argued that the whole has that property. However, a property that applies to the parts or to individual members may not be transferable to the whole thing or to the collection. Some examples illustrate composition:

> This Little League team has the best pitcher, catcher, and short stop in the country.
> So, it must be the best team in the country.
> The atoms of the table are invisible to the naked eye. Hence, the table must be invisible.

Sometimes, a property that applies to the parts also applies to the whole. Such is the case with the statement: "Every picket of this fence is white; therefore, the picket fence is white." This statement does not commit the fallacy of composition.

In contrast, the fallacy of **division** takes a property that is true of the whole or group and applies it to the parts.

> This Little League team is the best in the country. So, its pitcher must be the best in the country.
>
> The pizza pie is circular. It follows that every slice of the pizza is round.

Although the team taken collectively is the best, its pitcher may not be ranked as the best. Similarly, circular pizzas are usually sliced across the middle, leaving us with triangular-shaped slices. In the fallacy of division, we must be careful not to attribute the properties of the whole to its component parts. It should be apparent that composition and division are basically the flip sides of one another. We can rework the previous examples of composition, and by reversing the conclusion and premise, we create examples of division.

Exercise 3-A: Fallacies of Ambiguity

Identify the fallacy of ambiguity: equivocation, amphiboly, grouping ambiguity, composition, division.

1. Moby Dick is a long novel. Therefore, its author, Herman Melville must have used very long words.
2. Jane: I told my dad and little brother that I want to go to Las Vegas for the weekend. *He* said *he* would seriously consider it. I am hoping *he* will let me go!

   Scott: That's weird! Why does your little brother get to decide where you can go?
3. Police officers save more lives than firefighters.
4. Each of the parts of this airplane is very light. So, the airplane itself is very light.
5. This chocolate cake is very sweet. Thus, the ingredients that went into the cake such as eggs, flour, and baking soda must all be very sweet.
6. My house is closer to Grandma's house than my uncle's house.
7. My psychiatrist told me I was crazy, and I said I want a second opinion. He said okay you're ugly, too. (Rodney Dangerfield)
8. In this village, camels transport more crops than elephants.
9. Rita said that after she removed the gift wrapping from her birthday presents, she threw *them* into the trash bin. Apparently, she did not appreciate her gifts if she threw them away.
10. Water can quench your thirst. Therefore, its two components, hydrogen and oxygen, can quench your thirst.
11. The sign read, "Wanted: Man to take care of cow that does not smoke or drink." How odd! A cow certainly does not smoke but must take a drink sometime.
12. Betty spends more money on rings than necklaces.

13. Each member of this English class has a Social Security number. Therefore, the English class has a Social Security number.
14. Jan's boyfriend is a *shrimp*. But if he's a shrimp then he is a crustacean that belongs in the sea.
15. Wendy: I have a photo of Brad Pitt on my bed.

    Bert: I don't believe it! What would Brad Pitt be doing on your bed?
16. My wife's jealousy is getting ridiculous. The other day, she looked at my calendar and wanted to know who "May" was.
17. I like sports cars more than my girlfriend.
18. Everything in the universe has a cause. Therefore, the universe has a cause.
19. In this neighborhood, coyotes kill more pets than bobcats.
20. Jim: Weren't you planning to ask out the girl from chemistry class?

    Dex: Yeah, I did but she said she could not go out with me because she had *class*. What a stuck-up snob! She thinks she is too *classy* to go out with the likes of me!

Definitions

Vagueness is different from ambiguity, although both are impediments to clarity and an obstacle to effective argumentation. As we have already mentioned, a vague claim lacks precision and is excessively inexact. In ordinary speech, we often cannot help but use vague terms, but in our writing, we should strive to be more precise. The term "good" for example is vague when describing subjects such as moral agents, the weather, friends, arguments, etc. In later chapters, we will learn how to be more precise about evaluating an argument. Instead of assessing an argument as good, we will specify how the argument is valid, sound, strong, or cogent. Instead of saying that someone's reasoning is "bad," we will identify the exact problem as appeal to pity, straw man, slippery slope, hasty generalization, weak analogy, or a number of other fallacies. In doing so, we will avoid vagueness.

To effectively communicate an argument, we might start by making sure our terms are clear. When delivering our arguments, we should make sure that our language is free from ambiguity and vagueness. The most persuasive arguments are those that are easy to understand because of organized and clear communication. We can avoid problems with clarity by defining key terms from the start. Depending on the topic and the terms upon which an argument hinges, we can choose from a myriad number of ways to define our terms.

We can also be more precise with our meaning by defining our terms from the start. One group of definitions is categorized as **denotative definitions**. When we ask what a given word denotes, we are asking for a list of the things to which the word applies. Denotative definitions pick out the members of the class that a given term denotes. One type of denotative definition is an **enumerative definition**. An enumerative definition identifies individual members or specific instances of a term. For example, we could define "dog" as Lassie, Toto, and Benji. The name "Lassie" picks out one unique and single dog. Another type of denotative definition is **definition by subclass,** which names smaller classes or subgroups contained in the larger class being defined. For example, "dog" means collies, terriers, and pit bulls. Definitions by subclass do not pick out individual members; there are several members within the subclass collies, whereas Lassie is one instance of a dog. Denotative definitions are sometimes referred to as definitions by example.

> **Definitions for "Canine"**
> - comes from Latin word "canis" meaning dog
> - my neighbor's dog named Taquito
> - man's best friend
> - dog
> - a domesticated animal resembling a wolf
> - beagles and poodles

There are also **connotative definitions**. Connotative definitions name the qualities or properties that a term connotes or implies. One type of connotative definition is a synonymous definition. A **synonymous definition** is a single word that has the same intentional meaning as the word being defined. For example, "round" means circular, or "feline" means cat. The words "round" and "circular" can be used interchangeably in most contexts and thus are synonymous. A second type of connotative definition is an **etymological definition,** which refers to the root meaning of the word according to the language from which the term is originally derived. For example, the word "philosophy" derives from the Greek words *philo* and *sophia* meaning love of wisdom. A third type of denotative definition is an **analytical definition**. "Precipitation" is water that reaches the earth's surface from the atmosphere as the result of meteorological causes. The preceding sentence is an analytical definition that specifies (a) the type of thing (the genus) the term applies to, and (b) the difference (differentia) between the things the term applies to and other things of the same type (species).

While we may choose to define our terms in a few of these different ways, one type of definition to avoid is persuasive definitions. A **persuasive definition** is value-laden and intended to arouse either positive or negative emotions. Persuasive definitions are widely used by advertisers to sell their products or by politicians to disparage the opposing side. For example, Wheaties is defined by commercials as "the breakfast of champions." To defend his political ideology, Winston Churchill disparaged "socialism" as "the philosophy of failure, the creed of ignorance and the gospel of envy." While it may prove effective in sales and politics, we generally ought to avoid emotionally charged definitions when we define our terms. When writing about a controversial issue, it is best to use neutral language and stick to definitions that are mutually acceptable to all parties.

A good definition should pick out all and only those things to which a term applies. A definition may be too **broad** if it includes things that it shouldn't. For example, consider the definition "a means of transportation" for the term "automobile." This would be a definition that is too broad because it could include skateboards, bicycles, trains, planes, etc. For, these things fit the definition since they are means of transportation, but you would not call them "automobiles."

Another problem with definitions is that they can be too narrow. A **narrow** definition excludes items that should belong to the class of things denoted by the term. Defining an "artist" as someone who can draw or paint leaves out some types of artists, including sculptors, graphic designers, composers, etc.

In Plato's dialogue, *The Meno*, a definition of virtue is offered which is both too broad and too narrow. The definition of "virtue" offered by Meno is "the power of ruling others." Can you think of how this definition is too broad because it includes people who are not virtuous? That is, can you think of someone who rules others but is not virtuous? How might this definition be narrow? Are there virtuous people who do not have the power to rule others?

Exercise 3-B: Kinds of Definition

Identify the kind of definition (enumerative, subclass, synonymous, etymological, analytical, and persuasive). The term being defined is enclosed by quotation marks.

1. "Beverages" are coffees, teas, sodas, and beers.
2. An "appeaser" is one who feeds a crocodile, hoping it will eat him last. (Churchill)
3. "Teleological" comes from the Greek word "telos" meaning order, design, or purpose.
4. Pitchers, quarterbacks, and gymnasts are "athletes."
5. "Enormous" means big, large, or gigantic.
6. A "square" is a rectangle with four equal sides.
7. Atlanta, Nashville, and Sacramento are "state capitals."
8. "Affluent" means rich, wealthy, or well-off.
9. "Faith" is not wanting to know what is true. (Friedrich Nietzsche)
10. Spoons and forks are "utensils."
11. "Primary colors" are red, blue, and yellow.
12. A "marathon" is a long-distance race.
13. "Carpe diem" originates from the Latin words meaning seize the day.
14. "Furniture" means tables, chairs, beds, and sofas.
15. "Humorous" means funny and hilarious.
16. "Artists" include Michelangelo, Raphael, Picasso, and da Vinci.
17. A "fetus" is an innocent unborn person with a right to life.
18. "Novels" are *Moby Dick*, *Grapes of Wrath,* and *Jane Eyre*.
19. "Caffeinated drinks" are beverages that contain stimulants.
20. A "banker" is a fellow who lends you his umbrella when the sun is shining but wants it back the minute it begins to rain. (Mark Twain)
21. "Intractable" means not easily governed, obstinate, unruly, not disposed to being taught.
22. "Diadem" means an ornamental headband worn as a badge of royalty.
23. "Fastidious" means fussy.
24. "Stalagmites" are rock formations that rise from the floor of a cave.
25. Barbra Streisand and Celine Dion are "singers."

Exercise 3-C: Broad and Narrow Definitions

Determine whether the definition is too broad, too narrow, or both.

1. A "bachelor" is an unmarried person.
2. A "doctor" is a person who has earned an advanced medical degree.
3. A "human" is a being with ten fingers and ten toes.
4. A "chair" is a piece of furniture that you sit on.
5. "Toys" are things that children play with.
6. "Virtue" is the power of governing. (In *The Meno* by Plato)

For problems 7–10, please write your own definitions for these terms:

7. A broad definition for "birds."
8. A narrow definition for "criminal."
9. A broad definition for "natural disasters."
10. A narrow definition for "teacher."

Hume and the Problem of Evil

Scottish philosopher David Hume questioned the existence of God. Some people claim that there is no rational argument to prove that God exists. Hume goes further and argues that there is good reason to believe that God does not exist given the extent of evils in the world. The presence of evils (pain and suffering) in the world seems to contradict the attributes that theists often assign to God. Hume offers an *a posteriori* argument based on his observations of the amount of unnecessary suffering that humans experience. Assuming God is omnipotent (all-powerful), omniscient (all-knowing), and benevolent (all-loving), why is there evil in the world? If God is perfectly all-loving, he must wish to abolish evil. If God is all-powerful, he must be able to abolish evil. If God is all-knowing, he must know in advance that an evil is going to occur.

1. If God is omnipotent, omniscient, and all-good, then evil would not exist.
2. There are evils (pain and suffering) in the world.
3. So, God cannot be omnipotent, omniscient, and all-good. (So, the Christian God does not exist.)

The following is an excerpt from David Hume's *Dialogues Concerning Natural Religion*, which he finished writing in 1776. In this excerpt, Hume identifies four sources or circumstances that give rise to evils in this world. Thus, he defines evils as composed of four major subclasses (definition by subclass). Hume doubts that all these evils are necessary and claims that a perfect God would not have created a world with so many imperfections and so much useless misery.

David Hume: *Dialogues* (The Problem of Evil)

[201] [Misery is not] what we expect from infinite power, infinite wisdom, and infinite goodness. Why is there any misery at all in the world? Not by chance surely. From some cause then. Is it from the intention of the Deity? But he is perfectly benevolent. Is it contrary to his intention? But he is almighty. Nothing can shake the solidity of this reasoning, so short, so clear, so decisive; except we assert, that these subjects exceed all human capacity ... But there is no view of human life, or of the condition of mankind, from which, without the greatest violence, we can infer the moral attributes, or learn that infinite benevolence, conjoined with infinite power and infinite wisdom, which we must discover by the eyes of faith alone.

[205] In short, I repeat the question: Is the world, considered in general, and as it appears to us in this life, different from what a man, or such a limited being, would, beforehand, expect from a very powerful, wise, and benevolent Deity?

There seems to be four circumstances, on which depend all, or the greatest part of the ills, that molest sensible creatures; and it is not impossible, but all these circumstances may be necessary and unavoidable ...

The **first circumstance** which introduces evil, is that contrivance or economy of the animal creation, by which **pains**, as well as pleasures, are employed to excite all creatures to action, and make them vigilant in the great work of self-preservation. Now pleasure alone, in its various degrees, seems to human understanding sufficient for this purpose. All animals might be constantly in a state of enjoyment: but when urged by any of the necessities of nature, such as thirst, hunger, weariness; instead of pain, they might feel a diminution of pleasure, by which they might be prompted to seek that object which is necessary to their subsistence. Men pursue pleasure as eagerly as they avoid pain; at least they might have been so constituted. It seems, therefore, plainly possible to carry on the business of life without any pain ...

[206] But a capacity of pain would not alone produce pain, were it not for the **second circumstance**, viz. the conducting of the world by **general laws** ... In short, might not the Deity exterminate all ill, wherever it were to be found; and produce all good, without any preparation, or long progress of causes and effects? ... A being, therefore, who knows the secret springs of the universe, might easily, by particular volitions, turn all these accidents to the good of mankind, and render the whole world happy, without discovering himself in any operation. A fleet, whose purposes were salutary to society, might always meet with a fair wind. Good princes enjoy sound health and long life. Persons born to power and authority, be framed with good tempers and virtuous dispositions. A few such events as these, regularly and wisely conducted, would change the face of the world ...

[207] If everything in the universe be conducted by general laws, and if animals be rendered susceptible of pain, it scarcely seems possible but some ill must arise in the various shocks of matter, and the various concurrence and opposition of general laws; but this ill would be very rare, were it not for the **third circumstance**, which I proposed to mention, viz. **the great frugality with which all powers and faculties** are distributed to every particular being. So

David Hume, *Dialogues Concerning Natural Religion*, 1779.

well-adjusted are the organs and capacities of all animals, and so well fitted to their preservation, that, as far as history or tradition reaches, there appears not to be any single species which has yet been extinguished in the universe. Every animal has the requisite endowments; but these endowments are bestowed with so scrupulous an economy, that any considerable diminution must entirely destroy the creature. Wherever one power is increased, there is a proportional abatement in the others. Animals which excel in swiftness are commonly defective in force. Those which possess both are either imperfect in some of their senses or are oppressed with the most craving wants. The human species, whose chief excellency is reason and sagacity, is of all others the most necessitous, and the most deficient in bodily advantages; without clothes, without arms, without food, without lodging, without any convenience of life, except what they owe to their own skill and industry. In short, nature seems to have formed an exact calculation of the necessities of her creatures; and, like a rigid master, has afforded them little more powers or endowments than what are strictly sufficient to supply those necessities. An indulgent parent would have bestowed a large stock, in order to guard against accidents, and secure the happiness and welfare of the creature in the most unfortunate concurrence of circumstances ...

[209] The **fourth circumstance**, whence arises the misery and ill of the universe, is the **inaccurate workmanship** of all the springs and principles of the great machine of **nature**. It must be acknowledged, that there are few parts of the universe, which seem not to serve some purpose, and whose removal would not produce a visible defect and disorder in the whole. The parts hang all together; nor can one be touched without affecting the rest, in a greater or less degree. But at the same time, it must be observed, that none of these parts or principles, however useful, are so accurately adjusted, as to keep precisely within those bounds in which their utility consists; but they are, all of them, apt, on every occasion, to run into the one extreme or the other. One would imagine that this grand production had not received the last hand of the maker; so little finished is every part, and so coarse are the strokes with which it is executed. Thus, the winds are requisite to convey the vapors along the surface of the globe, and to assist men in navigation: but how oft, rising up to tempests and hurricanes, do they become pernicious? Rains are necessary to nourish all the plants and animals of the earth: but how often are they defective? how often excessive? Heat is requisite to all life and vegetation; but is not always found in the due proportion. On the mixture and secretion of the humors and juices of the body depend the health and prosperity of the animal: but the parts perform not regularly their proper function. What more useful than all the passions of the mind, ambition, vanity, love, anger? But how oft do they break their bounds, and cause the greatest convulsions in society? There is nothing so advantageous in the universe, but what frequently becomes pernicious, by its excess or defect; nor has Nature guarded, with the requisite accuracy, against all disorder or confusion. The irregularity is never perhaps so great as to destroy any species; but is often sufficient to involve the individuals in ruin and misery.

[210] On the concurrence, then, of these four circumstances, does all or the greatest part of natural evil depend. Were all living creatures incapable of pain, or were the world administered

by particular volitions, evil never could have found access into the universe: and were animals endowed with a large stock of powers and faculties, beyond what strict necessity requires; or were the several springs and principles of the universe so accurately framed as to preserve always the just temperament and medium; there must have been very little ill in comparison of what we feel at present. What then shall we pronounce on this occasion? Shall we say that these circumstances are not necessary, and that they might easily have been altered in the contrivance of the universe? ...

[211] Look round this universe. What an immense profusion of beings, animated and organized, sensible and active! You admire this prodigious variety and fecundity. But inspect a little more narrowly these living existences, the only beings worth regarding. How hostile and destructive to each other! How insufficient all of them for their own happiness! How contemptible or odious to the spectator! The whole presents nothing but the idea of a blind Nature, impregnated by a great vivifying principle, and pouring forth from her lap, without discernment or parental care, her maimed and abortive children!

Exercise 3-D: Reading Questions on Hume's *Dialogues*, The Problem of Evil

1. According to Hume, why is it problematic that evil exists? What conclusion does he draw about God? (paragraphs 201 and 205)?
2. What is the first circumstance that gives rise to evil in Hume's view? Why does he state that pleasure should be sufficient enough motivator for humans (paragraph 205)?
3. What is the second circumstance that gives rise to evil? What laws could the creator of the universe have established to make this world a better place according to Hume (paragraph 206)?
4. What is the third circumstance that gives rise to evil? What strengths do humans have and what powers do they lack (paragraph 207)?
5. How does Hume define the fourth circumstance, i.e., the inaccurate workmanship of nature, by subclass (paragraph 209)?
6. Why does Hume liken the creator of the universe to blind nature (paragraph 211)?

Rhetoric and Loaded Language

Rhetoric uses language to affect its audience's beliefs without offering reasons for a claim. As a means of persuasion, rhetoric is often employed in place of good argumentation. Rhetoric often makes use of words that are emotionally charged or have subtle overtones. With respect to nonargumentative persuasion, we will refer to words or phrases that attempt to manipulate audiences as **rhetorical devices**. Rhetorical devices, also known as slanters, may sway audiences in a number of ways. Specially chosen words can glorify or belittle, exaggerate or downplay, or put a positive or negative spin on things.

Rhetoric can be used to make it appear that one is winning a debate or has provided actual proof. Rhetoric may also serve as distractors to change the subject or to hide embedded assumptions. Rhetorical devices can be a powerful tool of persuasion that the prudent listener should guard against. So as not to be taken in by these rhetorical devices, the critical thinker must learn how to identify them and not mistake them for well-supported arguments. When attempting to convince others, we should not depend simply on the use of psychologically appealing techniques, but we should offer supporting evidence and reasons for our conclusions. There is nothing wrong with using rhetoric to try to sound persuasive as long as you do not offer mere rhetoric as a substitute for good arguments.

One form of rhetoric seeks to strengthen or weaken a claim by praising or censuring its subject. **Euphemisms** and **dysphemisms** are expressions that are value-laden and produce positive or negative associations. A euphemism for "bodyguard" is escort, while "thug" would be a dysphemism. It is generally a good idea to employ euphemisms to be polite or diplomatic. In order to reduce hostility, we might call a heated fight merely "a difference of opinion." We could, on the other hand, disparage an opinionated person by calling her a "know-it-all" or "smarty-pants." Euphemisms and dysphemisms impart emotional associations intended to influence other people's perceptions of things.

Another rhetorical device, called a **weaseler,** helps give the speaker a way out in case the claim being made is challenged. Words like "perhaps" and "possibly," as well as qualifying phrases like "as far as we know" or "within reasonable limits" allow people to weasel out of their commitment or responsibility. If challenged, a person can deny that she made any definite claims or strong assertions. When making promises, people can escape criticism if they add the word "probably" or "maybe" to their statements. Thus, we ought to be wary of someone who says that they may or probably will do something for you. When it comes to compliments, the sky is the limit as long as you qualify your statement with weaselers.

> You are possibly the most talented person I have met lately.
> As far as I know, you may be my perfect soulmate, and my one true love.

Later, of course, the one who professed these claims can turn around and deny them. After all, there were carefully added qualifications concerning limited time frames and imperfect knowledge.

A **downplayer** is a rhetorical move intended to make something seem less important than it really is. Downplaying words include *mere, merely, just, only, so-called, supposed, alleged,* etc. Downplayers diminish the significance of the thing in question.

> Mr. Sebastian Peabody is *merely* the substitute teacher.
> Smith is a *purported* expert in the field, but he *just* has a minor in physics.

Sometimes, we can downplay something by enclosing a term under scrutiny within quotation marks.
Gregory raves about his latest "work of art" but it looks like the mere scribbling of a kindergartner.

Another technique that politicians like to employ is **horse laugh** or appeal to ridicule. This technique helps someone to make light of a situation and to avoid giving serious consideration to the issue at hand. With a horse laugh, people can give the impression of having won their point because of their appearance of joviality and cheeriness. The rhetorical device of horse laugh includes ridicule of all kinds. Horse laugh can include telling an unrelated joke, using sarcastic language, or simply laughing at the person one disagrees with.

> Winston Churchill once remarked to a woman, "I may be drunk, miss, but in the morning, I will be sober, and you will still be ugly."
> A politician might simply laugh at his opponent, "Candidate Jones the best man for the job? Har, har, har."

Hyperbole means exaggeration or extravagant overstatement. This rhetorical device represents something as being greater, bigger, worse, etc., than it really is. Calling one's parents "slave drivers" for imposing household chores would be hyperbole. Likewise describing a hangnail as a serious injury exaggerates the situation. Not all strong claims count as hyperbole. "Michael Jordan is the best professional basketball player of all time" may be close enough to the truth so as not to count as a hyperbole.

When a claim is made without any support except for the speaker's assurance that evidence or proof exists, a **proof surrogate** has been committed. Sometimes a proof surrogate occurs when the source is not specifically identified, or it may involve the use of words such as *clearly, it is obvious that, research shows, studies prove*, or *nine out of ten doctors agree*.

> A government official said today that the new tax plan will help the middle class.
> Experts agree the best way to educate children is through homeschooling.
> Studies show that flossing does not lead to healthier teeth and gums.
> Obviously, the Irish exchange student drinks beer.

Proof surrogates use words or phrases that make it seem like there is evidence for a claim without actually stating what the proof or evidence is. The best way to avoid proof surrogates is to carefully cite your sources and discuss the specific persons or studies you are referencing.

Exercise 3-E: Rhetorical Devices

Identify the rhetorical devices (dysphemism, euphemism, weaseler, downplayer, proof surrogate, horselaugh, hyperbole).

1. Larry is *merely* a freshman and doesn't know his way around the campus.
2. All teachers are *unreasonable dictators*!
3. *Studies suggest* that couples married before the age of 21 are more likely to stay together.

4. I have tons of work this weekend. It will be sheer torture!
5. Animal rights is an issue many *goofballs* and *hippie nutcases* feel strongly about.
6. Do I agree with your answer? Well, *sort of*. *Perhaps*, you have a good suggestion.
7. *Clearly,* the most reasonable compromise is taking a vacation to Hawaii rather than France.
8. I don't have to buy her a Valentine's Day gift. After all, we've *only* gone out on a few dates.
9. *Research shows* that children who eat a cup of oatmeal every morning concentrate better in school.
10. *As far as we can tell,* Grandma Betty is *possibly* the best cook in the state of Georgia.
11. My hairstylist Sally got her *"degree"* from beauty school. But is that really a degree?
12. It's true that my girlfriend weighs 300 pounds. However, I would describe her as *pleasantly plump* and *curvy*.
13. Los Angeles has got to be *the hottest place on Earth*. I literally *melt* when I visit that city.
14. If you want to be a total *nerd* and *loser*, then go ahead and stay home instead of going to the prom.
15. Mr. Jones claims that volunteering in the Peace Corps can teach young people to work hard and to take life seriously. But what does he know? He's *just* a high school teacher.
16. I would not call my new boyfriend old. Instead, he's rather *mature* and *distinguished*.
17. *Obviously,* the best way to balance the budget is to cut public spending.
18. You actually like logic? Well, I hope you have tons of fun with your Venn diagrams, truth tables, and proofs, Mr. Spock! Or should I call you Sherlock Holmes?
19. *Nine out of ten dentists claim* Wite-brite is a more effective brand of toothpaste than Aquashine.
20. My friend, Huang, is a so-called expert of fashion. Today, he is sporting a leather vest over his animal print kimono, socks with his golden sandals, round spectacles, a rosary, and a black beret.

Hume and Objections to the Teleological Argument

In Hume's *Dialogues*, fictional characters discuss the rationality of religious belief. In this dialogue, Cleanthes defends a version of the teleological argument for God's existence. Cleanthes claims that we can use reason and empirical evidence to prove that God exists. Philo, the philosophical skeptic, who most represents Hume's views, disagrees with Cleanthes. Philo denies that religious beliefs can be grounded in observed phenomena. In this excerpt, Philo argues that Cleanthes's reasoning is not cogent because he is drawing conclusions about the whole universe from the creation of its parts. Thus, Philo accuses Cleanthes of committing the fallacy of composition.

Dialogues Concerning Natural Religion

By David Hume

Excerpt I

If we see a house, CLEANTHES, we conclude, with the greatest certainty, that it had an architect or builder; ... But surely you will not affirm, that the universe bears such a resemblance to a house, that we can with the same certainty infer a similar cause, or that the analogy is here entire and perfect. The dissimilitude is so striking, that the utmost you can here pretend to is a guess, a conjecture, a presumption concerning a similar cause; and how that pretension will be received in the world, I leave you to consider ...

But can a conclusion, with any propriety, be transferred from parts to the whole? Does not the great disproportion bar all comparison and inference? From observing the growth of a hair, can we learn anything concerning the generation of a man? Would the manner of a leaf's blowing, even though perfectly known, afford us any instruction concerning the vegetation of a tree?

But, allowing that we were to take the operations of one part of nature upon another, for the foundation of our judgement concerning the origin of the whole, (which never can be admitted,) yet why select so minute, so weak, so bounded a principle, as the reason and design of animals is found to be upon this planet? What peculiar privilege has this little agitation of the brain which we call thought, that we must thus make it the model of the whole universe? Our partiality in our own favor does indeed present it on all occasions; but sound philosophy ought carefully to guard against so natural an illusion ...

Stone, wood, brick, iron, brass, have not, at this time, in this minute globe of earth, an order or arrangement without human art and contrivance; therefore, the universe could not originally attain its order and arrangement, without something similar to human art. But is a part of nature a rule for another part very wide of the former? Is it a rule for the whole? Is a very small part a rule for the universe? Is nature in one situation, a certain rule for nature in another situation vastly different from the former?

Excerpt II

And what shadow of an argument, continued PHILO, can you produce, from your hypothesis, to prove the unity of the Deity? A great number of men join in building a house or ship, in rearing a city, in framing a commonwealth; why may not several deities combine in contriving and framing a world? This is only so much greater similarity to human affairs. By sharing the work among several, we may so much further limit the attributes of each, and get rid of that extensive power and knowledge, which must be supposed in one deity, and which, according to you, can only serve to weaken the proof of his existence.

Excerpt III

Did I show you a house or palace, where there was not one apartment convenient or agreeable; where the windows, doors, fires, passages, stairs, and the whole economy of the building, were

David Hume, *Dialogues Concerning Natural Religion*, 1779.

the source of noise, confusion, fatigue, darkness, and the extremes of heat and cold; you would certainly blame the contrivance, without any further examination … You would assert in general, that, if the architect had had skill and good intentions, he might have formed such a plan of the whole and might have adjusted the parts in such a manner, as would have remedied all or most of these inconveniences. His ignorance, or even your own ignorance of such a plan, will never convince you of the impossibility of it. If you find any inconveniences and deformities in the building, you will always, without entering into any detail, condemn the architect.

Excerpt IV

The BRAHMINS assert, that the world arose from an infinite spider, who spun this whole complicated mass from his bowels, and annihilates afterwards the whole or any part of it, by absorbing it again, and resolving it into his own essence. Here is a species of cosmogony, which appears to us ridiculous; because a spider is a little contemptible animal, whose operations we are never likely to take for a model of the whole universe. But still here is a new species of analogy, even in our globe. And were there a planet wholly inhabited by spiders, (which is very possible,) this inference would there appear as natural and irrefragable as that which in our planet ascribes the origin of all things to design and intelligence, as explained by CLEANTHES. Why an orderly system may not be spun from the belly as well as from the brain, it will be difficult for him to give a satisfactory reason.

Exercise 3-F: Reading Questions on Hume's *Dialogues*, Objections

1. When one sees a house, what can one conclude? According to Philo, who is speaking to Cleanthes, one should not compare a house to what (Excerpt I)?
2. Hume claims that there is a great disproportion from some parts to the whole that it bars comparison. What other examples does he give of parts to whole that have great disproportion (Excerpt I)?
3. What point does Hume make about stone, wood, brick, iron, and brass (Excerpt I)?
4. Hume observes that sometimes "a great number of men join in building." What point is he trying to make about the creation of the universe (Excerpt II)?
5. Hume asks us to imagine a house that was noisy, confusing, dark, and extremely hot or cold. What thought would come to mind if he showed us such a house (Excerpt III)?
6. Hume also criticizes certain believers for committing the anthropomorphic fallacy—or the tendency to attribute human emotions and characteristics to inanimate objects or to the natural world. What does Hume say about the possibility of a world wholly inhabited by spiders (Excerpt IV)?

CHAPTER 4
Emotional Appeals

> In Chapter 4, we will discuss rhetorical devices that target the emotions of an audience and fallacious reasoning that rest on questionable presumptions. After completing the chapter, readers will be able to
> - identify different types of emotional appeal,
> - distinguish fallacies of presumption, and
> - analyze logical reasoning in passages of Pascal's *Pensees*, Russell's "Is There a God," and Plato's *Euthyphro*.

Another group of rhetorical devices that works on our feelings of pity, guilt, anger, fear, or hope is known as emotional appeals. Emotional appeals can be viewed as a type of fallacy or defect in an argument that may be psychologically persuasive but fails to offer legitimately relevant support for the conclusion. A good argument should provide justification for accepting its conclusion; emotional appeals fail to do this by only targeting people's emotions as a means of persuasion.

One type of emotional appeal is called an **"Argument" from Outrage** when it hides relevant issues by arousing anger. Anger is not an argument. Professing that one is angry might make others believe an argument has been given when it hasn't. Becoming angry because we see that something is wrong is sometimes appropriate; saying that something is wrong simply because you are angry does not constitute a good argument. An employee screams, "I should not be the one fired! I am so upset right now. I'm ready to blow a gasket!"

When the emotion appealed to is fear, we call this **Scare Tactics** or **Appeal to Force** (also called by the Latin phrase "ad baculum"). There can be justified appeals to fear such as, "You had better not smoke if you don't want to get lung cancer." The fallacy can occur when someone is threatened that an unpleasant consequence will occur if he or she does not comply. For example, the boss might demand, "You had better work late if you want to keep your job." A bully could threaten, "Give me your lunch money, or I'll beat you up." In these cases, the employer and the bully commit an appeal to force fallacy.

An **Appeal to Pity** (also known in Latin as "ad misericordiam") works like scare tactics, except it works on a person's feelings of compassion or pity. An appeal to pity attempts to persuade others to believe in something or to take action to improve a pathetic situation. A girlfriend might plead, "How can you break up with me? I just lost my job, and I have no friends or family to turn to." A job applicant might urge, "Please hire me. I've got five kids and a wife to support. We'll be homeless and hungry if I don't work soon."

When someone appeals to your vanity, the fallacy goes by the name of **apple polishing**. Note that this move can take subtle forms—for instance, "You are too smart to believe in telepathy." Apple-polishing appeals to people's feelings of vanity or pride. A salesman could compliment a shopper, "You really should buy that dress. It emphasizes your shapely figure. If you got it, show it off!"

Guilt Trip is yet another emotional appeal that works on feelings of guilt. The arguer tries to elicit feelings of guilt to persuade people to do something. Guilt trips often involve mentioning what you have done for others and claiming that they owe you for your sacrifice or help. Failure to fulfill one's duty or obligation should elicit feelings of guilt.

> Parent to child: "You won't do your mother this favor? Perhaps you forget everything I've done for you all these years!"

In the case of **Wishful Thinking,** you accept a claim because you want it to be true. The fallacy of wishful thinking happens when we accept a claim simply because it would be pleasant or gratifying if it were true. Some people, for example, may believe in God simply on the basis of wishful thinking or a desire for an afterlife.

Appeals to the People or **Ad Populum** arguments attempt to justify a belief or practice on the grounds that other people accept it. For example, imagine one college student says to another:

> Hey man, why aren't you drinking? If you want to be a college student, you gotta drink. You can't be a real college student if you don't drink. Come on, everyone in this house took at least two shots. You have to take a shot too.

An appeal to the people can come in many forms and can appeal to a majority, certain groups, or special individuals. Some of the subvarieties are as follows:

- **Argument from Popularity** or **Bandwagon Fallacy** observes that a certain claim is widely believed to be true by some sector of the population. This fallacy goes on to conclude that we also must accept the truth of the claim given that it is supported by others. Yet, there is no logical reason why mainstream ideas are correct. A prosecutor may argue, "You ought to believe the defendant is guilty. Almost everyone who has met him thinks that he is a cold-blooded killer."
- **Argument from Common Practice** also seeks to justify something on the grounds of its popularity. The fallacy tries to convince you to do something because it is the trend; you should do something because that is what most people are doing. It differs from the appeal to popularity by focusing on what people do instead of what people believe.

A friend might urge you to go to the movies by saying, "The latest James Bond movie is a big hit. You should watch it."

- **Appeal to Vanity or Snobbery** often associates the claim or product with someone who is admired, pursued, or imitated. Popular celebrities or elite groups may endorse a particular product or support some action. This kind of persuasive tactic plays on a person's vanity or ego. Appeal to vanity or snobbery implies that if you were to believe or act the same way as these special people, you can become like them or be associated with them. Appealing to vanity, the marine corps ad reads "The Few, The Proud, the Marines." Yet, another example: "Angelina Jolie uses Allegra face serum. You should, also."
- **Argument from Tradition** focuses on what has been done or thought in the past. Past beliefs or actions set the precedent, and it is presumed by this fallacy that we must follow the tradition. Deviations from the norm or custom are disapproved of. However, if there is a good reason why a convention or ritual should end, then appealing to tradition would be insufficient justification for the practice. For example, we can say that traditionally it was widely accepted that children should be seen and not heard. Today, we might think differently and value the participation of children in conversation.
- **Argument from Peer Pressure** puts all its weight on the approval of one's friends or peers. This fallacy is psychologically persuasive because people want to fit in and be accepted by their peers. The pressure to conform and be like your peers is hard to resist. People do not want to be excluded or miss out on the fun, so they go along with what their friends are doing. One's peers can also include colleagues or others who are similar in age, share the same profession, or live in the same community. Thus, peer pressure overlaps with the next subvariety, Group Think.
- **Group Think** fallacy also plays on group identification. The group that a person might want to please may be a club, fraternity, political group, etc. Membership in a group can encourage group thinking; members follow group consensus for fear of being ostracized. A species of group thinking is **Nationalism**, a powerful emotion that can lead to the absolute endorsement of all of a country's policies. An advertisement appealing to nationalism might read, "Buy X. It's made in America!"

Exercise 4-A: Emotional Appeals

Identify the emotional appeals (appeal to force, appeal to pity, appeal to outrage, apple polishing, guilt trip, wishful thinking, and appeal to the people) in these passages. For appeal to the people, more than one subvariety may apply.

1. The price of textbooks is around a hundred dollars. It makes me fuming mad! So, this is absolutely and completely wrong, and textbook prices should be lowered right away.
2. Wear the gold sweater instead of the red one, because it brings out your beautiful blue eyes. I know you'll agree because you have great taste and fine fashion sense. So, which will it be?

3. Steven: The truth is you need to accept my proposal of marriage. I mean how could you not accept my proposal after I took care of your dying mother these last five months?
4. You need to acquit this young man. Keep in mind that he came from a broken home, never knowing his father, and being abandoned by his mother. Think about the poverty he's known, the foster homes, the birthdays going unnoticed, and the Christmases he's never had.
5. I know that you are an intelligent and responsible person who really cares about people. Now, will you sign my petition?
6. You should write my paper for me. If not, something very bad could happen to you. I'll see to it.
7. Little girl: My little pet poodle has been missing for more than two years, but I know she's still alive. She just couldn't be dead.
8. Nick Arrow was voted off *American Idol*? Those *American Idol* judges infuriate me! I am so upset right now. It goes to show that those judges had no right to vote that singer off.
9. Polls show that the majority of Californians disagree with the legalization of marijuana for medical reasons, which is why you should vote to repeal Proposition 215.
10. There can't be a geography test tomorrow! It's not like I checked or anything, but it's such a nice day outside, and my boyfriend said that we could spend a few days on Catalina Island together.
11. Remember, I bought the movie tickets. The least you can do is pay for the popcorn and drinks!
12. No one in the marines wears flannel pajamas. If you want to fit in, soldier, get rid of the flannel!
13. Why don't you switch to diet soda? All the thin people have done so. If you switch to diet soda, you will be thin too.
14. "We can't tell Mom! Just look at Mr. Tibbles! He's just a cute, fluffy, and innocent little cat. If we tell Mom that Mr. Tibbles broke the mug, she'll take away his dinner. Do you want Mr. Tibbles not to get food and then starve and die?"
15. Son, I have to tell you that I strongly disapprove of your having long hair and wearing earrings. Men, especially in our family, just don't do that!
16. Do you mean after I bought you roses and candy, and I wined and dined you in the fanciest place in town, all I get is one little kiss goodnight? Maybe you should think again.
17. More and more people are buying sports utility vehicles. Isn't it time you bought one too?
18. If my boss wasn't such a "slave driver," I would perform better at work. He is impossible to please! I am literally at my wits' end.
19. Employee to boss: It's a real pleasure working with you sir. You are a brilliant person with great power in the business world. I am so glad to be working with you. Hopefully, you'll see me up in the ranks with your higher employees. From janitor to secretary, here I come!
20. Of course, you should take your husband's last name when you are married. Your mother and grandmother did. In fact, all the married women in our family changed their names.

21. Michael still hasn't asked me out yet, but I know it's just because he's waiting for the right moment which hasn't been available in the last five years. He secretly wants me.
22. If you tell Mom I shot the neighbor's dog, I'll accidentally shoot you!
23. A time-share broker: "You mean that after we flew you down here to Florida at no cost to you, put you up in a Gold Crown resort for three days with all meals provided, and took you to Disney World, you're not going to buy even one of our time-shares?"
24. You've got to see Tom Cruise's latest film right away. It's breaking all the box office records, and everyone I know is raving about it.
25. Student: I have two essays to write and three tests this week! This just pisses me off! I am furious at how much work I must do. It's totally wrong for teachers to assign so much work.
26. Obviously, we should buy IBM's computers whenever we need new computers. We have been buying IBM as far back as anyone can remember.
27. Sam: Let's go, Tim! You have to help me move into my new apartment.

    Tim: I can't. I've made other plans this weekend.

    Sam: But you have to. After all, you still owe me $500.
28. Sorry, officer. I know I was speeding but please don't give me a speeding ticket. I understand you are only doing your duty and trying to keep the streets safe. Our fine city owes upstanding and courageous police officers like you a huge debt of gratitude. Please don't give me a ticket!
29. We Target employees know that Target brand items are better than Walmart brand items because, well, they are from Target, aren't they? Go Target!
30. Johnny, of course I deserve the use of your bicycle for the afternoon. After all, I'm sure you wouldn't want your mother to find out that you played hooky today.

Exercise 4-B: Fallacy Letter

Identify the **rhetorical devices** (dysphemism, euphemism, weaseler, downplayer, proof surrogate, horse laugh, hyperbole) and **emotional appeals** (appeal to force, appeal to pity, appeal to outrage, apple polishing, guilt trip, wishful thinking) contained in the following letter.

Dear Senator Bradshaw,

Have you heard about the senseless murders of poor defenseless animals by allegedly "humane" researchers? There is no proof that animal research will lead to the cure of cancer, diabetes, or other human diseases. So, these poor animals are all being slaughtered in vain. Can you imagine once beloved pets huddled in the corner of their cage awaiting torture and mutilation at the hands of these Frankensteins all in the name of so-called science? Does anyone care that these animals are being butchered by the thousands, perhaps by the millions, merely to obtain useless data that may save just a handful of human lives? The thought of it makes my blood boil! Obviously, this has to stop! If researchers want to experiment, let them use computers or themselves. Then they'll see how much fun they can have with their surgical knives and experimental pills! Har! Har!

The real-life heroes who deserve our applause are the animal liberators! These brave souls time and again have stood up against an insensitive bureaucracy, and won, saving former pet animals. Polls show that a majority of Americans support animal liberators and their cause. Even top celebrities such as Brad Pitt, Beyoncé, and Paris Hilton have joined the crusade to free research animals.

I voted for you in the past two elections and contributed to your campaign funds because I know you are one of the few politicians out there with a moral backbone. I trust in your keen judgment and compassionate spirit. You can be assured of my continued support in the upcoming election so long as you do the right thing and help to stop animal research.

Sincerely,
Frank Reynolds

Fallacies of Presumption

A **False Dilemma** assumes that only two alternatives exist in a given situation. Limiting the possible choices to just two forces anyone who does not agree with one alternative to accept the second one. Sometimes the one alternative is an exaggerated or unlikely possibility. The false dilemma relies on a valid inference of disjunctive syllogism: when there are only two alternatives and the first one does not hold, the second one must. This is a valid move, but a false dilemma goes wrong by claiming a false disjunctive statement "either … or …" for one of its premises. This claim is false when the arguer has, either unintentionally or intentionally, overlooked alternative possibilities. Though there may be situations where it really is "black or white," most situations are much more complex, and choices should not be narrowed down to two—there are gray areas with several possible shades.

A false dilemma may also be expressed using a different grammatical form such as "if-then" or "unless." Any sentence with an "or" can easily be translated into a sentence with "if-then": "Either A or B" translates to "If not A, then B." Thus, a false dilemma like "either we balance the budget, or we all starve to death" becomes, "if we do not fix the problem, we will all suffer." Although the sentence structure may change, it remains the same fallacy of false dilemma.

False dilemma may also be called the either/or fallacy, false dichotomy, black or white fallacy, etc. The following examples demonstrate how a false dilemma presents a limited number of options (usually two) when there are actually more options.

Examples: (i) Either you're for me or against me. (ii) If you're not first, you're last! (iii) Either buy Girl Scout cookies or you are not an American patriot.

The **Perfectionist Fallacy** uses a false dilemma in a special way; it first assumes that the only two options for action are the perfect success for that action or nothing good at all, then it rejects any proposed action that will not work perfectly. In a perfectionist fallacy, a person argues that we either do something completely or not at all. It comes up when a plan or policy is under consideration, and it goes like this: If policy X will not meet our goals as well as we'd like them met (i.e., "perfectly"), then policy X should be rejected. This principle downgrades policy X simply because it says, in effect, "Either the policy is perfect, or else we must reject it." Example: It's a mistake to use videotape replays to make calls. For, no matter how many cameras you have following the action on the field, you're still going to miss some calls. There's no way to see everything that's going on.

Another variant of the false dilemma, the **Line-Drawing Fallacy**, arises when discussing vague concepts: If you can't draw a line to demarcate the edge of a concept it is dismissed as hopelessly unclear. The line-drawing fallacy insists that a line must be drawn at some precise point when in fact it is not necessary that such a line be drawn. Someone might criticize the Constitution's protection against excessive bail, falsely arguing that we don't know where to draw the line between excessive and nonexcessive amounts. The line-drawing fallacy can be seen as a version of false dilemma. It presents the following alternatives: either there is a precise place where we draw the line, or else there is no line to be drawn (no difference) between one end of the scale and the other, suggesting that the extremes must be the same.

With **Begging the Question Fallacy** (petitio principii), the truth of the conclusion is already assumed by the premises. One type of begging the question occurs when a key premise is left unstated. The type of begging the question that we will focus on includes the case in which the conclusion is simply restated in the premises in a slightly different form. Example: (i) Since I'm not lying, it follows that I'm telling the truth. (ii) I am taller than my brother because he is shorter than me.

Another type of begging the question is called **Circular Reasoning,** which involves a chain of inferences. At the beginning of that chain is the assumption of the truth of the conclusion. Example: We know that God exists since the Bible says God exists. What the Bible says must be true since God wrote it and God never lies. (Here, we must agree that God exists in order to believe that God wrote the Bible.) The arguer should give evidence or reasons to believe the conclusion. With circular reasoning, the arguer simply assumes the conclusion as given without doing the work to prove it is true.

A loaded question or **Complex Question** is a question that contains an unwarranted or questionable assumption. In this sense, it is "loaded" because the question has smuggled in certain assumptions that have not been justified. For example, the question "What is a nice girl like you doing in a place like this?" presumes certain ideas about the place, what it means to be "a nice girl," and that the girl is indeed "nice." The noncritical person may answer a loaded question too quickly and accept the embedded assumptions. A loaded question is also called a complex question because the question can be broken down into two simpler questions. The question "Why did you steal cash from my wallet?" presumes guilt and asks for an explanation. It is a complex question consisting of two separate simpler questions. First, we should establish the answer to the simpler question, "Did you steal cash from my wallet?" Second, "If you stole the cash, why did you do it?"

Exercise 4-C: Fallacies of Presumption

Identify the fallacies of presumption (false dilemma, perfectionist, line-drawing, begging the question/circular reasoning, and complex question) in the following passages.

1. Is there really any difference between an A and a B? Does 90 or 91 percent deserve to be an A? What about 89.9 percent or 89.8 percent? Maybe 89.5 percent is close enough for an A? It's difficult to figure out a good cutoff point. That's why I think grades are totally bogus!
2. Either you contribute to the American Cancer Foundation, or you don't care about finding a cure for cancer.
3. I know she's wrong because I don't trust her logic. I don't trust her logic because she's not very smart. She isn't smart because she's incorrect.
4. All this talk about secondhand smoke causing cancer! I just don't believe it. How does it happen? When does it happen? The first time you take a breath in a smoky room? The second time? The third? You can never pin it down exactly!
5. The shirt I just bought is unquestionably fashionable because it is in style.
6. You show me when a fetus wasn't a person, just show me! Tell me exactly when it is. When the baby is born? Well, why not just a day before that? Or the day before that? Or the day before that? You just cannot mark exactly when! We have to say that life begins at conception.
7. Laws against teenagers drinking? They are a total waste of time, frankly. No matter how many laws we pass, there are always going to be some teens who will drink anyway.
8. Either you want to go out on another date with me, or you must be racist.
9. Which is it Senator Rushmore lied about, whether he used cocaine, when he used cocaine, or how much cocaine he used?
10. Philosophers are highly intelligent individuals because if they weren't highly intelligent, they wouldn't be philosophers.
11. No one can say just exactly how much sex has to be in a movie before you call it pornographic. It seems to me the whole concept makes no sense.
12. I am popular because I am the best football player. If I was not, I would not be so popular.
13. We can either save the environment or we can save jobs. Take your pick!
14. I can safely say that no law, no matter how stiff the consequence is, will completely stop illegal drug use. So, outlawing drugs is simply a waste of time.
15. Capital punishment is morally acceptable since murderers should be put to death.
16. It's a complete waste of time trying to learn a foreign language. After some years of study, you might be able to hold a simple conversation, but you'll never be as good as native speakers.
17. I will not commit this act because it is unjust, I know it is unjust because my conscience tells me so, and my conscience tells me so because the act is wrong.
18. Why are students in this class so much smarter than other classes at this university?
19. In this town, if you're not somebody, then you are nobody!
20. Alien life forms must exist because there are definitely extraterrestrial beings inhabiting other regions of the universe.

Exercise 4-D: Fallacy Letters

Identify the **rhetorical devices** (dysphemism, euphemism, weaseler, downplayer, proof surrogate, horselaugh, hyperbole) and **emotional appeals** (appeal to force, appeal to pity, appeal to outrage, apple polishing, guilt trip, wishful thinking) contained in the following letters.

Fallacy Letter from Crazy Ex-Girlfriend

My dearest Thomas,

You have not returned any of my phone calls in over six months, but I know that you still care about me. I also know that your new girlfriend forced you to get a restraining order because of my mere 138 phone calls in one week and my so-called stalking of her whenever she leaves the house. Obviously, your new girlfriend is the psycho one. I mean, what type of girlfriend would be that ridiculously possessive and crazed with jealousy to force her boyfriend to get a restraining order against the woman he truly loves? I may have gone over the top when we broke up, but that's only normal ... Of course, your new girlfriend tells you that my behavior is insane and dangerous, but what would she know? She has blond hair and drives a convertible Mustang!

I told the pizza delivery guy about this situation, and he agreed that you should take me back. If the pizza delivery guy (who was taken back by his third wife after they broke up) said this, obviously it must be true. Besides, so many people we know have gone back out with their girlfriends or boyfriends after they were cheated on. Take Sienna Miller and Jude Law, for instance. If it worked for them, it would work for us.

The only problem blocking our infinite happiness is your new girlfriend. Since you won the lottery before meeting her at a bar, it is obvious that she is only a gold-digging booze hound. Also, the little fairy tales she tells you about my stalking her are completely false. So, we happen to be at the post office, grocery store, gym, and mall at the same time—you try and prove that I stalk her! As far as we know, she and I may have the same schedule and may simply be in the same place at the same time. I know that you are not happy with her.

I know that since you are such a kind, forgiving, and generous person, you will admit that you love me and want to take me back. After all, I did buy you a new cell phone, Rolex, and iPod before we broke up. Those things were symbols of my love for you, and I know you would not keep them if you did not still feel the same. Either you take me back or your life will be filled with constant unhappiness and regret. Before you make your final decision, picture waking up to my sweet, caring face every morning, and I know that you will do the right thing.

Love always and forever,
Hannah

Fallacy Letter from Pleading Daughter

Dear Mom and Dad,
 College is going great, and I'm doing really well in all of my classes so far. Thank you so much for the care package; you are possibly the best parents ever! So, I am sure you will say yes to my one little request. The other night, some of the girls on my floor were talking about spring break and going to Cabo San Lucas. Now, I know you don't want me to go to Mexico during my freshman year of college, but everyone is going, and I will be a total loser if I don't go. Plus, I did work hard to graduate with honors from high school. You owe me this fun trip.

Studies show that going to a different country is a great educational opportunity and life experience, so there must be many things I can learn on my trip. Besides, it's not as if I am flying to the other side of the world. Mexico is only the next country over, a mere hundred miles away.

It is clear that I am a very responsible daughter, and I won't get myself into any trouble. I just want to have fun with my friends and have a good spring break. I talked to an upperclassman who had fun in Cabo, and she said she felt safe while she was there, so it must be a good place for me to visit where you won't have to worry. Also, a fantastic trip to Cabo will rejuvenate my spirits, and I will be even more motivated to study hard and get good grades. You wouldn't want a freshman like me flunking out in my very first year, would you? If I don't go, I will just die! So, I leave it to your wise judgment. Do you really want me to have a miserable spring break and miss out on a safe and educational trip with my friends?

Love,
Lauren

Pascal and the Wager

Pascal was a seventeenth-century French philosopher who presented an argument to motivate people to believe in God. This argument is now famously known as **Pascal's Wager**. While Pascal acknowledges that one can never know for certain whether God really exists, he states there is an equal chance of God's existing as not existing. He compares the odds of God's existing to the toss of a coin with a 50 percent chance of heads (God's existing) and 50 percent chance tails (God's not existing). Nonetheless, every person must make a decision either to believe or not believe in God.

Pascal offers pragmatic reasons for believing in God. One should choose to believe in God, for nothing could be lost, but only gained. Pascal believes it is a win/win situation for the believer. For, if God exists, then the believer will win infinite happiness in heaven. Even if God does not exist, then the deluded will still enjoy a happier life on Earth than would the atheist.

Pensées (Thoughts)

By Blaise Pascal

If there is a God, He is infinitely incomprehensible, since, having neither parts nor limits, He has no affinity to us. We are then incapable of knowing either what He is or if He is …

Let us then examine this point, and say, "God is, or He is not." But to which side shall we incline? Reason can decide nothing here. There is an infinite chaos which separates us. A game is being played at the extremity of this infinite distance where heads or tails will turn up. What will you wager? … according to reason, you can defend neither of the propositions (i.e., "God is" or "God is not").

Yes; but you must wager. It is not optional. You are embarked. Which will you choose then? Let us weigh the gain and the loss in wagering that God is. Let us estimate these two chances.

Blaise Pascal, *Pensees*, E. P. Dutton and Co., 1958.

If you gain, you gain all; if you lose, you lose nothing. Wager then without hesitation that He is. ... there is here an infinity of an infinitely happy life to gain, a chance of gain against a finite number of chances of loss, and what you stake is finite ...

Endeavour, then, to convince yourself, not by increase of proofs of God, but by the abatement of your passions. You would like to attain faith and do not know the way; you would like to cure yourself of unbelief and ask the remedy for it. Learn of those who have been bound like you, and who now stake all their possessions. These are people who know the way which you would follow, and who are cured of an ill of which you would be cured. Follow the way by which they began; by acting as if they believed, taking the holy water, having masses said, etc. Even this will naturally make you believe ...

Now what harm will befall you in taking this side? You will be faithful, honest, humble, grateful, generous, a sincere friend, truthful. Certainly, you will not have those poisonous pleasures, glory and luxury; but will you not have others? I will tell you that you will thereby gain in this life, and that, at each step you take on this road, you will see so great certainty of gain, so much nothingness in what you risk, that you will at last recognize that you have wagered for something certain and infinite, for which you have given nothing ...

The heart has its reasons, which reason does not know. We feel it in a thousand things. I say that the heart naturally loves the Universal Being, and also itself naturally ... It is the heart which experiences God, and not the reason. This, then, is faith: God felt by the heart, not by the reason. Faith is a gift of God; do not believe that we said it was a gift of reasoning ...

We know truth, not only by the reason, but also by the heart. And reason must trust these intuitions of the heart, and must base them on every argument ... And it is as useless and absurd for reason to demand from the heart proofs of her first principles, before admitting them, as it would be for the heart to demand from reason an intuition of all demonstrated propositions before accepting them ... The heart has its own order; the intellect has its own, which is by principle and demonstration. The heart has another. We do not prove that we ought to be loved by enumerating in order the causes of love; that would be ridiculous.

Exercise 4-E: Reading Questions on Pascal's *Pensées*

1. According to Pascal, can we know what God is or whether God is? Why or why not?
2. Is the choice to believe or not to believe in God optional? That is, does everyone have to make a wager, or can one refuse to play?
3. What good consequences might a person gain in believing in God? Does Pascal think that a believer risks losing anything if God does not exist?
4. How does Pascal describe pleasures, glory, and luxury? Are these things we should seek?
5. How does Pascal define "faith"? What is the difference between what is known by the heart versus what is known by reason?
6. Some critics argue that Pascal's Wager is an argument that commits several fallacies and emotional appeals. Can you detect some of these fallacies or emotional appeals?

Russell and the Teapot

In this excerpt from his essay, "Is There a God?" Russell compares the widespread belief in God to the belief in a certain china teapot.

Russell: "Is There a God"

Many orthodox people speak as though it were the business of sceptics to disprove received dogmas rather than of dogmatists to prove them. This is, of course, a mistake. If I were to suggest that between Earth and Mars there is a china teapot revolving about the sun in an elliptical orbit, nobody would be able to disprove my assertion provided I were careful to add that the teapot is too small to be revealed even by our most powerful telescopes. But if I were to go on to say that, since my assertion cannot be disproved, it is an intolerable presumption on the part of human reason to doubt it, I should rightly be thought to be talking nonsense. If, however, the existence of such a teapot were affirmed in ancient books, taught as the sacred truth every Sunday, and instilled into the minds of children at school, hesitation to believe in its existence would become a mark of eccentricity and entitle the doubter to the attentions of the psychiatrist in an enlightened age or of the Inquisitor in an earlier time. It is customary to suppose that, if a belief is widespread, there must be something reasonable about it. I do not think this view can be held by anyone who has studied history.

Exercise 4-F: Reading Questions on Russell

1. What fallacy is being committed by those who believe in the existence of the teapot?
2. How does Russell's view compare with the opinions of orthodox people, skeptics, dogmatists, and doubters?

Plato and Piety

Euthyphro and Socrates are represented as meeting on King Archon's porch. Both have legal business at hand. Socrates is a defendant in a suit for impiety and corruption of youths, which Meletus has brought against him, and Euthyphro too is a plaintiff in an action for murder, which he has brought against his own father. The latter originated in the following manner: A poor dependent of the family had slain one of their domestic slaves in Naxos. The guilty person was bound and thrown into a ditch by the command of Euthyphro's father, who sent a messenger to the interpreters of religion at Athens to ask what should be done with him. Before the messenger came back, the criminal had died from hunger and exposure.

This is the origin of the charge of murder that Euthyphro brings against his father. Socrates is confident that before he could have undertaken the responsibility of such a prosecution, Euthyphro must have been perfectly informed of the nature of piety and impiety, and as Socrates is going to be tried for impiety himself, Socrates thinks that he cannot do better than learn from Euthyphro (who will be admitted by everybody, including the judges, to be an unimpeachable authority) what piety is and what impiety is. What then is piety?

Euthyphro

By Plato; trans. Benjamin Jowett

Euthyphro and Socrates are represented as meeting in the porch of the King Archon. Both have legal business in hand. Socrates is the defendant in a suit for impiety and corruption of youths which Meletus has brought against him; and Euthyphro too is plaintiff in an action for murder, which he has brought against his own father. The latter originated in the following manner: —A poor dependent of the family had slain one of their domestic slaves in Naxos. The guilty person was bound and thrown into a ditch by the command of Euthyphro's father, who sent to the interpreters of religion at Athens to ask what should be done with him. Before the messenger came back, the criminal had died from hunger and exposure.

This is the origin of the charge of murder which Euthyphro brings against his father. Socrates is confident that before he could have undertaken the responsibility of such a prosecution, Euthyphro must have been perfectly informed of the nature of piety and impiety; and as Socrates is going to be tried for impiety himself, Socrates thinks that he cannot do better than learn from Euthyphro (who will be admitted by everybody, including the judges, to be an unimpeachable authority) what piety is, and what is impiety. What then is piety?

SOCRATES: **And what is piety, and what is impiety?**

EUTHYPHRO: <u>Piety is doing as I am doing; that is to say, prosecuting anyone who is guilty of murder, sacrilege, or of any similar crime—whether he be your father or mother, or whoever he may be—that makes no difference; and not to prosecute them is impiety</u>. And please consider, Socrates, what notable proof I will give you of the truth of my words, a proof which I have already given to others: —of the principle, I mean, that the impious, whoever he may be, ought not to go unpunished. For do not men regard Zeus as the best and most righteous of the gods? —and yet they admit that he bound his father (Cronos) because he wickedly devoured his sons, and that he too had punished his own father (Uranus) for a similar reason, in a nameless manner. And yet when I proceed against my father, they are angry with me. So inconsistent are they in their way of talking when the gods are concerned, and when I am concerned.

SOCRATES: May not this be the reason, Euthyphro, why I am charged with impiety—that I cannot away with these stories about the gods? and therefore I suppose that people think me wrong. But, as you who are well informed about them approve of them, I cannot do better than assent to your superior wisdom. What else can I say, confessing as I do, that I know nothing about them? Tell me, for the love of Zeus, whether you really believe that they are true.

Plato, *Euthyphro*, trans. Benjamin Jowett, 1891.

EUTHYPHRO: Yes, Socrates; and things more wonderful still, of which the world is in ignorance.

SOCRATES: And do you really believe that the gods fought with one another, and had dire quarrels, battles, and the like, as the poets say, and as you may see represented in the works of great artists? The temples are full of them; and notably the robe of Athene, which is carried up to the Acropolis at the great Panathenaea, is embroidered with them. Are all these tales of the gods true, Euthyphro?

EUTHYPHRO: Yes, Socrates; and, as I was saying, I can tell you, if you would like to hear them, many other things about the gods which would quite amaze you.

SOCRATES: I dare say; and you shall tell me them at some other time when I have leisure. But just at present I would rather hear from you a more precise answer, which you have not as yet given, my friend, to the question, What is 'piety'? When asked, you only replied, Doing as you do, charging your father with murder.

EUTHYPHRO: And what I said was true, Socrates.

SOCRATES: No doubt, Euthyphro; but you would admit that there are many other pious acts?

EUTHYPHRO: There are.

SOCRATES: Remember that I did not ask you to give me two or three examples of piety, but to explain the general idea which makes all pious things to be pious. Do you not recollect that there was one idea which made the impious impious, and the pious pious?

EUTHYPHRO: I remember.

SOCRATES: Tell me what is the nature of this idea, and then I shall have a standard to which I may look, and by which I may measure actions, whether yours or those of any one else, and then I shall be able to say that such and such an action is pious, such another impious.

EUTHYPHRO: I will tell you, if you like.

SOCRATES: I should very much like.

EUTHYPHRO: <u>Piety, then, is that which is dear to the gods, and impiety is that which is not dear to them.</u>

CHAPTER 4 Emotional Appeals | 65

SOCRATES: Very good, Euthyphro; you have now given me the sort of answer which I wanted. But whether what you say is true or not I cannot as yet tell, although I have no doubt that you will prove the truth of your words.

EUTHYPHRO: Of course.

SOCRATES: Come, then, and let us examine what we are saying. That thing or person which is dear to the gods is pious, and that thing or person which is hateful to the gods is impious, these two being the extreme opposites of one another. Was not that said?

EUTHYPHRO: It was.

SOCRATES: And well said?

EUTHYPHRO: Yes, Socrates, I thought so; it was certainly said.

SOCRATES: And further, Euthyphro, the gods were admitted to have enmities and hatreds and differences?

EUTHYPHRO: Yes, that was also said ...

SOCRATES: [The gods] have differences of opinion, as you say, about good and evil, just and unjust, honorable and dishonorable: there would have been no quarrels among them, if there had been no such differences—would there now?

EUTHYPHRO: You are quite right.

SOCRATES: Does not every man love that which he deems noble and just and good, and hate the opposite of them?

EUTHYPHRO: Very true.

SOCRATES: But, as you say, people regard the same things, some as just and others as unjust,—about these they dispute; and so there arise wars and fighting among them.

EUTHYPHRO: Very true.

SOCRATES: Then the same things are hated by the gods and loved by the gods, and are both hateful and dear to them?

EUTHYPHRO: True.

SOCRATES: And upon this view the same things, Euthyphro, will be pious and also impious?

EUTHYPHRO: So, I should suppose.

SOCRATES: Then, my friend, I remark with surprise that you have not answered the question which I asked. For I certainly did not ask you to tell me what action is both pious and impious: but now it would seem that what is loved by the gods is also hated by them. And therefore, Euthyphro, in thus chastising your father you may very likely be doing what is agreeable to Zeus but disagreeable to Cronos or Uranus, and what is acceptable to Hephaestus but unacceptable to Here, and there may be other gods who have similar differences of opinion.

EUTHYPHRO: But I believe, Socrates, that all the gods would be agreed as to the propriety of punishing a murderer: there would be no difference of opinion about that ...

SOCRATES: Well then, my dear friend Euthyphro, do tell me, for my better instruction and information, what proof have you that in the opinion of all the gods a servant who is guilty of murder, and is put in chains by the master of the dead man, and dies because he is put in chains before he who bound him can learn from the interpreters of the gods what he ought to do with him, dies unjustly; and that on behalf of such an one a son ought to proceed against his father and accuse him of murder. How would you show that all the gods absolutely agree in approving of his act? Prove to me that they do, and I will applaud your wisdom as long as I live.

EUTHYPHRO: It will be a difficult task; but I could make the matter very clear indeed to you.

SOCRATES: I understand; you mean to say that I am not so quick of apprehension as the judges: for to them you will be sure to prove that the act is unjust, and hateful to the gods.

EUTHYPHRO: Yes indeed, Socrates; at least if they will listen to me.

SOCRATES: But they will be sure to listen if they find that you are a good speaker. There was a notion that came into my mind while you were speaking; I said to myself: 'Well, and what if Euthyphro does prove to me that all the gods regarded the death of the serf as unjust, how do I know anything more of the nature of piety and impiety? for granting that this action may be hateful to the gods, still piety and impiety are not adequately defined by these distinctions, for that which is hateful to the gods has been shown to be also pleasing and dear to them.' And therefore, Euthyphro, I do not ask you to prove this; I will suppose, if you like, that all the gods condemn and abominate such an action. <u>But I will amend the definition so far as to say that what all the gods hate is impious, and what they love pious or holy; and what some of them love and others hate is both or neither. Shall this be our definition of piety and impiety?</u>

EUTHYPHRO: Why not, Socrates?

SOCRATES: Why not! certainly, as far as I am concerned, Euthyphro, there is no reason why not. But whether this admission will greatly assist you in the task of instructing me as you promised, is a matter for you to consider.

EUTHYPHRO: Yes, I should say that what all the gods love is pious and holy, and the opposite which they all hate, impious.

SOCRATES: Ought we to enquire into the truth of this, Euthyphro, or simply to accept the mere statement on our own authority and that of others? What do you say?

EUTHYPHRO: We should enquire; and I believe that the statement will stand the test of enquiry.

SOCRATES: We shall know better, my good friend, in a little while. The point which I should first wish to understand is whether the pious or holy is beloved by the gods because it is holy, or holy because it is beloved of the gods.

EUTHYPHRO: I do not understand your meaning, Socrates ...

SOCRATES: And what do you say of piety, Euthyphro: is not piety, according to your definition, loved by all the gods?

EUTHYPHRO: Yes.

SOCRATES: Because it is pious or holy, or for some other reason?

EUTHYPHRO: No, that is the reason.

SOCRATES: It is loved because it is holy, not holy because it is loved?

EUTHYPHRO: Yes.

SOCRATES: And that which is dear to the gods is loved by them, and is in a state to be loved of them because it is loved of them?

EUTHYPHRO: Certainly.

SOCRATES: Then that which is dear to the gods, Euthyphro, is not holy, nor is that which is holy loved of God, as you affirm; but they are two different things.

EUTHYPHRO: How do you mean, Socrates?

SOCRATES: I mean to say that <u>the holy has been acknowledged by us to be loved of God because it is holy, not to be holy because it is loved.</u>

EUTHYPHRO: Yes.

SOCRATES: <u>But that which is dear to the gods is dear to them because it is loved by them, not loved by them because it is dear to them.</u>

EUTHYPHRO: True.

SOCRATES: But, friend Euthyphro, if that which is holy is the same with that which is dear to God, and is loved because it is holy, then that which is dear to God would have been loved as being dear to God; but if that which is dear to God is dear to him because loved by him, then that which is holy would have been holy because loved by him. But now you see that the reverse is the case, and that they are quite different from one another. For one (Theophiles) is of a kind to be loved because it is loved, and the other (osion) is loved because it is of a kind to be loved. Thus, you appear to me, Euthyphro, when I ask you what is the essence of holiness, to offer an attribute only, and not the essence—the attribute of being loved by all the gods. But you still refuse to explain to me the nature of holiness. And therefore, if you please, I will ask you not to hide your treasure, but to tell me once more what holiness or piety really is, whether dear to the gods or not (for that is a matter about which we will not quarrel); and what is impiety?

EUTHYPHRO: I really do not know, Socrates, how to express what I mean. For somehow or other our arguments, on whatever ground we rest them, seem to turn round and walk away from us.

SOCRATES: Your words, Euthyphro, are like the handiwork of my ancestor Daedalus; and if I were the sayer or propounder of them, you might say that my arguments walk away and will not remain fixed where they are placed because I am a descendant of his. But now, since these notions are your own, you must find some other gibe, for they certainly, as you yourself allow, show an inclination to be on the move.

EUTHYPHRO: Nay, Socrates, I shall still say that you are the Daedalus who sets arguments in motion; not I, certainly, but you make them move or go round, for they would never have stirred, as far as I am concerned.

SOCRATES: Then I must be a greater than Daedalus: for whereas he only made his own inventions to move, I move those of other people as well. And the beauty of it is that I would rather not. For I would give the wisdom of Daedalus, and the wealth of Tantalus, to be able to detain them and keep them fixed. But enough of this. As I perceive that you are lazy, I will myself endeavor to show you how you might instruct me in the nature of piety; and I hope that you will not grudge your labor. Tell me, then—Is not that which is pious necessarily just? ...

SOCRATES: And when you say this, can you wonder at your words not standing firm, but walking away? Will you accuse me of being the Daedalus who makes them walk away, not perceiving that there is another and far greater artist than Daedalus who makes them go round in a circle, and he is yourself; for the argument, as you will perceive, comes round to the same point. Were we not saying that the holy or pious was not the same with that which is loved of the gods? Have you forgotten?

EUTHYPHRO: I quite remember.

SOCRATES: And are you not saying that what is loved of the gods is holy; and is not this the same as what is dear to them—do you see?

EUTHYPHRO: True.

SOCRATES: Then either we were wrong in our former assertion; or, if we were right then, we are wrong now.

EUTHYPHRO: One of the two must be true.

SOCRATES: Then we must begin again and ask, What is piety? That is an enquiry which I shall never be weary of pursuing as far as in me lies; and I entreat you not to scorn me, but to apply your mind to the utmost, and tell me the truth. For, if any man knows, you are he; and therefore, I must detain you, like Proteus, until you tell. If you had not certainly known the nature of piety and impiety, I am confident that you would never, on behalf of a serf, have charged your aged father with murder. You would not have run such a risk of doing wrong in the sight of the gods, and you would have had too much respect for the opinions of men. I am sure, therefore, that you know the nature of piety and impiety. Speak out then, my dear Euthyphro, and do not hide your knowledge.

EUTHYPHRO: Another time, Socrates; for I am in a hurry, and must go now.

SOCRATES: Alas! my companion, and will you leave me in despair? I was hoping that you would instruct me in the nature of piety and impiety; and then I might have cleared myself of Meletus and his indictment. I would have told him that I had been enlightened by Euthyphro, and had given up rash innovations and speculations, in which I indulged only through ignorance, and that now I am about to lead a better life.

Exercise 4-G: Reading Questions on Plato's *Euthyphro*

1. Who is Euthyphro? Under what circumstances does Socrates encounter Euthyphro?
2. How does Euthyphro first define piety? Why is Socrates dissatisfied with this first definition?
3. What is Euthyphro's second definition? What problem does Socrates see in the second definition?
4. What is Euthyphro's third definition? How does the third definition provide a merely accidental attribute of piety?
5. What question (Euthyphro's dilemma) does Socrates ask in reply? How does Euthyphro's response to the dilemma lead Socrates to find fault with the third definition?
6. What is Socrates looking for in a good definition? What kinds of problems does Socrates find in people's definition of piety?
7. At the end of the dialogue, what does Euthyphro say when Socrates continues to ask for a definition for piety?

CHAPTER 5
Deductive Reasoning

In Chapter 5, we will learn how to evaluate deductive arguments and what it means for a deductive argument to be valid, invalid, sound, or unsound. We will pay careful attention to the structure of arguments as we distinguish particular valid argument forms from formal fallacies. After completing the chapter, readers will be able to

- identify valid and invalid argument forms;
- evaluate deductive arguments as valid, invalid, sound, and unsound;
- draw valid inferences; and
- analyze logical reasoning in passages of Anselm's *Proslogion* and Epicurus's *Letters*.

Let us now turn to the task of evaluating whether a deductive argument succeeds in providing necessary support for the conclusion. At the most general level we call an argument good if it can provide support for a particular claim, the conclusion. Instead of calling arguments "good" and "bad," we will rate arguments by more specific evaluative terms. We will evaluate deductive arguments by the terms valid or invalid, and sound or unsound.

One way an argument can be good is by being valid. An argument is logically **valid** if and only if the conclusion must be true if all the premises are true. For an invalid argument, it is possible for all the premises to be true while the conclusion is false. This possibility is often known as a counterexample demonstrating the invalidity of a deductive argument. More informally, we may say that the conclusion of a valid argument must follow from its premises or that the premises provide support for the necessary truth of the conclusion. Validity concerns the inferential relationship between the premises and the conclusion, and not the actual truth-values of the component statements. The premises do not all have to be true for an argument to be valid, validity also does not guarantee a true conclusion. For example, a valid argument may consist of only false claims such as the following:

> All humans are cold-blooded.
> <u>Lassie is human.</u>
> Therefore, Lassie is cold-blooded.

While both the premises and the conclusion are false, the argument is valid because if we assume that the premises as true, then the conclusion must be true. There is a necessary inferential link or logical connectedness between the premises and the conclusion. Except for the truth-value combination of all true premises and a false conclusion, a valid argument may have all sorts of truth-value combinations: true premises and true conclusion, false premises and false conclusion, false premises and a true conclusion, a mix of true and false premises and either a true or false conclusion. Furthermore, it is important to note that the term "valid" applies to arguments, not to statements. Although we often hear people say that a certain claim is valid, we will restrict our use of the terms "valid" and "invalid" to arguments, while claims or statements are "true" or "false."

The best kind of deductive argument is not only valid, but it is also sound. An argument is **sound** if and only if it is valid and all its premises are true. This means that the conclusion necessarily follows from the premises and that all the premises are true. Not only does a sound argument have true premises, but given the definition of validity, it follows that a sound argument always has a true conclusion. Example One is a sound argument because it meets the two requirements of being valid and having all true premises. An argument is unsound if any of its premises are false or if it is not valid.

Example One	Example Two
(valid, sound)	(valid, unsound)
All dogs are mammals (T).	All dogs are reptiles (F).
Lassie is a dog (T).	Shamu is a dog (F).
So, Lassie is a mammal (T).	So, Shamu is a reptile (F).

These examples are valid because if one were to assume the truth of the premises, then the conclusion would necessarily be true. To test for validity, begin by pretending that all the premises are true, and then determine whether the conclusion would have to be true based on your assumptions. Consider Example Two: if you pretend that all dogs are reptiles and that Shamu is a dog, would it necessarily follow from these statements that Shamu is a reptile? The answer would be yes; it is a valid argument. We can compare these valid arguments to the next two examples of invalid arguments.

Example Three	Example Four
(invalid, unsound)	(invalid, unsound)
All dogs are mammals (T).	All dogs are amphibians (F).
Lassie is a dog (T).	Shamu is an amphibian (F).
So, Shamu is a killer whale (T).	So, Shamu is a dog (F).

For Examples Three and Four, the conclusion does not follow from the information given in the premises. Even though all the statements in Example Three are true (all dogs are mammals, Lassie is a dog), it is not valid because the conclusion is not logically supported by the premises. Moreover, an argument's having all true statements is not sufficient to make it a good one.

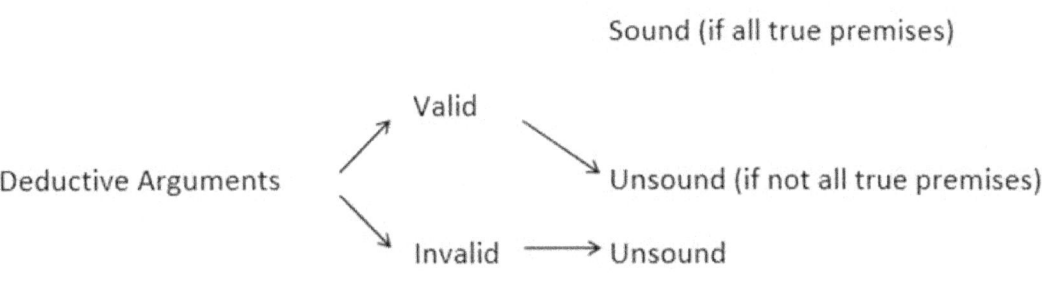

IMG 5.1

We see that the evaluative terms for deductive arguments correspond to the evaluative terms for inductive arguments. When evaluating an argument as valid or invalid, begin by assuming or pretending that all the premises are true. Then ask whether the conclusion must be true based on that assumption. For a valid argument, the conclusion must be true if the premises are assumed true.

By definition, all invalid arguments are unsound. Valid arguments with true premises are sound, while valid arguments with one or more false premises are unsound.

Valid Argument Forms and Formal Fallacies

There are special deductive argument forms related to disjunctive syllogisms and hypothetical syllogisms that are always valid or invalid owing to their form or structure. These valid argument forms are so common and distinctive in logical discourse that they have been given special names such as modus ponens and modus tollens.

Consider the following argument made in the philosophy of religion.

> If God is maximally perfect, then God actually exists.
> God is maximally perfect.
> Therefore, God actually exists.

In this argument, the second premise is the antecedent of the first premise, a conditional statement. It goes on to infer the consequent of the conditional. This inference is called Modus Ponens, and it is made by any argument having this structure:

> If X, then Y. X. Therefore, Y. **Modus Ponens**

In yet another argument in the philosophy of religion, philosopher David Hume argues that God's existence is incompatible with all the evil in the world. Hume's argument against God's existence can be formulated as having a modus tollens structure. A *Modus Tollens* argument form begins with a conditional statement and the negation of the consequent as its premises. The conclusion drawn is the negation of the antecedent.

> If God is all-good, omniscient, and omnipotent, then evil would not exist.
> <u>Evil exists (pain, suffering, disease, natural disasters, crimes).</u>
> Therefore, it is not the case that God is all-good, omniscient, and omnipotent.
> If X, then Y. Not Y. Therefore, not X. **Modus Tollens**

Another deductively valid argument form involving conditionals is called the **Chain Argument** or simply **Hypothetical Syllogism**. In a more general sense, the term "hypothetical syllogism" can mean a deductive argument with two premises and a conclusion where at least one of the premises is a conditional statement. This term may have a different meaning when "hypothetical syllogism" refers to the valid inference. As a valid argument form, hypothetical syllogism consists of three conditional statements. The two conditionals in the premises are such that the antecedent of one of the premises is the consequent of the other premise. The conclusion drawn is another conditional statement. Here is an example:

> If I am doubting, then I am thinking.
> <u>If I am thinking, then I exist.</u>
> Therefore, if I am doubting, then I exist.
> If X, then Y. If Y, then Z. Therefore, if X, then Z. **Hypothetical Syllogism**

Disjunctive Syllogism can also refer specifically to the valid argument form. The structure of this valid argument begins with a disjunctive statement as one of its premises. The other premise denies or negates one of the disjuncts, and the conclusion drawn is that the other disjunct is true. Our example of a disjunctive statement is as follows:

> The Ontological Argument is either inductive or deductive.
> <u>The Ontological Argument is not inductive.</u>
> Therefore, the Ontological Argument is deductive.

> Either X or Y. Not X. Therefore, Y. **Disjunctive Syllogism**
> Either X or Y. Not Y. Therefore, X. **Disjunctive Syllogism**

Another valid argument form is called **Constructive Dilemma**. The premises of a constructive dilemma include a disjunctive statement and two conditional statements. The disjuncts of the one premise appear in the antecedents of the two conditional premises. The conclusion of a constructive dilemma is a disjunctive statement whose disjuncts are the consequents of the two conditionals. For example, a couple expecting a baby might reason as follows:

> If the baby is a boy, we will name him Gilbert.
> If the baby is a girl, we will name her Ursula.

Either our baby will be a boy or a girl.
Therefore, the baby will be named either Gilbert or Ursula.

If W, then X.
If Y, then Z.
Either W or Y.
Therefore, either X or Z. **Constructive Dilemma**

In philosophical literature, constructive dilemmas abound. Pascal's Wager can be reformulated as a constructive dilemma.

If God exists, then the believer will be happier in Heaven than the nonbeliever.
If God does not exist, then the believer will be happier on Earth than the nonbeliever.
Either God exists or does not exist.
Therefore, the believer will be happier in Heaven or on Earth than the nonbeliever.

If G, then H.
If not G, then E.
Either G or not G.
Therefore, either H or E.

Destructive Dilemma is similar to constructive dilemma, but the disjunctive statement in the premises contains the negation of the consequents as its disjuncts. The conclusion is likewise a disjunctive statement with the negation of the antecedents as its disjuncts. For both constructive and destructive dilemmas, there are two conditionals. A constructive dilemma involves inferences that resemble two applications of modus ponens since the disjunction of the antecedents leads to the disjunction of the consequents. On the other hand, a destructive dilemma is comparable to a modus tollens inference applied twice: the negation of the consequents leads to the negation of the antecedents. The following example illustrates the destructive dilemma argument form.

If Joe marries Martha, then he will enjoy home-cooked meals.
If Joe marries Barbie, then he will enjoy stimulating conversations.
Either Joe will not enjoy home-cooked meals or not enjoy stimulating conversations.
Therefore, either Joe will not marry Martha or not marry Barbie.

If M, then H.
If B, then S.
Either not H or not S.
Therefore, either not M or not B. **Destructive Dilemma**

TABLE 5.1 Valid and Invalid Argument Forms

Valid Argument Forms	
Disjunctive Syllogism (DS) 1. Either A or B 2. Not A 3. B	**Hypothetical Syllogism** (HS) 1. If A, then B 2. If B, then C 3. If A, then C (Also called the "Chain Argument")
Modus Ponens (MP) 1. If A, then B 2. A 3. B	**Modus Tollens** (MT) 1. If A, then B 2. Not B 3. Not A
Constructive Dilemma (CD) 1. If A, then C. 2. If B, then D. 3. Either A or B. 4. Either C or D.	**Destructive Dilemma** (DD) 1. If A, then C. 2. If B, then D. 3. Either not C or not D. 4. Either not A or not B.
Invalid Argument Forms	
Affirming the Consequent (AC) 1. If A, then B 2. B 3. A	**Denying the Antecedent** (DA) 1. If A, then B 2. Not A 3. Not B

Just as there are argument forms that are valid, there are also argument forms that are invalid by their very structure. These invalid argument forms are known as the **Fallacy of Affirming the Consequent and the Fallacy of Denying the Antecedent.**

The structure of affirming the consequent looks very similar to modus ponens. Consider the following:

> If I am in San Diego, then I am in California.
> I am in California.
> Therefore, I am in San Diego.

> If X, then Y. Y. Therefore, X. **Affirming the Consequent**

One of the premises is a conditional statement, while the other asserts that the consequent is true. The conclusion states that the antecedent is true. This is invalid because the premises could be true, and yet I may not be in San Diego. I could be in Sacramento, for example. This fallacy is called "affirming the consequent" because one of the premises (in this case, the second premise) affirms that the consequent (e.g., "I am in California") is true.

Similarly, the formal fallacy of denying the consequent is similar to modus tollens.
Two examples:

If I am in San Diego, then I am in California.
<u>I am not in San Diego.</u>
Therefore, I am not in California.

If the diver went swimming, then her swimsuit would be wet.
<u>The diver did not go swimming</u>.
Therefore, her swimsuit is not wet.

If X, then Y. Not X. Therefore, Not Y. **Denying the Antecedent**

Both of these examples contain a premise that denies the antecedent of a conditional statement. Hence, the fallacy committed by these arguments is called "denying the antecedent." "I am in San Diego" is the antecedent of the first conditional, and its negation appears as the second premise. Likewise, "the diver went swimming" is denied as being true by a premise.

Why are these two examples that deny the antecedent invalid? If we assume both of the premises to be true, the conclusion will not have to be true. Let's suppose it is true that if the diver went swimming, then her swimsuit would be wet. Also, let's suppose that the diver's swimsuit is wet. Does the conclusion that the diver went swimming have to be true? No. The diver's swimsuit may be wet for other reasons (e.g., rain).

Exercise 5-A: Deductive Validity and Soundness

For each deductive argument, determine whether it is valid or invalid and sound or unsound. The truth-values of the premises are indicated in parentheses. Also, indicate whether the argument exemplifies modus ponens, modus tollens, the fallacy of affirming the consequent or denying the antecedent. Please note that not all passages commit MP, MT, AC, or DA.

1. All violinists are South Americans (F). Rita is a violinist (T). So, Rita is South American.
2. If Stalin was Swedish, then Stalin was a dictator (F). Stalin was a dictator (T). So, it follows that Stalin was Swedish.
3. If Patrick is Scottish, then Pierre is Chinese (F). Patrick is not Scottish (T). So, Patrick is not Chinese.
4. If Ted is baking cookies, then he needs flour (T). Ted does not need flour (T). Hence, Ted is not baking cookies.
5. Larry is Joe's friend (T). Joe is Tina's friend (F). It follows that Tina is certainly Larry's friend.
6. Either tomatoes are fruits or vegetables (T). Tomatoes are not vegetables (T). Consequently, tomatoes are fruits.
7. This sentence is a statement (T). Therefore, this sentence has a true value.
8. Odd numbers are divisible by two (F). Twelve is an odd number (F). Therefore, it must be the case that twelve is divisible by two.

9. If Napoleon is French, then Napoleon is a European (T). Napoleon is not French (F).

   So, it follows that Napoleon is not European.

10. If Eva Peron is Argentinian, then she is South American (T). Eva Peron is Argentinian (T). Hence, Eva Peron is South American.
11. If the moon landing was not a hoax, then Neil Armstrong was the first man on it (T). The moon land was real (T). Therefore, Neil Armstrong was the first man on the moon.
12. Every collie is a dog (T). Lassie is a dog (T). This entails that Lassie is a collie.
13. If Tony is from New York, then he is an American (T). Tony is an American (F). Therefore, Tony is from New York.
14. All men are mortal (T). Socrates is a man (T). Therefore, Socrates is mortal (T).
15. If you eat fast food, then you will be taking in more calories than you should (T). If you take in more calories than you need, then you will gain weight (T). Therefore, if you eat fast food, then you will gain weight.
16. The sum of 5 and 7 is 12 (T). The sum of two odd numbers must be odd (F). Five and 7 are odd numbers (T). It follows that 12 is an odd number.
17. Every reptile is cold-blooded (T). My cat Jewels is cold-blooded (F). Therefore, my cat is a reptile.
18. An octagon has six sides (F). The sign in front of my house is octagonal (F). Accordingly, the sign in front of my house has six sides.
19. All mammals are warm-blooded (T). Zebras are mammals (T). So, zebras are warm-blooded.
20. If I go to the concert, I won't wake up for school on time (F). I won't go to the concert (F). Therefore, I will wake up on time for school.
21. Dolores is meticulous (T). This means Dolores is very detail-oriented and precise.
22. Either I will have tacos or a burrito for lunch (T). I didn't have tacos (T). Therefore, I had a burrito.
23. If it rains, the ground is wet (T). If the ground is wet, the soles of my shoes are wet (F). If it rains, the soles of my shoes are wet.
24. Either you vote or don't vote (T). If you vote, you are exercising your right as a citizen (T). If you don't vote, you are wasting your right as a citizen (T). Therefore, you are either exercising or wasting your right as a citizen.
25. All koalas are amphibians (F). All amphibians are crustaceans (F). Thus, all koalas are crustaceans.
26. Some animals are horses (F). Some animals are giraffes (T). This implies that some horses are giraffes.
27. The lengths of the sides of a rectangle are 5 inches and 10 inches (T). Therefore, the area of the rectangle is 15 inches.
28. The kids in school are hyper today (F). So, they must be overactive and have a hard time keeping still.

29. Greg is taller than Sue (T). Sue is taller than Laura (T). Thus, Greg is taller than Laura.
30. Some melons are (T). Some fruits are melons (T). So, some fruits are cantaloupes. (Hint: Some X are Y. Some Z are X. So, some Z are Y.)

Exercise 5-B: Types of Deductive Arguments

For the problems in Exercise 5-A, identify the type of deductive argument (math, definition, categorical, disjunctive, or hypothetical syllogism). In some cases, the argument may be deductive but may not fit one of these five types.

Exercise 5-C: True or False Questions

1. A deductive argument must have two premises and one conclusion.
2. The following is an argument from the definition: Cholesterol is endogenous in humans. Therefore, it is manufactured inside the human body.
3. Disjunctive syllogisms contain a statement of the form "Either ... or ..."
4. All sound deductive arguments are valid.
5. All deductive arguments have a necessarily true conclusion.
6. A sound argument may be invalid.
7. A sound argument may have a false conclusion.
8. A valid argument must have a true conclusion.
9. If an argument has true premises and a true conclusion, we know that it is a perfectly good argument.
10. A statement may legitimately be spoken of as "valid" or "invalid."

Exercise 5-D: Valid Argument Forms

Identify the argument form (MP, MT, HS, DS, CD, DD).

1. If grandma baked strudel, then she had purchased some apples. Grandma did not purchase some apples. Therefore, she did not bake strudel.
2. If we remain on standard time, then the grass will get one hour less sunlight. If the grass gets one hour less sunlight, then it will stay greener. Therefore, if we remain on standard time, then the grass will stay greener.
3. The inmate has a choice of lethal injection or the gas chamber in California. The inmate does not choose lethal injection. So, the inmate chooses the gas chamber.
4. Either we keep fighting or we surrender. If we keep fighting, then more people will die. If we surrender, then we will lose our freedom. Thus, either more people will die, or we will lose our freedom.

5. If truth is no "harlot" as Schopenhauer claims, then truth is coy and elusive. If truth is coy and elusive, then no man may ever grasp the truth fully. Hence, if truth is no "harlot" as Schopenhauer claims, then no man may ever grasp the truth fully.
6. If it is Monday, then Jack has baseball practice; however, if it is Tuesday, then Jack has soccer practice. Either Jack does not have baseball practice, or he does not have soccer practice. It follows that either it is not Monday, or it is not Tuesday.
7. If the families and friends of innocent victims have the right to see effective retribution, then the death penalty is justified. The families and friends of innocent victims do have the right to see effective retribution. Therefore, the death penalty is justified.
8. The rock star will either cancel the concert or perform tonight. The rock star will not cancel the concert. Consequently, the rock star will perform tonight.
9. If Superman and Batman teamed up, then they must have defeated the Joker and saved Gotham City from destruction. Superman and Batman did team up. Consequently, they must have defeated the Joker and saved Gotham City from destruction.
10. If the sale of marijuana has been legalized in Alabama, then Connie can legally buy marijuana in Birmingham. It is not the case that Connie can legally buy marijuana in Birmingham. Hence, the sale of marijuana has not been legalized in Alabama.
11. Either both Steve and Rick go to the party or both Greg and Sue go to the party. It is not the case that both Steve and Rick go to the party. So, both Greg and Sue go to the party.
12. If we visit the farm in the summer, then we can see fireworks. If we visit the farm in the winter, then we can play in the snow. Either we cannot see fireworks, or we cannot play in the snow. Thus, either we don't visit the farm in the summer or in the winter.
13. If terminating the life of a killer is more economical than keeping him in jail at the taxpayer's expense, then the death penalty is justified. Terminating the life of a killer is more economic than keeping him in jail at the taxpayer's expense. Therefore, the death penalty is justified.
14. If the criminal is executed in Nebraska, then that criminal is electrocuted. If the criminal is executed in Mississippi, then the criminal is lethally injected. The criminal is executed in Nebraska or Mississippi. It follows that the criminal is electrocuted or lethally injected.
15. If your pets are not spayed or neutered, then they will reproduce. If your pets reproduce, then you may end up with more animals than you can care for. Thus, if your pets are not spayed or neutered, then you may end up with more animals than you can care for.

Exercise 5-E: Valid Inferences

Applying the valid forms (MP, MT, HS, DS, CD), what conclusion can you infer from the following premises? If no conclusion can be validly inferred using these rules of inference, briefly explain why.

1. If the pirate found the map, then the pirate ship sailed to Jamaica. If the pirate ship sailed to Jamaica, then the governor's daughter was kidnapped.
2. If the captain found the map, then the sailor sailed to Jamaica. The captain found the map.
3. Either the butler or the housekeeper murdered the guest. The housekeeper did not murder the guest.
4. Either Charlie Brown or Peppermint Patty went to the pumpkin patch. If Charlie Brown went, then Snoopy did also. If Peppermint Patty went, then Woodstock went, too.
5. If the nanny went home, then the butler and the housekeeper stayed at the mansion. It is not the case that both the butler and the housekeeper stayed at the mansion.
6. If the clown was not arrested for the crime, then the magician did not tell the truth. The magician told the truth.
7. Either Count Dracula or Frankenstein is hiding in Transylvania. Frankenstein is not hiding in Transylvania.
8. If Rudolph does not pull Santa's sleigh, then Prancer and Blitzen will pull Santa's sleigh. Rudolph does not pull Santa's sleigh.
9. Either Holmes or Watson found the fingerprints. If Holmes found the fingerprints, then Holmes will solve the mystery. If Watson found them, then he will be running tests in the laboratory.
10. Either Captain Hook or Peter Pan knows the whereabouts of Tinkerbell. Captain Hook does not know the whereabouts of Tinkerbell.
11. If Robin Hood and Maid Marian had a picnic, then Little John and Friar Tuck went hunting. Robin Hood and Maid Marian had a picnic.
12. If both Kubla Khan and Alexander the Great were brave warriors, then either Marc Antony or Brutus was a traitor. It is not the case that Marc Antony or Brutus was a traitor.

Exercise 5-F: Complex Arguments

The following passages are complex arguments. Answer the question at the beginning of each problem. To help you answer the question, first translate the sentences in the passage. Also, identify the valid argument forms that allow you to infer the conclusion from the premises. The valid forms may include modus ponens, modus tollens, hypothetical syllogism, disjunctive syllogism, constructive dilemma, or destructive dilemma. For each passage, you should identify two or more valid forms. (For the sake of uniformity in translations, we have underscored a letter for each component statement.)

Sample Question:
1. **Did the cow jump over the moon?** If the c̲ow jumped over the moon, then the little d̲og laughed. If the little d̲og laughed, then the dish r̲an away with the spoon. The dish did not r̲un away with the spoon.

First, translate each sentence:

1. If C, then D.
2. If D, then R.
3. Not R.

Then, apply rules MP, MT, HS, DS, CD, or DD to these statements:

4. If C, then R. By 1, 2 HS
5. Not C. By 3, 4 MT

Answer to question: No, the cow did not jump over the moon.

2. **Did the spider sit down beside Little Miss Muffet?** Either Humpty Dumpty sat on the wall or Little Miss Muffet sat on her tuffet. If Humpty Dumpty sat on the wall, then he had a great fall. If Little Miss Muffet sat on her tuffet, then the spider sat down beside her. Humpty Dumpty did not have a great fall.

3. **Is Tinkerbell happy?** If Captain Hook kidnaps Wendy, then Peter Pan will rescue her. If Tinkerbell is happy, then Peter Pan stays with her. If Peter Pan stays with Tinkerbell, then Peter Pan will not rescue Wendy. Captain Hook kidnapped Wendy.

4. **Does Nod go fishing for the herring fish?** Either Wynken or Blynken sailed off in a wooden shoe. Wynken did not sail off in a wooden shoe. If Blynken sailed off in a wooden shoe, then the old moon will not sing a song. If Nod goes fishing for the herring fish, then the old moon will sing a song.

5. **Will the farmer in the dell have to go to the market?** If the farmer in the dell takes a wife, then the wife will have a child. If the farmer in the dell does not take a wife, then he will adopt a dog. Either the farmer in the dell takes a wife or not. If the wife will have a child or the farmer adopts a dog, then the farmer will have to go to the market.

6. **Will the master be pleased?** Either the black sheep has wool for the dame or for the little boy who lives down the lane. If the black sheep has wool for the dame, then she will weave a winter cloak. If the black sheep has wool for the little boy who lives down the lane, then the boy will have new trousers. If either the dame will weave a winter cloak or the boy will have new trousers, then the master will be pleased.

7. **Will the old witch lure Hansel or Gretel into her house?** Either Jack and Jill went up the hill to fetch a pail of water, or Hansel or Gretel were left in the woods to starve. It is not the case that Jack and Jill went up the hill to fetch a pail of water. If Hansel or Gretel were left in the woods to starve, then the old witch will lure them into her house. (There is also a more precise way to symbolize the first premise so that the disjuncts are compound formulas, but we will learn that in the next chapter).

8. **Did Georgie Porgie make the girls cry?** Either Georgie Porgie ate pudding, or he ate gooseberry pie. Georgie Porgie will try to kiss the girls if he ate gooseberry pie. If he tries to kiss the girls, then he will make the girls cry. Georgie Porgie did not eat pudding.

9. **Are the three little kittens naughty or good?** If the three little kittens lose their mittens, then they shall have no pie. If the three little kittens soil their mittens, then they will wash

them. Either the three little kittens will have pie or will not wash their mittens. If either the three little kittens do not lose or do not soil their mittens, then they are good kittens.
10. **How many fiddlers did Old King Cole call for?** If Old King Cole was a merry old soul, then he called for his pipe and bowl. If he called for his pipe and bowl, then he did not call for just a single fiddler. Either Old King Cole called for three fiddlers or for just a single fiddler. Indeed, Old King Cole was a merry old soul.

Anselm and the Ontological Argument

In the medieval era (eleventh century) Anselm, an archbishop, formulated an intriguing argument for the existence of God. Although followers of the faith may assume the existence of God as true by revelation, Anselm claims that others can be convinced of it by means of rational argument. Anselm's Ontological Argument is his attempt to prove the existence of the Christian god. His argument is called "ontological" after the Greek word "ontos," which means being, essence, or nature. Anselm claims that the nature or essence of God necessarily entails God's existence. Anselm defended the existence of God by an *a priori* (nonempirical) logical analysis of what he took to be the definition of God: "that than which nothing greater can be thought or conceived." Given this definition, Anselm argues that the existence of God is a statement that cannot be logically denied; denying the statement would lead to a contradiction. For Anselm, God's existence is absolutely certain. He observes that it is only a "fool" who would doubt or deny the existence of God. An excerpt from Anselm's writings is included toward the end of this chapter. First, let us examine the mode of argumentation employed by Anselm: reductio ad absurdum.

Reductio Ad Absurdum

One way to formalize Anselm's argument is as a reductio ad absurdum argument. **Reductio ad absurdum** (RAA or reductio for short) is a method of proof that begins with an assumption. If we can show that this assumption leads to a contradiction of the form "p and not p," then we have proven that the assumption must be false. Thus, the strategy behind a reductio is to begin with the negation of the conclusion that we are trying to prove and then proceed to show how this negation leads to contradictory statements. If we are able to derive a contradiction, we have proven that our assumption is false, and hence the conclusion we had wanted to prove is true. Thus, a reductio is an indirect way of proving a statement is true by showing that the negation of the statement logically implies a contradiction or some ridiculous conclusion.

When Pigs Fly Example

Before we introduce Anselm's Ontological Argument, a few examples of reductio proof may help. We are all probably familiar with idioms such as "when pigs fly," "when Hell freezes over," or "a snowball's chance in Hell." Suppose Fred asks the head cheerleader, Kelly, for a date. After laughing hysterically, Kelly responds, "When pigs fly!" Kelly has just set the stage for an RAA argument. We would need to make the premises and the conclusion explicit, of course, but the reductio would go something like this:

1. If Kelly goes out with Fred, then pigs fly. (Kelly's response)
2. Pigs do not fly. (A fact about the world)

To prove that Kelly will not go out with Fred, we assume the opposite.

3. Kelly goes out with Fred. (Assumption for RAA)
4. Pigs fly. (Modus Ponens on 1 and 3)
5. Hence, Kelly does not go out with Fred. (RAA, 2 and 4 contradict each other)

We have shown that if we assume that Kelly goes out with Fred, we can derive the statement that "pigs fly." This statement is absurd because it contradicts a fact in the world that no pigs fly.

The House-Building Example

Another example is one we previously encountered in Hume's response to the Teleological Argument. Hume writes,

> And what shadow of an argument, continued PHILO, can you produce, from your hypothesis, to prove the unity (oneness) of the Deity? A great number of men join in building a house or ship, in rearing a city, in framing a commonwealth; why may not several deities combine in contriving and framing a world? This is only so much greater similarity to human affairs. By sharing the work among several, we may so much further limit the attributes of each, and get rid of that extensive power and knowledge, which must be supposed in one deity, and which, according to you, can only serve to weaken the proof of his existence.

In this excerpt, Hume argues that God should not be compared to a builder of a house or master architect as some versions of the Teleological Argument do. For this characterization of God would entail unacceptable consequences for the Christian. The reductio would proceed as follows:

1. There is only one God who created the world (Christian premise).
2. A house is created by a number of builders (a fact in the world).
3. Assume the world is like a house, and God is like a builder (assumption).
4. So, the world could have been built by a number of builders or gods (by 2 & 3).
5. So, there can be more than one God (by 4).
6. So, it is false that the world is like a house, and God a builder (RAA, 5 contradicts 1).

Moreover, the argument form of RAA has this basic structure that we can informally divide into four steps:

1. Premises: list your premises.
2. Assumption: assume the negation of the conclusion you wish to prove.
3. Contradiction: show the assumption, along with premises, leads to a contradiction.
4. Conclusion: you have proven that your assumption is false.

The assumption we will begin with for Anselm's Ontological Argument is the fool's claim "there is no God." Additionally, Anselm takes as a given the definition that God is "something greater than which cannot be thought" (GNT). Anselm also claims that "existing in reality as well" as existing in thought alone is "greater." That is, existence in reality is greater than existing in the thought alone.

1. God is something greater than which cannot be thought (GNT) (premise, definition).
2. Existence in reality is greater than existence in the thought alone (premise).
3. Suppose God exists in the thought alone but not in reality (assumption).
4. If God exists in the thought alone but not in reality, then there is something greater than God, something just like God but who exists in reality (by 2 and 3).
5. So, there is something greater than God (by 3, 4, MP).
6. So, it is false that God exists in the thought alone but not in reality (RAA, 5 contradicts 1).

We can abbreviate this argument to make its structure more apparent:

1. God is GNT (premise).
2. Actually existing is better than not (premise).
3. Suppose that God does not actually exist (assumption).
4. If God does not actually exist, then He is not GNT (by 2 and 3).
5. God is not GNT (by 3, 4, MP).
6. So, God actually exists (RAA, 5 contradicts 1).

Exercise 5-G: Reductio Ad Absurdum

Who Dunnit Example

Try to prove by reductio ad absurdum (RAA) that the butler did NOT do it! Here are the facts of the case:

> The millionaire was murdered in Dallas on New Year's Eve. If the butler murdered the millionaire, then the butler was in Dallas on New Year's Eve. If the butler watched a Broadway play on New Year's Eve, then he was not in Dallas on that day. The butler did watch a Broadway play on New Year's Eve.

The Infanticide Example

On a more serious note, we find the RAA technique in literature concerning abortion. Pro-life philosopher, Don Marquis, defends his theory on abortion against pro-choice personhood theories. Unlike Marquis, those who offer personhood theories on abortion claim that the moral permissibility or wrongness of abortion depends on the moral status of the fetus. Once the fetus is a person, then it is wrong to kill it. Thus, it would be morally wrong for a woman to have an abortion after the stage of fetal development when the fetus has become a person. Often, different personhood theories will identify a set of properties that makes something a person.

In the following excerpt, Marquis argues that many personhood theories lead to the justification of infanticide, an act unacceptable to most people. Reconstruct the following passage as an RAA argument.

> The account of the wrongness of killing defended in this essay does straightforwardly entail that it is prima facie seriously wrong to kill children and infants, for we do presume that they have future of values. Since we do believe that it is wrong to kill defenseless little babies, it is important that a theory of the wrongness of killing easily accounts for this. Personhood theories of the wrongness of killing on the other hand, cannot straightforwardly account for the wrongness of killing infants and young children.

Proslogion

By Anselm; trans. Sidney Norton Deane

Chapter 2: That God Really Exists

And so, Lord, do thou, who dost give understanding to faith, give me, so far as thou knowest it to be profitable, to understand that thou art as we believe; and that thou art that which we believe. And indeed, we believe that thou art a being than which nothing greater can be conceived. Or is there no such nature, since the fool hath said in his heart, there is no God? (Psalms 14:1). But, at any rate, this very fool, when he hears of this being of which I speak a being than which nothing greater can be conceived understands what he hears, and what he understands is in his understanding; although he does not understand it to exist.

For, it is one thing for an object to be in the understanding, and another to understand that the object exists. When a painter first conceives of what he will afterwards perform, he has it in his understanding, but he does not yet understand it to be, because he has not yet performed it. But after he has made the painting, he both has it in his understanding, and he understands that it exists, because he has made it.

Hence, even the fool is convinced that something exists in the understanding, at least, than which nothing greater can be conceived. For, when he hears of this, he understands it. And whatever is understood, exists in the understanding. And assuredly that, than which nothing greater can be conceived, cannot exist in the understanding alone. For, suppose it exists in the understanding alone: then it can be conceived to exist in reality; which is greater.

Therefore, if that, than which nothing greater can be conceived, exists in the understanding alone, the very being, than which nothing greater can be conceived, is one, than which a greater can be conceived. But obviously this is impossible. Hence, there is no doubt that there exists a being, than which nothing greater can be conceived, and it exists both in the understanding and in reality.

Anselm, Selections from "Proslogion," *Works of St. Anselm*, trans. Sidney Norton Deane, Open Court Publishing Company, 1903.

Chapter 3: That God Cannot be Thought Not to Exist

God cannot be conceived not to exist. God is that, than which nothing greater can be conceived. That which can be conceived not to exist is not God.

And it assuredly exists so truly, that it cannot be conceived not to exist. For, it is possible to conceive of a being which cannot be conceived not to exist; and this is greater than one which can be conceived not to exist. Hence, if that, than which nothing greater can be conceived, can be conceived not to exist, it is not that, than which nothing greater can be conceived. But this is an irreconcilable contradiction. There is, then, so truly a being than which nothing greater can be conceived to exist, that it cannot even be conceived not to exist;. and this being thou art, O Lord, our God.

So truly, therefore, dost thou exist, O Lord, my God, that thou canst not be conceived not to exist; and rightly. For, if a mind could conceive of a being better than thee, the creature would rise above the Creator; and this is most absurd. And, indeed, whatever else there is, except thee alone, can be conceived not to exist. To thee alone, therefore, it belongs to exist more truly than all other beings, and hence in a higher degree than all others. For, whatever else exists does not exist so truly, and hence in a less degree it belongs to it to exist. Why, then, has the fool said in his heart, there is no God (Psalms 14:1), since it is so evident, to a rational mind, that thou dost exist in the highest degree of all? Why, except that he is dull and a fool?

Exercise 5-H: Reading Questions on Anselm's *Proslogion*

1. What is Anselm's argument and why is it classified as deductive?
2. Why has Anselm's argument been named "ontological"?
3. How does Anselm define God? Does "a being than which nothing greater can be conceived" mean the same thing as "the highest" or "the supreme" being?
4. What kinds of properties does God possess in Anselm's view?
5. How does Anselm differentiate between "existing in the understanding alone" and "existing in reality"? Which is better in Anselm's judgment?
6. What property of existence must God possess according to Anselm?
7. Why does Anselm think that only a "fool" would deny God's existence?
8. What are the premises and conclusion of Anselm's argument?

Epicurus and Death

These excerpts were written by Epicurus, an ancient philosopher who lived in Samos, Greece, between 341 and 270 BC. He wrote a few famous letters to his students. His *Letter to Menoeceus* presents Epicurus's ethical views regarding pleasure, friendship, love, security, the fear of death, happiness, and the value of philosophy. Epicurus believed that the people should seek "ataraxia," i.e., tranquility of mind and body. In his Letter to Herodotus, we learn some of Epicurus's theory of the physical world.

1. (1) Let no one be slow to seek wisdom when he is young nor weary in the search of it when he has grown old. (2) For no age is too early or too late for the health of the soul. (3) And to say that the season for studying philosophy has not yet come, or that it is past and gone, is like saying that the season for happiness is not yet or that it is now no more.
2. (1) Accustom yourself to believing that death is nothing to us, for (2) good and evil imply the capacity for sensation, and (3) death is the privation of all sentience.
3. Pleasure is our first and kindred good. It is the starting-point of every choice and of every aversion, and to it we come back, inasmuch as we make feeling the rule by which to judge of every good thing.
4. (1) Death, therefore, the most awful of evils, is nothing to us, seeing that, (2) when we are, death is not come, and, (3) when death is come, we are not.
5. So, (1) we must exercise ourselves in the things which bring happiness, since, (2) if that be present, we have everything, and, (3) if that be absent, all our actions are directed towards attaining it.
6. (1) Nothing can be created out of that which does not exist. We conclude this to be true because (2) if things could be created out of that which did not exist, we would see all things being created out of everything, with no need of seeds, and (3) our experience shows us that this is not true.

Exercise 5-I: Reading Questions on Epicurus's *Letters*

1. In passage I, what is the conclusion? When should someone seek wisdom? What analogy does Epicurus make regarding the season for studying philosophy?
2. What is the conclusion of passage II? What does Epicurus say happens to us when we die?
3. How are we to judge "every good thing" according to Epicurus in passage III?
4. Passage IV can be written as a constructive dilemma if we include the implicit premise "Either we are alive or dead." The argument would look something like this:

    Premise i: If you are alive, then your death does not exist.
    Premise ii: If you are dead, then you do not exist.
    Premise iii: Either you are dead or alive (implied in the passage).
    Conclusion: Either your death does not exist, or you do not exist.
    How do the statements in Passage IV correspond to premises A and B in the above argument?

5. What is the conclusion of passage V? According to Epicurus, what happens when we do not have happiness?
6. What valid argument form (MP, MT, HS, DS, CD, DD) does passage VI commit? What conclusion does Epicurus draw in passage VI?

CHAPTER 6
Sentence Logic

> In Chapter 6, we will learn a symbolic language called sentence logic and use this language to assess deductive arguments. After completing the chapter, readers will be able to
> - understand negations, conjunctions, disjunctions, and conditionals;
> - translate an English statement into a sentence logic statement;
> - use a truth table to ascertain possible truth values of a proposition;
> - differentiate between necessary and sufficient conditions;
> - identify logically equivalent statements; and
> - identify the premises and conclusion of an argument and assess validity.

The validity of deductive arguments can be proven by employing various logical methods. To do this, first, we must learn how to express our statements in a truth-functional language called sentence or propositional logic. Then by understanding the truth-functional definitions of logical connectives or operators and by applying laws of natural deduction, we can generate logically equivalent statements, as well as infer conclusions from premises. Examining the logical structure of sentences can help with the analysis and critique of deductive arguments.

Propositional logic is a truth-functional language because it breaks up a complex sentence into its constituent parts such that the truth value of the complex sentence will depend on the truth values of its component parts or atomic sentences. An **atomic statement** is the simplest kind of sentence in propositional logic and will be symbolized by a capital letter.

Conjunctions, Disjunctions, and Negations

One type of sentence in propositional logic is conjunctions. Let us examine this conjunction:

(C & R)   My **c**ountry is the world, and my **r**eligion is to do good. —Thomas Paine

This quote may be broken down into two component parts, each atomic part expressing its own complete thought. The first atomic statement is "My country is the world," which we may symbolize as C, and the second statement "My religion is to do good" may be symbolized by R. We use the ampersand symbol & as the logical connective to express the word "and." A logical connective or logical operator forms more complex sentences from simpler ones. In this case, the ampersand joins the two atomic statements to form a compound statement. Thus, our translation reads (C & R). Although it can be stated in many different ways, the word "and" is the standard way to express a conjunction. A **conjunction** is true only if both atomic sentences, called the conjuncts, are true. A logical connective of propositional logic is truth-functional because the truth value of the compound sentence is a function of or depends on the simpler atomic statements. We can express the truth-functional definition of a conjunction by way of a truth table:

X	Y	(X & Y)
T	T	T
T	F	F
F	T	F
F	F	F

This truth table lists all the possible truth-value combinations for the atomic statements X and Y. Then for the final column, we see the truth value of the conjunction for each possible case. So, in Row 1, the only case in which the sentence (X & Y) is true occurs when X is true and Y is true. That is, a conjunction is true just in case both of its conjuncts are true.

Other words in our English language also express conjunctions. These include words such as "but," "although," "though," "yet," "despite," "however," "nevertheless," and "while." When we see simpler statements joined by these words, we will most likely use the & connective.

(D & M)   **D**eath smiles at us all, but all a **m**an can do is smile back. —Marcus Aurelius

This quote by the Stoic philosopher involves two atomic statements: "Death smiles at us all," and "All a man can do is smile back." Let's use the capital letters D and M in our translation. Thus, an acceptable translation for this sentence can be (D & M).

Sometimes, punctuation such as a comma or a semicolon can express conjunction. The following examples leave out the conjunctive word such as "and," "but," or "yet." We may translate them nevertheless as a conjunction using the "&" logical connective.

(V & M)   Virtue has a **v**eil, vice a **m**ask. —Victor Hugo
(C & P)   **C**leverness is good, **p**atience is better. —Hermann Hesse
(P & A)   **P**rosperity is a great teacher; **a**dversity a greater. —William Hazlitt

There are two kinds of logical connectives: **unary** versus **binary** connectives. The & of the conjunction is a binary connective because it requires two component parts that are joined together. On the other hand, a unary connective only requires one statement. For propositional logic, there is one unary connective, and we will use the tilde symbol ~ to express negation. The tilde goes in front of a statement that it is negating. These sentences are negations, and the translations consist of a tilde preceding a capital letter:

~T   I will not be **t**riumphed over. —Cleopatra
~C   **C**ommon sense is not so common. —Voltaire
~P   **P**olitics have no relation to morals. —Niccolò Machiavelli
~W   It is un**w**ise to be too sure of one's own wisdom.—Mahatma Gandhi

In the third statement, we have chosen P to stand for the simple statement "Politics have no relation to morals." The insertion of "no" in the middle of the sentence negates P. Prefixes such as "un-," "il-," or "im-" also may be treated as negations as in the last quote by Gandhi. Unlike formulas formed by binary connectives, no parentheses surround a negation. So, a sentence of the form (X & Y) requires parentheses to serve as punctuation, indicating that it is one complete sentence. However, ~X does not need parentheses.

The truth table for negation gives a truth value for the compound sentence ~X that is opposite to the truth value of the sentence X which it negates:

X	~X
T	F
F	T

At this point, we will present the formation rules for well-formed formulas of propositional logic. In doing so, we are concerned with the syntax of a logical system. The syntax lays out the set of rules that determine whether a sentence is a well-formed formula of a given logical system.

1. Capital letters (A, B, C, …) are well-formed formulas of propositional logic.
2. If X is a well-formed formula of propositional logic, then ~X is a well-formed formula.
3. If X and Y are well-formed formulas of propositional logic, then (X & Y), (X ∨ Y), and (X ⊃ Y), are well-formed formulas.
4. No other formula except those formed by these rules are well-formed formulas of propositional logic.

These formation rules introduce two additional logical connectives: ∨ and ⊃. In other logical systems, a fifth logical operator called the triple bar ≡ is included to express biconditional statements, but we will omit it in our treatment of propositional logic. The ∨ symbol is called the "wedge" or "vel." In Latin, "vel" means a combination of and/or; it stands for the inclusive sense of "or" rather than the exclusive sense of "or." Our English word "or" is rather ambiguous because in certain contexts, we may mean the inclusive sense and in other contexts we are intending the exclusive sense of the word. For instance, at a dinner party, a host may serve several side dishes, including green bean casserole and mashed potatoes. It is up to the guest to select either the green beans or the potatoes, and this choice involves the inclusive sense of "or." The guest may opt for the green beans or the potatoes, or both.

On the other hand, a parent may offer a child a choice of dessert such as either a slice of chocolate cake or apple pie. Most likely, in this context, the child is permitted either a slice of cake or of pie, but not both. Choosing one dessert excludes the possibility of having the other. This illustrates the exclusive sense of "or" which we can express as "X or Y, but not both X and Y." The "vel" symbol or wedge in the formula (X ∨ Y) means "X or Y, or both X and Y."

The formula (X ∨ Y) is a disjunctive statement, joining two simpler formulas called the disjuncts. Just like a conjunction, a disjunction may be defined by a truth table with four rows that give the four possible cases. In the truth table for (X ∨ Y), we see that Row 1 allows for both disjuncts to be true since the logical connective ∨ stands for the inclusive sense of "or." The only case in which the disjunctive statement is false occurs in Row 4 when both disjuncts are false. This truth table shows that the "∨" is also a truth-functional connective since the truth value of the whole sentence is a function of its component parts.

X	Y	(X ∨ Y)
T	T	T
T	F	T
F	T	T
F	F	F

Some examples of disjunctive statements include the following:

(S ∨ P) You're either part of the **s**olution or you're part of the **p**roblem. —Eldridge Cleaver
(P ∨ R) Art is either **p**lagiarism or **r**evolution. —Paul Gauguin
(R ∨ H) You can be **r**ight, or you can be **h**appy. —Gerald Jampolsky

A sentence of propositional logic can also combine two or more logical connectives. If there is more than one logical connective, then it is important to establish the main connective or operator. The main operator is the last logical connective applied when building the well-formed formula. Between a unary and a binary connective, the binary connective is the main operator unless the unary connective is the only one in the formula or the only connective that lies outside of the parentheses.

The placement of parentheses is very important in establishing the grouping order of a compound sentence. It is a common convention when working with propositional logic to omit the outermost parentheses, and this is a shortcut that we will now take. For example, the earlier sentence (R ∨ H) may simply be written as R ∨ H, where we omit the outermost parentheses although it is understood to be there. The following examples leave out the outermost parentheses, and the main operator of the formula is identified.

Formula	Main Operator
~A & B	&
C ∨ ~D	∨

~E ∨ ~F	∨
~(G & H)	~
~(~I ∨ ~J)	~
(~K & L) ∨ M	∨
~N & ~(O ∨ P)	&
(Q ∨ ~R) ∨ (S & T)	∨
~[G ∨ ~(S & ~D)]	~
~[S & {(P ∨ A) & ~M}] & ~G	&

In the last well-formed formula, the subformulas are grouped using parentheses ( ) for the innermost formulas and then braces { } and brackets [ ] may also be used. It is perfectly fine, however, to use only parentheses, but for clarity, braces and brackets make the grouping easier to spot in longer formulas.

In an English sentence, the punctuation and the order of the words can often help us to identify the main operator and to determine how to group the simpler statements. For Example 1, the punctuation is a semicolon that breaks the sentence into two parts; it is a conjunction with a negated statement in the second conjunct. There is no comma in Example 2, but the "either … or … " structure reveals what the two options or disjuncts should be. In Example 3, the comma divides the main parts of the sentence; the "and" symbolized by & is the main connective.

Example 1:	All the rivers **r**un into the sea; yet the sea is not **f**ull. —King Solomon
Translation 1:	R & ~F Main operator is &.
Example 2:	Either we are **a**lone in the universe or we are not. —Arthur C. Clarke
Translation 2:	A ∨ ~A Main operator is ∨.
Example 3:	Life **o**pens up opportunities to you, and you either **t**ake them or you stay **a**fraid of taking them. —Jim Carrey
Translation 3:	O & (T ∨ A) Main operator is &.
Example 4:	Tis neither **h**ere nor **t**here. —William Shakespeare
Translation 4a:	~H & ~T Main operator is &
Translation 4b:	~(H ∨ T) Main operator is ~

There are two common ways to translate Example 4. Shakespeare's quote "Tis neither here nor there" can be understood as a conjunction of two negated statements meaning "It is not here and it is not there." Another acceptable translation is the negation of a disjunctive statement: "It is not the case that either it is here or it is there." The phrase "neither X nor Y" is a shortened version of "It is not the case that either X or Y." The word "neither" is formed by combining the words "not" and "either," while "nor" results from combining "not" and "or." We will learn that translations 4a and 4b are equivalent by a law called De Morgan's Rule.

Let's consider a few special compound sentences related to negations, conjunctions, and disjunctions by translating these variants of the Shakespeare quote.

Example 5:	~(H ∨ T)	It is not the case that it is either here or there.
Example 6:	~(H & T)	It is not the case that it is both here and there.
Example 7:	~H ∨ ~T	It is not here or it is not there.
Example 8:	~H & ~T	It is not here and it is not there.

At first glance, Examples 5 and 7 may appear to be equivalent as well as Examples 6 and 8. However, these logical connectives are not mathematical operations but truth-functional operators. By De Morgan's Rule, Examples 5 and 8 are logically equivalent. Also, Examples 6 and 7 are logically equivalent. De Morgan's Rule has two formulations:

~(X & Y) is logically equivalent to ~X ∨ ~Y
~(X ∨ Y) is logically equivalent to ~X & ~Y

When constructing longer translations, grouping is important in order to convey a precise meaning. For example, suppose your family decides to go on a vacation. You are told that "you will go to Hawaii and Paris or Rome." This is a puzzling proposition and the ambiguity arises due to the lack of proper punctuation. One interpretation is that you will go to both Hawaii and Paris, or you will go to Rome only. Another plausible interpretation is that you will go to Hawaii, and additionally you will go to a second place, either to Paris or to Rome. The following formulas translate these three sentences, respectively.

H & P ∨ R	Ambiguous and not a well-formed formula; there is no main operator.
(H & P) ∨ R	Precise meaning; a well-formed formula; the main operator is ∨.
H & (P ∨ R)	Precise meaning; a well-formed formula; the main operator is &.

Since the last two formulas include ∨ which expresses the inclusive sense of "or," it turns out both sentences allow for the possibility that you will go to all three places. For one of the two formulas, you are definitely going to Hawaii. Which one? That's right, H & (P ∨ R) means you will go to Hawaii.

We must first interpret what a sentence in ordinary language is saying before we can translate it into propositional logic. There may be sentences, for example, that contain the word "not" but do not imply negation. The following sentence includes the word "not" and yet there is no tilde in the translation.

| W & Y | Not only can I **w**histle but I can **y**odel, too. |
| M | Laura and Peter are **m**iles apart. |

Sometimes the word "and" appears, such as in the previous example, yet we cannot translate it as a conjunction. This is because the verb "are miles apart" does not apply to Laura and Peter individually. Ultimately, there is no substitute for a careful examination of what the claims are saying.

CHAPTER 6 Sentence Logic | 95

Exercise 6-A: Propositional Translation with ~, &, ∨

Translate the following English sentences into well-formed formulas of propositional logic. The suggested letter to use for atomic sentences is bold-faced and underlined. Consider what simple statement each capital letter symbolizes. Also, words such as "not" or "no" or prefixes such as "un-," "il-," or "im-" suggest negation.

1. My optimism wears heavy **b**oots and is **l**oud. —Henry Rollins
2. Mankind is made **g**reat or **l**ittle by its own will. —Friedrich Schiller
3. **C**orrection does much, but **e**ncouragement does more. —Goethe
4. Friends are **b**orn, not **m**ade. —Henry Adams
5. I want to be with those who know **s**ecret things or else **a**lone. —Rainer Maria Rilke
6. Despite wearing a **R**olex, I have no **t**ime. —Faraaz Kazi
7. Life is 10 percent **w**hat you make it, and 90 percent **h**ow you take it. —Irving Berlin
8. **S**uccess comes when people act together; **f**ailure tends to happen alone. —Deepak Chopra
9. Doubt is an un**c**omfortable condition, but certainty is a **r**idiculous one. —Voltaire
10. I know I am but **s**ummer to your heart, and not the **f**ull four seasons of the year. —Edna St. Vincent Millay
11. I'm not the one-night-stand **k**ind of girl, despite the **r**umors. —Kim Kardashian
12. Kind words do not **c**ost much, yet they **a**ccomplish much. —Blaise Pascal
13. I am neither a **m**an nor a **w**oman but an **a**uthor. —Charlotte Brontë
14. Maybe I am **r**ight and maybe I'm **w**rong; nevertheless, I am in **l**ove with you. —Bert Palmer
15. I don't need a friend who **c**hanges when I change and who **n**ods when I nod; my **s**hadow does that much better. —Plutarch
16. Yesterday is not ours to **r**ecover, but tomorrow is ours to **w**in or **l**ose. —Lyndon B. Johnson
17. Though we **t**ravel the world over to find the beautiful, we must **c**arry it with us or we **f**ind it not. —Ralph Waldo Emerson
18. **H**ealth is the number one thing on the planet; however, I am quite **p**artial to rum and raisin ice cream. –Chris Eubank Sr.
19. Marriage is neither heave**n** nor hel**l**; it is simply **p**urgatory. —Abraham Lincoln
20. A fanatic is one who can't change his **m**ind and won't change the **s**ubject. —Winston Churchill
21. You can either **f**it in or **s**tand out. Not both. —Seth Godin

Conditional Statements

Another logical connective is the horseshoe, which is symbolized by ⊃ and it forms a conditional statement. Conditional statements are perhaps the most challenging translations in propositional logic. A **conditional statement** is a compound sentence that combines two simpler statements, to be found in the antecedent and in consequent. The antecedent typically comes after the word "if" and is placed in front of the horseshoe, while the consequent follows "then" and is placed after the horseshoe. Thus, (X ⊃ Y) is the translation for the standard conditional of the form "If X, then Y."

The truth value of a conditional claim is false when its antecedent is true and its consequent is false. This appears in Row 2 of the following truth table, where X is true, and Y is false. In all other cases, the conditional is true.

X	Y	(X ⊃ Y)
T	T	T
T	F	F
F	T	T
F	F	T

Conditional statements are perhaps the most challenging to translate because of the variety of ways the same proposition can be expressed in English. The following five rules can guide this translation.

Rule 1
When "**if**" appears by itself, what immediately follows is the **antecedent of the conditional.** In other words, the formula that immediately follows the "if" should go before the horseshoe. Thus, the statements "If **B**ill goes to work, **S**am plays golf," and "**S**am plays golf if **B**ill goes to work" are both translated (B ⊃ S).

Rule 2
When "**only if**" appears, what immediately follows is the **consequent of the conditional.** Therefore, when you see the phrase "only if," and this phrase is not contained in the longer phrase "if and only if," you should put the formula that follows "only if" after the horseshoe. The phrase "if and only if" is translated with a triple bar ≡ to create a biconditional statement.

Some examples can help illustrate Rules 1 and 2.

(K ⊃ J)   **J**ohn goes to the dance if **K**ate accompanies him.
(K ⊃ P)   **K**ate accompanies John only if her **p**arents let her.
(~T ⊃ M) If **T**ed does not have to work, then **M**eg will go to the movies with him.

Rule 3
"**Provided**," "**provided that**," "**given that**," "**on condition that**," "**assuming that**" are sometimes used in place of "if." The same rule that governs the word "if" (Rule 1) applies to these phrases. That is, these phrases are followed by the antecedent of a conditional.

(T ⊃ W)   The Dodgers win the **W**orld Series provided that they win **t**oday's game.
(P ⊃ N)   Given that the **p**lane arrives on time, we can be home by **n**oon.

Rule 4

The phrases **"entails that"** and **"implies that"** also express conditional statements. These phrases are followed by the consequent and hence are treated in the same way that the phrase "only if" is treated by applying Rule 2.

(R ⊃ M)   **R**ob's being happy entails that (or implies that) **M**egan is happy.
(W ⊃ Q)   Being a **w**riter usually entails a fairly **q**uiet life. —Jill Paton Walsh

Implied in the quotes are two simple statements. We will use W to stand for "I am a writer," and Q to mean "I live a fairly quiet life." Walsh's quote may be reexpressed as a standard conditional statement, "If I am a writer, then I live a fairly quiet life." In the next example, we will need to convert the words into simple statements in order to translate it into a well-formed formula of propositional logic. Capital letters stand for simple statements, but the words "equality" and "individuality" are not statements that have truth values. However, we can understand "equality" to mean "there is equality;" "individuality" to mean "there is individuality." Hence, the sentence "Equality implies individuality" is equivalent to saying, "That there is equality implies that there is individuality" or as a conditional, "If there is equality, then there is individuality."

(E ⊃ I)   **E**quality implies **i**ndividuality. —Trey Anastasio

Rule 5: S ⊃ N Sufficient Condition ⊃ Necessary Condition

Another way to express a conditional statement is by the phrase **"is a sufficient condition for"** and **"is a necessary condition for."** Let us consider this example of a true conditional statement:

(E ⊃ S)   If today is **E**aster, then today is **S**unday."

The antecedent of this conditional, "today is Easter," is a sufficient condition for the consequent "today is Sunday." That is, it is enough to know that it is Easter to infer that it is Sunday. Furthermore, the consequent is said to be a necessary condition for the antecedent. In this case, it is necessary that it be Sunday, for today to be Easter. The next section will explain more about necessary and sufficient conditions.

Exercise 6-B: Propositional Translation with ⊃

Translate the following English sentences into well-formed formulas of propositional logic. The suggested letter to use for atomic sentences is bold-faced and underlined. Consider what simple statement each capital letter symbolizes. Also, words such as "not" or "no" or prefixes such as "un-," "in-," or "im-" suggest negation.

1. If there is no **G**od, **e**verything is permitted. —Fyodor Dostoevsky
2. **F**aith is necessary to **v**ictory. —William Hazlitt

3. You **f**ail only if you **s**top writing. —Ray Bradbury
4. I believe in a **b**enevolent dictatorship provided **I** am the dictator. —Richard Branson
5. **L**ove as an emotion is sufficient for a girl and a boy to be **t**ogether. —Sara Khan
6. **F**ar away is far away only if you don't **g**o there. —George Otis
7. To understand **s**cience, it is necessary to know its **h**istory. —Auguste Comte
8. It is amazing what you can **a**ccomplish if you do not care who gets the **c**redit. —Harry S. Truman
9. If you're not **m**aking mistakes, then you're not **d**oing anything. —John Wooden
10. Americans will **p**ut up with anything provided it doesn't **b**lock traffic. —Dan Rather
11. Only if you have been in the deepest **v**alley, can you ever know how magnificent it is to be on the highest **m**ountain. —Richard M. Nixon
12. A very small degree of **h**ope is sufficient to cause the birth of **l**ove. —Stendhal
13. It is necessary to have **w**ished for death in order to **k**now how good it is to live. —Alexandre Dumas
14. Three can keep a **s**ecret, if two of them are **d**ead. —Benjamin Franklin
15. This is im**p**ossible only if you **b**elieve it is. —Lewis Carroll
16. There is no such thing as a **w**orthless conversation, provided you know what to **l**isten for. —James Nathan Miller
17. The ability of discerning high **q**uality unavoidably implies the ability of identifying **s**hortcomings. —Esdger Dijkstra
18. If you're **t**eaching today what you were teaching five years ago, either the **f**ield is dead or **y**ou are. —Noam Chomsky
19. I **s**wear like a sailor, assuming the sailor in question **d**ied in 1800 and was **r**eally square. —Alexandra Petri
20. Either **l**ife entails **c**ourage, or it ceases to **b**e life. —E.M. Forster (Let L: there is life, C: there is courage, and B: life is life.)
21. A **c**hange in the weather is sufficient to recreate the **w**orld and **o**urselves. —Marcel Proust
22. If you tell the **t**ruth, you don't have to **r**emember anything. —Mark Twain
23. All is **w**ell, provided the **l**ight returns and the eclipse does not become endless **n**ight. —Victor Hugo
24. Assuming either the **L**eft Wing or the **R**ight Wing gained control of the country, it would probably fly around in **c**ircles. —Pat Paulsen
25. Increasing **j**obs more than output implies a fall in **p**roductivity and **s**tandards of living. —Alan Greenspan
26. It is not **f**ailure if you **e**njoyed the process. —Oprah Winfrey
27. True **f**aith is faith only if the actions of your life are in **h**armony with it and never **c**ontradict it. —Leo Tolstoy
28. **D**emocracy is necessary to **p**eace and to **u**ndermining the forces of terrorism. —Benazir Bhutto
29. If you have a **g**arden and a **l**ibrary, you have **e**verything you need. —Cicero
30. If he doesn't **f**ollow through with actions, he's either **s**elfish or a **l**iar. —Matthew Hussey

Exercise 6-C: Complex Propositional Translation

These sentences are more complicated than the previous exercises. Translate the following English sentences into well-formed formulas of propositional logic. The suggested letter to use for atomic sentences is bold-faced and underlined. Consider what simple statement each capital letter symbolizes. Also, words such as "not" or "no" or prefixes such as "un-," "in-," or "im-" suggest negation.

1. If you have a **p**ositive attitude and constantly strive to give your best **e**ffort, eventually you will **o**vercome your immediate problems and find you are **r**eady for greater challenges. —Pat Riley
2. Life is a series of **c**ollisions with the future; it is not the **s**um of what we have been, but what we **y**earn to be. —Jose Ortega y Gasset
3. **P**anic implies that there is no **r**ational thought taking place, that we are **f**rozen and in**c**apable of adjusting. —Anthony Scaramucci
4. The two basic items necessary to sustain **l**ife are **s**unshine and **c**oconut milk. —Dustin Hoffman
5. If you aren't in the **m**oment, you are either looking **f**orward to uncertainty, or back to **p**ain and **r**egret. —Jim Carrey
6. **W**riting for TV entails saying every **d**umb idea that comes into your head to a room of people and doing so with **c**onfidence. —Taylor Jenkins Reid
7. In this world, either you're **v**irtuous or you **e**njoy yourself. Not both. —Ayn Rand
8. **D**emocracy is timelessly human, and **t**imelessness always implies a certain amount of potential **y**outhfulness. —Thomas Mann
9. **E**mpathy is a necessary step for **t**ruth and **r**econciliation. —Simon Baron-Cohen
10. All honest work is good **w**ork; it is capable of leading to **s**elf-development, provided the doer seeks to **d**iscover the inherent lessons and **m**akes the most of the potentialities for such growth. —Paramahansa Yogananda
11. If I had loved you **l**ess or **p**layed you slyly, I might have **h**eld you for a summer more, but at the cost of **w**ords I value highly, and no such **s**ummer as the one before. —Edna St. Vincent Millay
12. A party of **o**rder or **s**tability, and a party of **p**rogress or **r**eform, are both necessary elements of a **h**ealthy state of political life. —John Stuart Mill
13. It is easy to **t**alk about development; however, it entails **p**ainstaking efforts to actually make it happen. —Arvind Kejriwal
14. Man must make his choice between **e**ase and **w**ealth; either may be his, but not both. —Newell Dwight Hillis
15. Three things are necessary for the **s**alvation of man: to know what he ought to **b**elieve; to know what he ought to **d**esire; and to know what he **o**ught to do. —Thomas Aquinas
16. Either God **w**ants to abolish evil, and **c**annot; or he **c**an and does not **w**ant to. —Epicurus
17. If God **w**ants to, but **c**annot, he is im**p**otent. —Epicurus

18. Going back to being a **h**ead coach entails a full-time commitment to that **j**ob and I would not **g**o into it for any amount of money and **d**o it halfway. —Bill Cowher
19. While some people may think being a **c**hef only entails making enticing **d**ishes and pushing culinary **b**oundaries, being a part of the food industry involves much **m**ore. —Marcus Samuelsson
20. If a projectile were deprived of the force of **g**ravity, it would not be **d**eflected toward the earth but would go off in a straight line into the **h**eavens and so with **u**niform motion, provided that the resistance of the **a**ir were removed. —Isaac Newton

Sentence Logic and Passage Analysis

By Nathan Huffine

The concepts and skills of logic may help us to analyze and critique arguments. Given a philosophical passage, we may start by translating the English sentences into formulas of sentence logic. As we translate the logical structure of the sentences, it may be useful to number and underline the simple statements in the passage to distinguish them from the others. We can more readily understand the relation between the component parts of an argument by paying attention to the indicator words for the premises and conclusion (such as "because," "since," "therefore," "so," "consequently") and the logical operators (such as "and," "or," "only if"). Sometimes, we may need to supply the implicit premises that are not directly asserted but are nonetheless intended by the speaker.

Let us demonstrate these steps as we analyze the following line from Epicurus:

> "Accustom yourself to believing that death is nothing to us, for good and evil imply the capacity for sensation, and death is the privation of all sentience."
>
> "(1) Accustom yourself to believing that death is nothing to us, **for** (2) good and evil **imply** the capacity for sensation, **and** (2) death is the privation of all sentience."

The word "for" indicates a premise, and the words "imply" and "and" act as logical operators combining component parts of the sentences. For added clarity, if the conclusion is not already at the end, we may place it last in the series of numbered sentences. So, you can reformulate the argument as:

> (1) Good and evil **imply** the capacity for sensation,
> **and** (2) death is the privation of all sentience.
> (3) So, death is nothing to us.

Converting and eliminating the connectives and indicator words further, we are almost ready to translate the argument into well-formed formulas of sentence logic.

> (1) **If** there exists good and evil, **then** there exists the capacity for sensation.
> (2) Death is the privation of all sentience.
> (3) Death is nothing to us.

For our translations, we shall use the following translation scheme, replacing all atomic statements with capital letters:

G = There exists good and evil.
S = There exists the capacity for sensation.
D = Death is the privation of all sentience.
N = Death is nothing to us.

(1) G > S
(2) D
(3) N

So far, as translated, this argument is not yet complete until we include the implicit premises in Epicurus's reasoning. One premise that underlies his argument is "If good and evil do not exist (~G), then death is nothing to us (N)." Let us refer to this as (1a). Furthermore, another implied premise for Epicurus is "If death is the privation of all sentience (D), then there is no capacity for sensation (~S)." Let us number this second claim as (2a) and add it to the premises.

(1) G > S
(1a) ~G > N
(2) D
(2a) D > ~S
(3) N

At this point, the argument has been translated into sentence logic and can be proven to be deductively valid. By the deductive rules of inference, Epicurus's argument is valid because the conclusion must be true if all the premises are assumed true. This argument works out neatly as a single deductive argument rather than an extended argument that combines both deductive and inductive subarguments. Deductively, the validity of this argument may be shown by applying the deductive rules in this sequence: MP, MT, and MP. ...

For our next example, we turn to the following argument presented by Plato through the character Glaucon in Book VII of *The Republic*:

> "And this we may truly affirm to be a great proof that a man is just, not willingly or because he thinks that justice is any good to him individually, but of necessity, for wherever anyone thinks that he can safely be unjust, there he is unjust. For all men believe in their hearts that injustice is far more profitable to the individual than justice."
>
> (1) [...] a man is just, **not** willingly **or** because he thinks that justice is any good to him individually, **but** of necessity, **for** (2) wherever anyone thinks that he can safely be unjust, there he is unjust. **For** (3) all men believe in their hearts that injustice is far more profitable to the individual than justice.

The words "or" and "but" act as logical operators, and the term "for" appearing in both sentences indicates that a premise follows. Also, in the first sentence, there is a negation expressed by the word "not." Similar to the previous passage, the conclusion is at the beginning of the passage, but for clarity, we will again place it at the end of the argument following the premises:

(1) <u>a man is just,</u> **not** <u>willingly</u> **or** <u>because he thinks that justice is any good to him individually,</u> **but** <u>of necessity,</u>
for (2) <u>wherever anyone thinks that he can safely be unjust, there he is unjust.</u>
For (3) <u>all men believe in their hearts that injustice is far more profitable to the individual than justice.</u>
(1) <u>Wherever anyone thinks that he can safely be unjust, there he is unjust.</u>
(2) <u>All men believe in their hearts that injustice is far more profitable to the individual than justice.</u>
(3) So, it is **not** the case that either a <u>man is just willingly,</u> **or** <u>a man is just because he thinks that it is any good for him individually,</u> **but** <u>a man is just out of necessity.</u>

Replacing all atomic statements with capital letters, we will apply this translation scheme:

U = Everyone is unjust wherever he thinks that he can safely be unjust.
P = Everyone believes in his heart that injustice is far more profitable to the individual than justice.
W = Everyone is just willingly.
G = Everyone is just because justice is good for everyone individually.
N = Everyone is just out of necessity.
(1) U
(2) P
(3) ~(W v G) & N

So far, as translated, this argument is not complete until we include the implicit premises in Glaucon's reasoning. One implicit premise that underlies his argument is "if everyone is unjust wherever he thinks that he can safely be unjust (U), then everyone is just out of necessity (N)." Let us refer to this as (1a) and add it to the premises. You can also infer that "if everyone is just out of necessity (N), then it is not the case that everyone is just willingly (~W)." This implied premise may be numbered (1b). Lastly, Glaucon assumes that "if everyone believes in his heart that injustice is far more profitable to the individual than justice, then it is not the case that everyone is just because justice is good for everyone individually." Let us include this as the third implicit premise which we will number (2a):

(1) U
(1a) U > N
(1b) N > ~W
(2) P
(2a) P > ~G
~(W v G) & N

The validity of this argument can be proven by first applying the rules of deduction, MP to (1) and (1a), and then again to the resulting statement and (1b). Alternatively, we can deduce ~W by applying HS to (1a) and (1b), followed by MP to the resulting statement and (1). We can also apply MP to lines (2) and (2a) to derive ~G. We then can conclude that ~W & ~G & N. By De Morgan's Rule, ~W & ~G is logically equivalent and may be replaced by the formula ~(W ∨ G).

Therefore, given the explicit and implicit premises, the conclusion ~(W ∨ G) & N is necessarily true. Having translated Glaucon's argument into sentence logic, we have employed deductive logic to demonstrate the validity of his argument. Whether it is sound is another question depending on the truth values of his premises, both the explicit and implicit ones. Socrates and other philosophers would disagree with a number of Glaucon's assumptions and reject the soundness of his argument, despite its validity.

Exercise 6-D: Translation and Validity of Arguments

Translate the following arguments from English into sentence logic formulas by (1) numbering and underlining each sentence and (2) marking all words indicating premises, conclusions, and logical operators. In some passages, (3) identifying missing or implicit premises may be needed.

1. You are delusional only if you are a thinking agent. If you are a thinking agent, then you exist. You are delusional. So, you exist.
2. Either God is dead, or God is alive. It is not the case that God is alive. If God is dead, then humans need new meaning in their lives. Humans need new meaning in their lives.
3. Clearly, the right amount of food and exercise for a professional wrestler is not the same as for a child. If the Golden Mean is absolute, then the right amount of food and exercise is the same for everyone. So, the Golden Mean is not absolute.
4. The God of Delphi is right to say that no one is wiser than Socrates. For, Socrates interrogated Athenians to disprove the God of Delphi, and Socrates could not find anyone who was wiser than himself.
5. It is better to be a dissatisfied Socrates than a satisfied fool. The fact that being a dissatisfied Socrates is better than being a satisfied fool implies that there is more to life than just satisfaction. Therefore, not only the quantity but also the quality of pleasure matters.

Necessary versus Sufficient Conditions

A conditional statement also expresses sufficient and necessary conditions. To clarify these terms, we will begin with an example. Suppose one morning, your car will not start, and you conclude that your car battery must be dead. What you would be thinking is the following conditional (C1):

  C1 If my car won't start, then my battery is dead.

But is this conditional statement true? Is the battery necessarily the cause of your car not starting? The antecedent of the conditional is "my car won't start," and the consequent is "my battery is dead." In any given conditional, the antecedent is the sufficient condition, and the consequent is the necessary condition. When you claim C1, you are stating that the car's not starting is a sufficient condition or enough information to establish that your battery is dead. Furthermore, you are claiming that the battery's being dead is the necessary condition or must be the case for your car's not to start.

The **sufficient condition** is the part of the conditional statement that immediately follows "if." Knowing the sufficient condition is true, should be "sufficient" or "enough"—all you need to know—to infer that the other part of the conditional is true. Knowing that Pierre is in Paris is enough information to know that Pierre is in France. "Being in Paris" is a sufficient condition for "being in France." On the other hand, the **necessary condition** is the part of the conditional that immediately follows the "then." The necessary condition is "necessary" or "required"—must be the case—whenever the sufficient condition is true. For example, being in France is required for "being in Paris." In other words, "being in France" is a necessary condition for "being in Paris."

Returning to example C1, your mechanic might respond that the battery being dead is one possible cause for your car not starting, but it is not the only reason why your car won't start. The problem could be caused by battery corrosion, a bad starter motor, a cracked distributor cap, a bad ignition coil, a clogged fuel filter, a broken timing belt. What your mechanic would be saying is that a dead battery is not the necessary condition for your car to start, since it is not the required cause for your car not starting. Also, the car not starting is not a sufficient condition for the battery to be dead because your car not starting is not enough information for you to infer that your battery is dead. Therefore, statement C1 is false.

With respect to truth values, we can define a **sufficient condition** as follows:

> For a conditional of the form "If X, then Y," condition X is sufficient for condition Y if and only if the truth of X guarantees (necessitates, brings about) the truth of Y.

For example, riding on an airplane is one way to travel to Canada. Thus, an airplane ride is a sufficient condition for reaching Canada. However, it is not necessary because there are other modes of travel. You could take the bus, drive a car, take a train, ride your bike, or hitch hike. Any of these means are sufficient means for getting you to Canada.

Just as we had defined a sufficient condition in terms of the truth value of its component parts, we can define a **necessary condition**:

> For a conditional of the form "If X, then Y," condition Y is necessary for condition X if and only if the falsity of Y guarantees (necessitates, brings about) the falsity of X.

There are quite a number of ways to express that something is a necessary condition. Let's suppose the surgeon says that you must have an operation to stay alive. Your surgeon can tell you any of the following statements.

> *Having the operation is necessary for you to stay alive.*
> *Without the operation, you will die.*

You must have the operation to live.
If you don't have the operation, then you will die.
The operation is needed to keep you alive.
You cannot live unless you have the operation.

After your surgeon breaks the news, you might then ask her, "Doctor, do you mean that the operation guarantees that I will continue to live?" Here, if the doctor is honest in her prognosis, she should say no. Regrettably, the operation is a necessary but not a sufficient condition for staying alive. Even if you have the operation, many things could still go wrong, thereby ending your life. You could have a heart attack; you might develop a fatal reaction to the anesthesia; you may die from infection; you could be bitten by a poisonous spider; lightning might strike you; you might be run over by a runaway trolley. Alas, the list of the possible causes that could lead to your untimely demise is almost endless.

Necessary conditions and sufficient conditions are **converse relations.** Given a conditional of the form "If X, then Y," Y is a necessary condition for X if and only if X is a sufficient condition for Y. Accordingly, with the converse relation, the terms of two statements are switched or trade places:

> Y is a **necessary** condition for X.
> X is a **sufficient** condition for Y.

This means that claiming that something is the necessary condition is equivalent to claiming that it is the sufficient condition as long as you change the order of the two terms, X and Y.

Exercise 6-E: Necessary versus Sufficient Condition

Determine if the condition given is necessary, sufficient, both, or neither.

1. "Being married" as a condition for "being a wife."
2. "Being married" as a condition for "being a father."
3. "Being an unmarried male" as a condition for "being a bachelor."
4. "Having four sides" as a condition for "being a square."
5. "Drinking coffee" as a condition for "consuming a beverage."
6. "Being first lady" as a condition for "being the wife of the current US president."
7. "Being a US citizen" as a condition for "being able to vote in presidential elections."
8. "Having a high IQ" as a condition for "being a billionaire."
9. "Being an elephant" as a condition for "being a mammal."
10. "Being younger than 20 years old" as a condition for "being a teenager."
11. "Being a woman" as a condition for "being a widow."
12. "Having a girlfriend" as a condition for "feeling happy."
13. "Being an odd number" as a condition for "being the number five."
14. "Being a rectangle" as a condition for "having four angles."
15. "Oxygen" as a condition for "having a fire."

Equivalent Expressions in Propositional Logic

Let us reconsider the surgeon's news expressed by this conditional statement, "If you do not have the operation, then you die." This proposition can be expressed in a number of different ways, each equivalent to the conditional statement. The surgeon could say the following:

P1   If you do not die, then you had the operation.
P2   Either you have the operation, or you die.

All three statements are equivalent to the conditional statement, "If you do not have the operation, then you will die." This equivalence is supported by three rules of inference.

One rule is called **Transposition** (Trans) or Contraposition. Transposition relates the conditional statement with P1. Transposition states:

"If X, then Y" is equivalent to "If not Y, then not X."

Recall that X is the antecedent and Y is the consequent of a conditional statement. The rule of Transposition allows you to switch the antecedent and the consequent as long as you take the negation of both. Here are more examples of Transposition:

If Spot is a dog, then Spot is not a reptile.	If Spot is a reptile, then Spot is not a dog.
If Al can tango, then Al can dance.	If Al cannot dance, then Al cannot tango.

Another rule is called **Material Implication** (Impl). This rule shows that the conditional statement is equivalent to P2. Material Implication expresses the following equivalence:

"If X, then Y" is equivalent to "Either not X or Y."

When applying Material Implication, the statement changes from a conditional statement (expressed by a horseshoe ⊃) to a disjunctive statement (expressed by a wedge ∨), or vice versa. Also, the antecedent and the first disjunct are negations of each other. Additional examples:

If you work, you earn some money.	Either you don't work, or you earn some money.
Either you are a minor or an adult.	If you are not a minor, then you are an adult.
Either an integer is odd or even.	If an integer is not odd, then it is even.

Thus, the conditional statement "If you do not have the operation, then you die" is equivalent to

P1   If you do not die, then you had the operation (by Trans).
P2   Either you have the operation, or you die (by Impl).

A third rule that establishes the equivalence of statements is **De Morgan's** (DM) **Law**. DM's Law relates conjunctions, statements formed with the ampersand &, with disjunctions, statements formed with the wedge ∨. There are two formulations of the DM's Law:

"It is not the case that both X and Y" is equivalent to "Either not X or not Y."
"It is not the case that either X or Y" is equivalent to "Both not X and not Y."

Due to lack of money, two friends might say to one another it is not the case that they can both go to the concert. This is logically equivalent to saying that either one friend cannot go, or the other friend cannot go. Some of us can truly say that it is not the case that I am either Polish or Brazilian. In other words, I am not Polish, and I am not Brazilian. Here are a few more pairs of statements that are equivalent by DM's Law:

It is not the case that either Jack is a child or a teen.
Jack is not a child, and he is not a teen.

It is not the case that Spain is both in Africa and Europe.
Spain is either not in Africa or not in Europe.

Either Max has a girlfriend, or he is unhappy.
It is not the case that both Max does not have a girlfriend and he is happy.

Exercise 6-F: Equivalent Statements

Translate each sentence into a well-formed formula of propositional logic. Identify the simple statements and choose the capital letters you will use to symbolize them. Then, apply the rule of inference to come up with an equivalent statement.

Example: Apply Impl: Either you have the operation, or you will die.
Answer: (O ∨ D) If you don't have the operation, then you will die.

1. Apply Impl: If Nina is Brazilian, then she is South American.
2. Apply Trans: If I drink wine, then I will not drink beer.
3. Apply Trans: If I do not go to the beach, then I do not need sunblock.
4. Apply DM: It is not the case that Gina is both a lawyer and a doctor.
5. Apply DM: It is not the case that either we are eating pizza or spaghetti for dinner.
6. Apply Impl: If I do not wake up now, I will be late for class.
7. Apply Impl: Either you marry me, or you'll be a spinster the rest of your life.
8. Apply DM: Either you will not go to the movies or you will not go to the party.
9. Apply Trans: If Bill gets a promotion, then he will not retire early.
10. Apply Impl: If I do not have enough money, then I will have to skip lunch.
11. Apply Trans: If Pat is not a male, then Pat is not a father.
12. Apply DM: It is not the case that either chemistry or algebra is an easy class.
13. Apply Trans: If I think, then I exist.
14. Apply Impl: If I am alive, then I am not dead.
15. Apply DM: I will not lie, and I will not steal.

Exercise 6-G: Equivalent Pairs of Sentences

Translate the following statements into sentence logic. Identify the simple statements and choose the capital letters you will use to symbolize them. Then, determine whether each pair of sentences are equivalent to one another. If they are equivalent, explain why: by Converse relation, by Transposition, by Implication, or by DM's Law. If they are not equivalent, explain why not.

1. It is not the case that Abby is both a waitress and she does not earn tips.

    Either Abby is not a waitress, or she earns tips.

2. If Barney plays basketball, then he wears shorts.

    If Barney does not wear shorts, then he does not play basketball.

3. If Camden does not take the trolley, then he borrowed his dad's car.

    Either Camden takes the trolley, or he borrows his dad's car.

4. Daniel graduating from high school is a necessary condition for him going to college.

    Daniel's going to college is a sufficient condition for graduating from high school.

5. Either Edward is right-handed or left-handed.

    If Edward is not right-handed, then he is left-handed.

6. If Frank dropped out of school, then he earns minimum wage.

    If Frank earns minimum wage, then he dropped out of school.

7. The rain is a sufficient condition for Gina to stay home.

    The rain is a necessary condition for Gina to stay home.

8. If Hannah travels to Spain, then she does not travel to Ireland.

    If Hannah travels to Ireland, then she does not travel to Spain.

9. It is not the case that both Irma had a bad day, and she won't eat ice cream.

    Either Irma had a good day, or she will eat a quart of ice cream.

10. If Jack mowed the lawn, then he raked the leaves.

    If Jack raked the leaves, then he mowed the lawn.

11. It is not the case that Ken either adopted some puppies or took in stray cats.

    Ken did not adopt some puppies, and he did not take in stray cats.

12. Laura's passing the final exam is a necessary condition for her to pass the class.

    Laura's passing the class is a sufficient condition for her passing the final exam.

CHAPTER 7
Ethical Reasoning

> In Chapter 7, we will focus on ethical philosophical theories, including relative versus objective moral theories, utilitarianism, duty ethics, and virtue-based ethics. After completing the chapter, readers will be able to
> evaluate ethical egoism in Plato's "Myth of Gyges,"
>
> - analyze Bentham's and Mill's utilitarianism,
> - understand Kant's categorical and hypothetical imperatives,
> - examine Rawls's social contract theory of justice,
> - analyze Aristotle's virtue ethics, and
> - identify moral fallacies.

Ethics is a field in philosophy that focuses on the right versus wrong action or the proper way to live one's life. Various ethical theories offer different moral principles or identify particular moral values or goals. Often, it is argued that these moral standards are objective and apply to all individuals. Before we discuss the three basic ethical theories, let us consider the view of **relativism,** which denies the objective truth of any ethical theory. Relativism claims that right and wrong depend on the beliefs held by society. Moreover, no same set of rules applies to every society or culture. Each society has its own set of moral rules, and an individual's belief is true if it conforms to the rules of his or her society. There is no overarching global standard by which one society's moral practices can be judged against another's. Thus, no culture has the right to criticize another culture's way of life or conventions. Relativism often observes that different groups hold different moral beliefs and values, and based on this observation, denies moral objectivity.

One extreme form of relativism is **subjectivism.** Instead of a society determining right from wrong, the individual makes the moral decisions, and whatever the individual decides is then right for that individual. Morality is in the eye of the beholder and becomes a matter of individual opinion, with one person's opinion being as true as any other's. When two people disagree, subjectivism provides no standard for settling moral disputes. Thus, subjectivism allows two individuals with contradictory moral beliefs to both be correct.

Objective Moral Theories

There are, however, three main schools of ethics that disagree with relativism and presuppose objective moral standards. The three approaches to ethics include consequentialism, nonconsequentialism or deontology, and virtue ethics. Some of these schools of thought emphasize the impacts of one's actions, while others require conformity to moral principles, and yet others recommend the cultivation of moral character traits to live a good life.

A **consequentialist** ethical theory claims that what makes an action wrong or right depends on the results. Whatever makes people better off (happy, healthy, etc.) is morally good, and whatever makes people worse off (pain, suffering) is morally bad. Nothing else needs to be considered in judging an action. In a situation where one must decide how to act, the agent must try to calculate the likely effects of various alternatives and pick the action that is most likely to produce the best results.

In contrast, a **nonconsequentialist** ethical theory denies that an action's consequences have any bearing on its rightness or wrongness. Instead, whether an action is good or bad depends on whether it is done according to duty, i.e., out of respect for the moral law. These nonconsequentialist theories are also called duty ethics or deontological theories. According to duty ethics, some things are simply wrong and may not be done even if they might produce good results. The only correct reason for performing a moral duty is because it is a duty, not because of what it might produce.

Third, **virtue ethics** is an approach that encourages people to cultivate virtues and keep away from vices. Instead of focusing on the actions of an agent, virtue ethics stresses the importance of character development. People should strive to follow the examples of moral ideals so that they themselves cultivate the right disposition to think and act well. In doing so, they will more likely flourish as humans and attain happiness.

Ethical Egoism

Consequentialism may be divided into two common theories: ethical egoism and utilitarianism. For ethical egoism, an action is morally right if it benefits you and wrong if it harms you. Sacrificing your interests to help others would be a morally wrong action. Promoting your welfare does not, however, mean you should give in to self-indulgence and momentary pleasures. Ethical egoists do not just do whatever they feel like doing because this may not advance their long-term self-interests. For both egoism and utilitarianism, you ought to be well-informed about the likely outcomes of an action and to perform the action that maximizes the best consequences.

In Plato's "The Myth of Gyges," the character Glaucon proposes the view of ethical egoism to Socrates and explores the concept of justice.

The Myth of Gyges

Plato; trans. Benjamin Jowett

Glaucon: Socrates, do you wish really to persuade us, or only to seem to have persuaded us, that to be just is always better than to be unjust? ... [pages omitted here] They say that to do injustice is, by nature, good; to suffer injustice, evil; but that the evil is greater than the good. And so, when men have both done and suffered injustice and have had experience of both, not being able to avoid the one and obtain the other, they think that they had better agree among themselves to have neither; hence there arise laws and mutual covenants; and that which is ordained by law is termed by them lawful and just. This they affirm to be the origin and nature of justice; —it is a mean or compromise, between the best of all, which is to do injustice and not be punished, and the worst of all, which is to suffer injustice without the power of retaliation; and justice, being at a middle point between the two, is tolerated not as a good, but as the lesser evil ...

Now that those who practice justice do so involuntarily and because they have not the power to be unjust will best appear if we imagine something of this kind: having given both to the just and the unjust power to do what they will, let us watch and see whither desire will lead them; then we shall discover in the very act the just and unjust man to be proceeding along the same road, following their interest, which all natures deem to be their good, and are only diverted into the path of justice by the force of law. The liberty which we are supposing may be most completely given to them in the form of such a power as is said to have been possessed by Gyges, the ancestor of Croesus the Lydian. According to the tradition, Gyges was a shepherd in the service of the king of Lydia; there was a great storm, and an earthquake made an opening in the earth at the place where he was feeding his flock. Amazed at the sight, he descended into the opening, where, among other marvels, he beheld a hollow brazen horse, having doors, at which he stooping and looking in saw a dead body of stature, as appeared to him, more than human, and having nothing on but a gold ring; this he took from the finger of the dead and reascended.

Now the shepherds met together, according to custom, that they might send their monthly report about the flocks to the king; into their assembly he came having the ring on his finger, and as he was sitting among them, he chanced to turn the collet of the ring inside his hand, when instantly he became invisible to the rest of the company, and they began to speak of him as if he were no longer present. He was astonished at this, and again touching the ring he turned the collet outwards and reappeared; he made several trials of the ring, and always with the same result—when he turned the collet inwards, he became invisible, when outwards he reappeared. Whereupon he contrived to be chosen as one of the messengers who were sent to the court; whereas soon as he arrived, he seduced the queen, and with her help conspired against the king and slew him and took the kingdom.

Suppose now that there were two such magic rings, and the just put on one of them and the unjust the other; no man can be imagined to be of such an iron nature that he would stand fast in justice. No man would keep his hands off what was not his own when he could safely take

Plato, Selections from "Book II," *The Republic*, trans. Benjamin Jowett, Clarendon Press, 1888.

what he liked out of the market or go into houses and lie with any one at his pleasure, or kill or release from prison whom he would, and in all respects be like a God among men. Then the actions of the just would be as the actions of the unjust; they would both come at last to the same point. And this we may truly affirm to be a great proof that a man is just, not willingly or because he thinks that justice is any good to him individually, but of necessity, for wherever anyone thinks that he can safely be unjust, there he is unjust. For all men believe in their hearts that injustice is far more profitable to the individual than justice, and he who argues as I have been supposing, will say that they are right. If you could imagine anyone obtaining this power of becoming invisible, and never doing any wrong or touching what was another's, he would be thought by the lookers-on to be a most wretched idiot, although they would praise him to one another's faces, and keep up appearances with one another from a fear that they too might suffer injustice. Enough of this.

Now, if we are to form a real judgment of the life of the just and unjust, we must isolate them; there is no other way; and how is the isolation to be effected? I answer: Let the unjust man be entirely unjust, and the just man entirely just; nothing is to be taken away from either of them, and both are to be perfectly furnished for the work of their respective lives. First, let the unjust be like other distinguished masters of craft; like the skillful pilot or physician, who knows intuitively his own powers and keeps within their limits, and who, if he fails at any point, is able to recover himself. So, let the unjust make his unjust attempts in the right way, and lie hidden if he means to be great in his injustice: (he who is found out is nobody) for the highest reach of injustice is, to be deemed just when you are not. Therefore, I say that in the perfectly unjust man we must assume the most perfect injustice; there is to be no deduction, but we must allow him, while doing the most unjust acts, to have acquired the greatest reputation for justice. If he has taken a false step, he must be able to recover himself; he must be one who can speak with effect, if any of his deeds come to light, and who can force his way where force is required by his courage and strength, and command of money and friends.

And at his side let us place the just man in his nobleness and simplicity, wishing, as Aeschylus says, to be and not to seem good. There must be no seeming, for if he seems to be just, he will be honored and rewarded, and then we shall not know whether he is just for the sake of justice or for the sake of honors and rewards; therefore, let him be clothed in justice only, and have no other covering; and he must be imagined in a state of life the opposite of the former. Let him be the best of men and let him be thought the worst; then he will have been put to the proof; and we shall see whether he will be affected by the fear of infamy and its consequences. And let him continue thus to the hour of death; being just and seeming to be unjust. When both have reached the uttermost extreme, the one of justice and the other of injustice, let judgment be given which of them is the happier of the two.

> Socrates: Heavens! My dear Glaucon, how energetically you polish them up for the decision, first one and then the other, as if they were two statues.

Glaucon: I do my best. And now that we know what they are like there is no difficulty in tracing out the sort of life which awaits either of them. This I will proceed to describe; but as you may think the description a little too coarse, I ask you to suppose, Socrates, that the words which follow are not mine.—Let me put them into the mouths of the eulogists of injustice: They will tell you that the just man who is thought unjust will be scourged, racked, bound—will have his eyes burnt out; and, at last, after suffering every kind of evil, he will be impaled: Then he will understand that he ought to seem only, and not to be, just ... In the first place, he is thought just, and therefore bears rule in the city; he can marry whom he will, and give in marriage to whom he will; also he can trade and deal where he likes, and always to his own advantage, because he has no misgivings about injustice; and at every contest, whether in public or private, he gets the better of his antagonists, and gains at their expense, and is rich, and out of his gains he can benefit his friends, and harm his enemies; moreover, he can offer sacrifices, and dedicate gifts to the gods abundantly and magnificently, and can honor the gods or any man whom he wants to honor in a far better style than the just, and therefore he is likely to be dearer than they are to the gods. And thus, Socrates, gods and men are said to unite in making the life of the unjust better than the life of the just ...

For what men say is that, if I am really just and am not also thought just profit there is none, but the pain and loss on the other hand are unmistakable. But if, though unjust, I acquire the reputation of justice, a heavenly life is promised to me. Since then, as philosophers prove, appearance tyrannizes over truth and is lord of happiness, to appearance I must devote myself. I will describe around me a picture and shadow of virtue to be the vestibule and exterior of my house; behind I will trail the subtle and crafty fox, as Archilochus, greatest of sages, recommends. But I hear someone exclaiming that the concealment of wickedness is often difficult; to which I answer, nothing great is easy. Nevertheless, the argument indicates this, if we would be happy, to be the path along which we should proceed. With a view to concealment, we will establish secret brotherhoods and political clubs. And there are professors of rhetoric who teach the art of persuading courts and assemblies; and so, partly by persuasion and partly by force, I shall make unlawful gains and not be punished. Still, I hear a voice saying that the gods cannot be deceived, neither can they be compelled. But what if there are no gods? Or suppose them to have no care of human things ...

On what principle, then, shall we any longer choose justice rather than the worst injustice? When, if we only unite the latter with a deceitful regard to appearances, we shall fare to our mind both with gods and men, in life and after death, as the most numerous and the highest authorities tell us. Knowing all this, Socrates, how can a man who has any superiority of mind or person or rank or wealth, be willing to honor justice; or indeed to refrain from laughing when he hears justice praised? And even if there should be someone who is able to disprove the truth of my words, and who is satisfied that justice is best, still he is not angry with the unjust, but is very ready to forgive them, because he also knows that men are not just of their own free will; unless, peradventure, there be someone whom the divinity within him may have inspired with a hatred of injustice, or who has attained knowledge of the truth—but no other man. He only blames injustice who, owing to cowardice or age or some weakness, has not the power of being unjust. And this is proved by the fact that when he obtains the power, he immediately becomes unjust ...

But I speak in this vehement manner, as I must frankly confess to you, because I want to hear from you the opposite side; and I would ask you to show not only the superiority which justice has over injustice, but what effect they have on the possessor of them which makes the one to be a good and the other an evil to him ... Now as you have admitted that justice is one of that highest class of goods which are desired indeed for their results, but in a far greater degree for their own sakes—like sight or hearing or knowledge or health, or any other real and natural and not merely conventional good ... And therefore, I say, not only prove to us that justice is better than injustice but show what they either of them do to the possessor of them, which makes the one to be a good and the other an evil, whether seen or unseen by gods and men.

Exercise 7-A: Reading Questions on Plato's "Myth of Gyges"

1. In "The Ring of Gyges," what happens to the shepherd Gyges?
2. In Glaucon's view, how would just and unjust people behave if they had the ring of invisibility?
3. Does Glaucon think people would naturally follow the laws if they knew they would not get caught?
4. Who tends to be happier, the just or unjust person, according to Glaucon? Why?
5. How does Glaucon argue that justice is established?
6. How are Glaucon's ideas on justice based on the theory of psychological egoism?

Utilitarianism

Another consequentialist theory is **utilitarianism**. According to utilitarianism, an action is morally right to the extent that it increases overall well-being and is morally wrong to the extent that it decreases overall well-being (increases suffering). 'Overall' refers to everyone likely to be affected by the action, policy, or rule being evaluated. Some utilitarians, notably Peter Singer, claim that the welfare of animals is also important and should be taken into consideration.

Utilitarians such as Jeremy Bentham and John Stuart Mill often use the word "utility" instead of "well-being." Utility refers to anything that provides some benefit, advantage, or pleasure, whatever contributes to the good life, such as happiness, health, self-respect, desire-satisfaction, etc. The morally right action maximizes the long-term good for everyone involved. Not only is utilitarianism inclusive, but it also demands impartiality. Everyone's happiness counts equally; your happiness matters but so does the happiness of strangers. Thus, you would not be justified in doing something that benefits just you and your friends if it causes others to suffer.

Jeremy Bentham: *An Introduction to the Principles of Morals and Legislation*

Chapter I: Of the Principle of Utility

I. Nature has placed mankind under the governance of two sovereign masters, *pain* and *pleasure.* It is for them alone to point out what we ought to do, as well as to determine what we shall do. On the one hand the standard of right and wrong, on the other the chain of causes and effects, are fastened to their throne. They govern us in all we do, in all we say, in all we think ...

II. The principle of utility is the foundation of the present work ... By the principle of utility is meant that principle which approves or disapproves of every action whatsoever according to the tendency it appears to have to augment or diminish the happiness of the party whose interest is in question ...

III. By utility is meant that property in any object, whereby it tends to produce benefit, advantage, pleasure, good, or happiness, (all this in the present case comes to the same thing) or (what comes again to the same thing) to prevent the happening of mischief, pain, evil, or unhappiness to the party whose interest is considered: if that party be the community in general, then the happiness of the community: if a particular individual, then the happiness of that individual ...

Chapter IV: Value of a Lot of Pleasure or Pain, How to be Measured

I. Pleasures then, and the avoidance of pains, are the *ends* ...

IV. To a *number* of persons, with reference to each of whom to the value of a pleasure or a pain is considered, it will be greater or less, according to seven circumstances: to wit, the six preceding ones; viz.,

1. Its *intensity.*
2. Its *duration.*
3. Its *certainty* or *uncertainty.*
4. Its *propinquity* or *remoteness.*
5. Its *fecundity.*
6. Its *purity.*

And one other; to wit:

7. Its *extent;* that is, the number of persons to whom it *extends;* or (in other words) who are affected by it.

What Utilitarianism Is

By John Stuart Mill

1 ... Those who know anything about the matter are aware that every writer, from Epicurus to Bentham, who maintained the theory of utility, meant by it, not something to be contradistinguished from pleasure, but pleasure itself, together with exemption from pain ... Yet the common herd, including the herd of writers, not only in newspapers and periodicals, but in books of weight and pretension, are perpetually falling into this shallow mistake. Having caught up the word utilitarian, while knowing nothing whatever about it but its sound, they habitually express by it the rejection, or the neglect, of pleasure in some of its forms; of beauty, of ornament, or of amusement. Nor is the term thus ignorantly misapplied solely in disparagement, but occasionally in compliment; as though it implied superiority to frivolity and the mere pleasures of the moment. And this perverted use is the only one in which the word is popularly known, and the one from which the new generation are acquiring their sole notion of its meaning. Those who introduced the word, but who had for many years discontinued it as a distinctive appellation, may well feel themselves called upon to resume it, if by doing so they can hope to contribute anything towards rescuing it from this utter degradation.

2 The creed which accepts as the foundation of morals, Utility, or the Greatest Happiness Principle, holds that actions are right in proportion as they tend to promote happiness, wrong as they tend to produce the reverse of happiness. By happiness is intended pleasure, and the absence of pain; by unhappiness, pain, and the privation of pleasure. To give a clear view of the moral standard set up by the theory, much more requires to be said; in particular, what things it includes in the ideas of pain and pleasure; and to what extent this is left an open question. But these supplementary explanations do not affect the theory of life on which this theory of morality is grounded- namely, that pleasure, and freedom from pain, are the only things desirable as ends; and that all desirable things (which are as numerous in the utilitarian as in any other scheme) are desirable either for the pleasure inherent in themselves, or as means to the promotion of pleasure and the prevention of pain.

3 Now, such a theory of life excites in many minds, and among them in some of the most estimable in feeling and purpose, inveterate dislike. To suppose that life has (as they express it) no higher end than pleasure- no better and nobler object of desire and pursuit- they designate as utterly mean and grovelling; as a doctrine worthy only of swine, to whom the followers of Epicurus were, at a very early period, contemptuously likened ...

4 When thus attacked, the Epicureans have always answered, that it is not they, but their accusers, who represent human nature in a degrading light; since the accusation supposes human beings to be capable of no pleasures except those of which swine are capable ... The comparison of the Epicurean life to that of beasts is felt as degrading, precisely because a beast's pleasures do not satisfy a human being's conceptions of happiness. Human beings have faculties more elevated than the animal appetites ... But there is no known Epicurean theory of life which does not assign to the pleasures of the intellect, of the feelings and imagination, and of the moral sentiments, a much higher value as pleasures than to those of mere sensation.

John Stuart Mill, Selections from "Chapter II: What Utilitarianism Is," *Utilitarianism*, Longmans, Green and Co., 1879.

It must be admitted, however, that utilitarian writers in general have placed the superiority of mental over bodily pleasures chiefly in the greater permanency, safety, uncostliness, etc., of the former- that is, in their circumstantial advantages rather than in their intrinsic nature ... It is quite compatible with the principle of utility to recognise the fact, that some kinds of pleasure are more desirable and more valuable than others. It would be absurd that while, in estimating all other things, quality is considered as well as quantity, the estimation of pleasures should be supposed to depend on quantity alone.

5 If I am asked, what I mean by difference of quality in pleasures, or what makes one pleasure more valuable than another, merely as a pleasure, except its being greater in amount, there is but one possible answer. Of two pleasures, if there be one to which all or almost all who have experience of both give a decided preference, irrespective of any feeling of moral obligation to prefer it, that is the more desirable pleasure. If one of the two is, by those who are competently acquainted with both, placed so far above the other that they prefer it, even though knowing it to be attended with a greater amount of discontent, and would not resign it for any quantity of the other pleasure which their nature is capable of, we are justified in ascribing to the preferred enjoyment a superiority in quality, so far outweighing quantity as to render it, in comparison, of small account.

6 Now it is an unquestionable fact that those who are equally acquainted with, and equally capable of appreciating and enjoying, both, do give a most marked preference to the manner of existence which employs their higher faculties. Few human creatures would consent to be changed into any of the lower animals, for a promise of the fullest allowance of a beast's pleasures; no intelligent human being would consent to be a fool, no instructed person would be an ignoramus, no person of feeling and conscience would be selfish and base, even though they should be persuaded that the fool, the dunce, or the rascal is better satisfied with his lot than they are with theirs. They would not resign what they possess more than he for the most complete satisfaction of all the desires which they have in common with him. If they ever fancy they would, it is only in cases of unhappiness so extreme, that to escape from it they would exchange their lot for almost any other, however undesirable in their own eyes. A being of higher faculties requires more to make him happy, is capable probably of more acute suffering, and certainly accessible to it at more points, than one of an inferior type; but in spite of these liabilities, he can never really wish to sink into what he feels to be a lower grade of existence. We may give what explanation we please of this unwillingness; we may attribute it to pride, a name which is given indiscriminately to some of the most and to some of the least estimable feelings of which mankind are capable: we may refer it to the love of liberty and personal independence, an appeal to which was with the Stoics one of the most effective means for the inculcation of it; to the love of power, or to the love of excitement, both of which do really enter into and contribute to it: but its most appropriate appellation is a sense of dignity, which all human beings possess in one form or other, and in some, though by no means in exact, proportion to their higher faculties, and which is so essential a part of the happiness of those in whom it is strong, that nothing which conflicts with it could be, otherwise than momentarily, an object of desire to them.

7 Whoever supposes that this preference takes place at a sacrifice of happiness- that the superior being, in anything like equal circumstances, is not happier than the inferior- confounds the two very different ideas, of happiness, and content. It is indisputable that the being whose capacities of enjoyment are low, has the greatest chance of having them fully satisfied; and a highly endowed being will always feel that any happiness which he can look for, as the world is constituted, is imperfect. But he can learn to bear its imperfections, if they are at all bearable; and they will not make him envy the being who is indeed unconscious of the imperfections, but only because he feels not at all the good which those imperfections qualify. It is better to be a human being dissatisfied than a pig satisfied; better to be Socrates dissatisfied than a fool satisfied. And if the fool, or the pig, are a different opinion, it is because they only know their own side of the question. The other party to the comparison knows both sides.

Exercise 7-B: Reading Questions on Bentham and Mill's *Utilitarianism*

1. Bentham claims that nature has placed mankind under the governance of what? What does he mean by this?
2. For Bentham, what does "utility" mean, and what is the "principle of utility"?
3. Prior to Mill, Jeremy Bentham offers hedonic calculus as a way of measuring the quantity of pleasures. What do Bentham's seven categories mean: intensity, certainty, duration, propinquity, fecundity, purity, and extent?
4. Do Bentham and Mill think that our happiness is any more important than the happiness of others? How do Bentham and Mill differ with respect to the quality of pleasures?
5. According to Mill, how have Epicureans been misunderstood by their critics or accusers? How does Mill respond to the objection that utilitarianism is a "doctrine worthy of swine"?
6. How does Mill determine that higher pleasures are more important to happiness than lower pleasures? How do we know some pleasures are qualitatively superior to others?
7. What point is Mill making when he brings up the reference to "Socrates dissatisfied"?

Divine Command Theory

Nonconsequentialist theories deny that the results produced by an action have anything to do with its rightness or wrongness. Rather, an action is morally right if it is consistent with the moral law; otherwise, it is wrong. We have certain moral duties, and we must perform them without regard to the consequences they may produce, simply because they are our duties.

What is the source of these moral laws? One type of nonconsequentialist theory is divine command theory, which states that the moral law is established by God. God gives us commands, and those commands determine what is right and wrong. If God commands us to do it, then it's our duty, and if God forbids it, then it's wrong. The objective moral standard can be found by consulting the scriptures and reading God's commands therein.

One problem with applying divine command theory is the difficulty of knowing just what God commands. Even if you accept a book (Bible, Koran) as God's word, it often needs to be interpreted. Then we have to agree on whose interpretation of the book is most accurate.

Another problem relates back to Euthyphro's dilemma: Is an action right because God commands it, or does God command it because it is right? On the first alternative, God's commands look arbitrary. It says that something is right because God commands it, simply because God's commanding it makes it right. But this would mean that there's no reason for right and wrong: God just happens to command and forbid certain things. God could just have easily decided that murdering babies is a moral obligation. It appears to reduce morality to the inexplicable whim of a supernatural being. On the second alternative, moral principles have their value whether or not God commands them, as if they stood above God. This is problematic for some theists because it seems to undermine God's authority as God would not be the source of morality.

Kant and Duty Ethics

Immanuel Kant offers probably the best-known nonconsequentialist theory. Kant's ethics is a **deontological moral theory** requiring that people fulfill their duties. Unlike the consequential theory of utilitarianism, Kant's ethics claims that the rightness or wrongness of actions does not depend on their consequences. Actions such as stealing, killing, or lying are morally wrong even when doing these actions can lead to greater net happiness. What matters is respecting the moral law and doing the right actions for the sake of principle.

Whereas utilitarianism may neglect human rights and downplay the relevance of the person's motive, duty theory bases morality on duty and makes rights inviolable. Furthermore, to be morally good, a human agent must not only do the morally right action but must do so with the appropriate motive. For an action to have moral worth, the agent must act for the sake of principle, out of duty.

Kant distinguishes between hypothetical and categorical imperatives, calling only the latter moral commands. An imperative is any claim about what we should do. **Hypothetical imperatives** tell us what we ought to do in order to reach some desired end. "You should fulfill contractual obligations if you want to get more clients." "If I desire to be a pharmacist, then I must learn chemistry." Hypothetical imperatives apply conditionally, relative to each person's desires and thus vary from individual to individual.

Kant defines a **categorical imperative** as the kind of imperative that is universal and morally binding on everyone. A categorical imperative is unconditional, and persons are obligated to obey them, regardless of what they want and independent of the consequences. Like a test of goodness for all actions, a categorical imperative is a supreme principle of morality that informs us which types of actions are morally right or wrong. If telling the truth is a moral rule that passes the categorical imperative, then this rule must be followed by everyone without exception no matter the circumstances. Since Kant believed that morality absolutely binds all rational agents, he claimed that morality must be based on categorical and not hypothetical imperatives.

According to Kant, the categorical imperative can be expressed by four formulations, each formulation he took to be basically equivalent to one another. Scholars see differences between the formulations and dispute this claim of equivalence. His **first formulation of the categorical imperative**, also known as the principle of universalizability, states, "We should act only on that maxim which we can at the same time will that it become universal law." A maxim is a rule that guides your action. For example, I might make it my maxim to say thank you whenever someone does me a favor. Thanking the person who helps you is a rule or maxim that might guide your action.

If I were to apply the first formulation of the categorical imperative, I need to ask myself whether I can rationally will that everyone act as I propose to act. That is, can I consistently will that the maxim of my action be universalized or become, as it were, the law of the land? If I can rationally will this, then the action is morally permissible. However, if I cannot rationally will that everyone do as I do, then the action is morally wrong and is prohibited. The first formulation of the categorical imperative commands you not to do anything that you would not be willing to allow everyone else to do as well. Thus, if you expect others to be honest, then you too have a duty to tell the truth. To be more precise, the first formulation of the categorical imperative requires that every maxim you act on must be such that you would authorize everyone always to act on that maxim in similar circumstances.

Some maxims do not pass this universalizability test because you cannot even conceive of universalizing the maxim. Kant's example of breaking promises illustrates this problem. In this example, Kant asks us to imagine a man desperate for money who makes a false promise to pay the money back but has no intention of ever doing so. The maxim of making false promises could not be universalized because one would have to will that everyone makes false promises in that same situation. But, if all promises in such situations are lies, then no one would believe alleged promises. The institution of promise-making would no longer exist since everyone would understand that all promises are shams, just vain pretenses.

Another way in which a maxim can fail the universalizability test involves a contradiction in the will. Kant's example about committing suicide involves a contradiction of the wills. Here, Kant describes a man living a miserable life who is contemplating suicide. Can one universalize the maxim of committing suicide? If so, then one should be able to consistently will that everyone in similar circumstances commit suicide when they are miserable with their lives. Kant identifies an interesting (though highly contestable) contradiction. He explains that people naturally want to survive and seek to preserve their lives. However, people who attempt to commit suicide are seeking to destroy their lives. It is irrational for people to pursue contradictory desires. One's will is thus involved in a contradiction wherein one seeks to stay alive and yet at the same time to die. Therefore, Kant concludes that no rational agent can consistently, without contradiction, have the will to commit suicide. As a result, suicide is never morally permissible for anyone.

The second formulation of the categorical imperative states that one should "act in such a way that you always treat humanity, whether in your own person or in the person of another, never simply as a means, but always at the same time as an end." This categorical imperative is sometimes known as the principle of respect for persons because it requires that we have an attitude of respect toward ourselves and toward other people. Respecting persons includes respecting ourselves as persons. We should not allow ourselves to be degraded or engage in actions that undermine our dignity.

Every rational being is an end in himself, not merely a means to be used by other persons. People have their own reasons for choosing their actions. Persons are "objective ends, i.e., beings whose existence in itself is an end." That is, human existence is its own purpose. According to Kant, humans are autonomous and thus have the capacity to be self-ruled. As persons, we make our own choices; we choose our life plans, our friends, our goals. It is fine to use things as a means to attain our goals, but it is never right to use persons as though they were completely at our disposal and lacked their own goals and a will of their own.

This does not imply, however, that we can never use people as a means to an end. We use one another all the time. We use the person who bags our groceries, delivers our pizza, collects our trash, etc. However, there are certain conditions that we must follow when we use people so that we still respect them as persons and do not merely treat them as means. First, we should never deceive, manipulate, or coerce someone so that we can achieve our personal desires. When soliciting the services of others, we should obtain their informed consent after having communicated what we are asking of them. Second, when we use persons, we should try to promote their rationality and autonomy, taking into consideration what their own personal goals or ends are. Slavery, sex trafficking, involuntary human experimentation, child labor, domestic abuse, etc. are examples of morally wrong actions prohibited by the second formulation of the categorical imperative.

In contrast to persons, things, including animals, have a conditional worth and have a value given to them by persons who are value-givers. Things may be bought and sold at a price. All material ends are relative, subjective, and worth pursuing only because of particular human desires. Every material thing has a purpose only as a means to an end, our end. Human beings are different. Humans should never be treated simply as a means. Even if a person seems useless or unloved by others, a person nonetheless has intrinsic worth, unlike things or animals, which have only an instrumental value. Although people have different abilities when it comes to their power to reason, we owe every person respect to the same degree because they are human beings who possess rationality. When applying the second formulation of the categorical imperative, you should ask yourself whether your action respects the goals of human beings rather than merely using them just for your own purposes. Kant explains how his four examples of breaking promises, committing suicide, wasting talents, and refusing to help others violate the second formulation of the categorical imperative. Each of these examples involves a person disrespecting himself or other people.

To be a good person in Kant's ethical theory requires not only doing the right action, but it demands the proper intention. A person has moral worth if she does the right thing with the proper intention or motivation. That is, a moral agent must have the right reason for doing the action. For Kant, the right reason or motivation is not emotions such as love, sympathy, or fear, and it is not the desire for rewards or happiness. An agent has moral worth if they are doing the right action for the sake of principle or out of duty. One should be motivated by morality, i.e., respect for the moral law. A good person always does their duty because it is their duty, just because that is what she is supposed to do. A person with moral worth must do good for goodness' sake regardless of the consequences. Kant describes the person who consistently acts for the sake of duty as someone who possesses "**the good will.**"

Fundamental Principles of Metaphysic of Morals

By Immanuel Kant; trans. Thomas Kingsmill Abbott

The First Formulation of the Categorical Imperative

There is therefore but one categorical imperative, namely, this: **Act only on that maxim whereby thou canst at the same time will that it should become a universal law.** … We will now enumerate a few duties …

    1. A man reduced to despair by a series of misfortunes feels wearied of life but is still so far in possession of his reason that he can ask himself whether it would not be contrary to his duty to himself to take his own life. Now he inquires whether the maxim of his action could become a universal law of nature. His maxim is: "From self-love I adopt it as a principle to shorten my life when its longer duration is likely to bring more evil than satisfaction." It is asked then simply whether this principle founded on self-love can become a universal law of nature. Now we see at once that a system of nature of which it should be a law to destroy life by means of the very feeling whose special nature it is to impel to the improvement of life would contradict itself and, therefore, could not exist as a system of nature; hence that maxim cannot possibly exist as a universal law of nature and, consequently, would be wholly inconsistent with the supreme principle of all duty.

    2. Another finds himself forced by necessity to borrow money. He knows that he will not be able to repay it but sees also that nothing will be lent to him unless he promises stoutly to repay it in a definite time. He desires to make this promise, but he has still so much conscience as to ask himself: "Is it not unlawful and inconsistent with duty to get out of a difficulty in this way?" Suppose, however, that he resolves to do so: then the maxim of his action would be expressed thus: "When I think myself in want of money, I will borrow money and promise to repay it, although I know that I never can do so." Now this principle of self-love or of one's own advantage may perhaps be consistent with my whole future welfare; but the question now is, "Is it right?" I change then the suggestion of self-love into a universal law, and state the question thus: "How would it be if my maxim were a universal law?" Then I see at once that it could never hold as a universal law of nature but would necessarily contradict itself. For supposing it to be a universal law that everyone when he thinks himself in a difficulty should be able to promise whatever he pleases, with the purpose of not keeping his promise, the promise itself would become impossible, as well as the end that one might have in view in it, since no one

Immanuel Kant, *Fundamental Principles of the Metaphysic of Morals*, trans. Thomas Kingsmill Abbott, 1873.

would consider that anything was promised to him but would ridicule all such statements as vain pretenses.

3. A third finds in himself a talent which with the help of some culture might make him a useful man in many respects. But he finds himself in comfortable circumstances and prefers to indulge in pleasure rather than to take pains in enlarging and improving his happy natural capacities. He asks, however, whether his maxim of neglect of his natural gifts, besides agreeing with his inclination to indulgence, agrees also with what is called duty. He sees then that a system of nature could indeed subsist with such a universal law although men (like the South Sea islanders) should let their talents rest and resolve to devote their lives merely to idleness, amusement, and propagation of their species- in a word, to enjoyment; but he cannot possibly will that this should be a universal law of nature or be implanted in us as such by a natural instinct. For, as a rational being, he necessarily wills that his faculties be developed, since they serve him and have been given him, for all sorts of possible purposes.

4. A fourth, who is in prosperity, while he sees that others have to contend with great wretchedness and that he could help them, thinks: "What concern is it of mine? Let everyone be as happy as Heaven pleases, or as he can make himself; I will take nothing from him nor even envy him, only I do not wish to contribute anything to his welfare or to his assistance in distress!" Now no doubt if such a mode of thinking were a universal law, the human race might very well subsist and doubtless even better than in a state in which everyone talks of sympathy and good-will, or even takes care occasionally to put it into practice, but, on the other side, also cheats when he can, betrays the rights of men, or otherwise violates them. But although it is possible that a universal law of nature might exist in accordance with that maxim, it is impossible to will that such a principle should have the universal validity of a law of nature. For a will which resolved this would contradict itself, inasmuch as many cases might occur in which one would have need of the love and sympathy of others, and in which, by such a law of nature, sprung from his own will, he would deprive himself of all hope of the aid he desires.

These are a few of the many actual duties, or at least what we regard as such, which obviously fall into two classes on the one principle that we have laid down. We must be able to will that a maxim of our action should be a universal law. This is the canon of the moral appreciation of the action generally. Some actions are of such a character that their maxim cannot without contradiction be even conceived as a universal law of nature, far from it being possible that we should will that it should be so. In others, this intrinsic impossibility is not found, but still it is impossible to will that their maxim should be raised to the universality of a law of nature, since such a will would contradict itself. It is easily seen that the former violates strict or rigorous (inflexible) duty; the latter only laxer (meritorious) duty. Thus, it has been completely shown how all duties depend as regards the nature of the obligation (not the object of the action) on the same principle ...

The Second Formulation of the Categorical Imperative

[This is a second formulation of Kant's categorical imperative] So act as to treat humanity, whether in thine own person or in that of any other, in every case as an end withal, never as means only. We will now inquire whether this can be practically carried out …

To abide by the previous examples:

Firstly, under the head of necessary duty to oneself: He who contemplates suicide should ask himself whether his action can be consistent with the idea of humanity as an end in itself. If he destroys himself in order to escape from painful circumstances, he uses a person merely as a mean to maintain a tolerable condition up to the end of life. But a man is not a thing, that is to say, something which can be used merely as means, but must in all his actions be always considered as an end in himself. I cannot, therefore, dispose in any way of a man in my own person so as to mutilate him, to damage or kill him. (It belongs to ethics proper to define this principle more precisely, so as to avoid all misunderstanding, e. g., as to the amputation of the limbs in order to preserve myself, as to exposing my life to danger with a view to preserving it, etc. This question is therefore omitted here.)

Secondly, as regards necessary duties, or those of strict obligation, towards others: He who is thinking of making a lying promise to others will see at once that he would be using another man merely as a mean, without the latter containing at the same time the end in himself. For he whom I propose by such a promise to use for my own purposes cannot possibly assent to my mode of acting towards him and, therefore, cannot himself contain the end of this action. This violation of the principle of humanity in other men is more obvious if we take in examples of attacks on the freedom and property of others. For then it is clear that he who transgresses the rights of men intends to use the person of others merely as a means, without considering that as rational beings they ought always to be esteemed also as ends, that is, as beings who must be capable of containing in themselves the end of the very same action …

Exercise 7-C: Reading Questions on Kant's *Metaphysics of Morals*

1. How are categorical imperatives distinguished from hypothetical imperatives?
2. Kant states the only good without qualification is the "*good will.*" What does he mean by this?
3. What does Kant mean that people are autonomous?
4. Why should we help other people, according to Kant? What should motivate us if our actions are to be morally worthy? Are sympathy and love good motives?
5. What is Kant's **first** formulation of the categorical imperative (universalizability)? How do the examples of committing suicide, breaking promises, wasting talents, and not helping others fail under the first formulation?
6. What is Kant's second formulation of the categorical imperative (respect for persons)? How do these examples fail under the second formulation?

7. According to Kant's second formulation, why does Kant add the word "merely" when stating that it is wrong to treat humanity "merely as a means"? How do you treat persons as ends?

Rawls and Justice

Building on a conception of justice as fairness, American philosopher John Rawls advocates for political liberalism. He was concerned about finding the fairest principles for a society, ones that could justly allocate the primary goods such as wealth, property, and power among its citizens. While the utilitarians favored policies that maximized the total net happiness for the whole society, Rawls worried that such a goal ignores fair distribution and allows for the sacrifice of minority rights for the good of the majority. Utilitarianism could justify, for example, the institution of slavery if it meant the prosperity of a nation and the greatest net happiness for the rest. In his book *The Theory of Justice*, Rawls writes,

> Justice is the first virtue of social institutions, as truth is of systems of thought. A theory however elegant and economical must be rejected or revised if it is untrue; likewise, laws and institutions no matter how efficient and well-arranged must be reformed or abolished if they are unjust. Each person possesses an inviolability founded on justice that even the welfare of society as a whole cannot override. For this reason, justice denies that the loss of freedom for some is made right by a greater good shared by others. It does not allow that the sacrifices imposed on a few are outweighed by the larger sum of advantages enjoyed by many. Therefore, in a just society the liberties of equal citizenship are taken as settled; the rights secured by justice are not subject to political bargaining or to the calculus of social interests.

In the tradition of political philosophers such as Locke and Rousseau, Rawls justifies his theory of justice on a social contract theory. The fairest principles are those that free and equal citizens would adopt. Rawls considers an original position in which everyone serves as legislators involved in choosing the laws of the land that they would agree upon for their society. The original position does not actually occur but is hypothetical, serving as a kind of thought experiment for coming up with the most just laws. A condition that Rawls adds to citizens in the original position is the veil of ignorance. All citizens acting as legislators must vote for laws behind a veil of ignorance that blinds them to particulars about themselves. In his book *The Theory of Justice*, Rawls describes the veil of ignorance:

> Among the essential features of this situation is that no one knows his place in society, his class position or social status, nor does anyone know his fortune in the distribution of natural assets and abilities, his intelligence, strength, and the like. I shall even assume that the parties do not know their conceptions of the good or their special psychological propensities. The principles of justice are chosen behind a veil of ignorance.

Based on the notion that "justice is blind," impartial citizens are ignorant of their personal characteristics, interests, and circumstances that might bias them to choose laws for their own advantage. The vote of citizens would not be influenced by their socioeconomic standing, age, gender, ethnicity, talents, conceptions of the good, religion, education, familial ties, occupations, etc.

Ignorant of particular details about their identity, citizens in the original position can know general facts about the state of the world and human nature. It is known that the state of the world is one of moderate scarcity such that there are enough primary goods in the society for everyone to survive and live fairly comfortably given social cooperation, although there is not so much wealth as to make everyone billionaires. Despite the veil of ignorance, citizens in the original position realize general facts about human nature. They can know that humans are social and rational beings with the instinct to survive, the need for food, the desire for friends, and the love of children, etc. They also know that individuals have different conceptions of the good life, including different religious beliefs or philosophical viewpoints; however, members of society operate on a reasonable pluralism, allowing them to respect or at least tolerate opposing views. Rawls also assumes that humans have a natural interest in acquiring more primary goods yet tend to be risk averse so that their desire for gain may be moderated by their fear of loss. Rawls claims that such free and equal citizens in the original position under the veil of ignorance would choose these two basic principles that would be fair for everyone and not just for themselves and their particular circumstances:

> **First Principle**: Each person is to have an equal right to the most extensive liberty compatible with similar liberty for others.
>
> **Second Principle**: Social and economic inequalities are to satisfy two conditions:
> 1. They are to be attached to offices and positions open to all under conditions of *fair equality of opportunity*.
> 2. They are to be to the greatest benefit of the least-advantaged members of society (the *difference principle*).

In Rawls's view, these two principles of justice are established by social contract hypothetically through the original position. Like Immanuel Kant, Rawls conceives human beings as rational agents who are self-legislating and autonomous. Both of these principles are the correct ones because they are the ones that rational agents would agree to adopt as the fairest for all without any arbitrary bias toward their own individual interests. Rawls also claims that people will prioritize the first principle over the second. He maintains that there is a lexical ordering such that the first principle has priority over the second, and the fair equality of opportunity principle has priority over the difference principle. Given the first principle, often known as the liberty principle, each person is to have equal basic rights such as the right to life, liberty of the person, right to vote, freedom of religion, freedom of speech, right to due process, etc. Each person is to have the maximum number of liberties as is compatible with others having an equal number of liberties. No one's liberty can be violated for the sake of socioeconomic goods. Thus, Rawls's theory of justice would not allow for the enslavement of a minority for the sake of the greater happiness of the majority, a serious objection against utilitarian theory.

Second in priority is the principle that allows for social and economic inequalities given two conditions. Rawls claims that we would agree to an unequal distribution of goods such as wealth, income, and power as long as everyone has an equal opportunity to compete for these goods, and this inequality is beneficial to everyone or to the least advantaged. Having a fair and equal opportunity to offices and positions of power would mean that no one with the requisite talent and motivation is excluded due to irrelevant factors, such as gender, age, race, or wealth. So, the fair equality of opportunity would require access to education for everyone regardless of wealth. It would mandate equal opportunity and consideration of all qualified applicants for a job or office.

The other condition that must be met to justify social and economic inequalities is the difference principle. Instead of an egalitarian distribution where everyone has equal shares of primary goods, the difference principle allows for inequalities where some members of society have more income or more power than others as long as this inequality will benefit everyone or those who are least advantaged. According to Rawls, citizens in the original position would agree to this principle because, under the veil of ignorance, they would not know their particular place in society—that is, whether they would be fortunate, blessed with wealth and talents, or among the unlucky poor and disadvantaged. If an individual happens to be born among the worst-off in society, at least the difference principle offers some protection by requiring that the fortune of others benefits the worst-off. For example, physicians are entitled to higher incomes, but others cannot complain for they know that they may one day fall sick and when they, upon falling sick, would benefit from medical expertise. Likewise, governmental subsidies to farmers seem fair if this economic support to the agricultural sector promotes the public good, perhaps by reducing the cost of produce. The difference principle is also justified according to Rawls because who we are is a matter of luck; we are all subject to a kind of natural and social lottery. We did nothing to merit being born intelligent, attractive, athletic, or wealthy. Conversely, the poor, unhealthy, disabled, etc., were born into disadvantaged circumstances without doing anything to deserve these either. In a sense, it is unfair that certain individuals are randomly born into rich families, have all sorts of advantages, and are well-endowed with talents and traits valued by society. The difference principle takes this into account and obligates those who are more fortunate to contribute to the good of the less advantaged.

Rawls justifies these two principles of justice by claiming that these are the very principles that people indifferent to their own special interests would choose for society. Assuming that people are rational and risk averse, Rawls characterizes them as following a maximin reasoning. Given a maximin strategy, an individual will, under uncertainty, choose the option that maximizes the worst possible outcome. That is, people will take the conservative approach when it comes to selecting various alternatives, opting for the alternative with the best worst outcome. For example, given the maximin strategy, Pete may choose to invest his money in secure municipal bonds rather than in high-risk stocks with potentially greater returns because the worst-case outcome for the former is a smaller return, but for the latter, the worst-case outcome can be loss of his money. Let us consider three hypothetical societies, each society consisting of three groups A, B, and C, with each group having an equal number of members. Let us also specify the economic distributions of wealth according to the following graph such that each member of a group in a given society has the following annual income.

	Group A	Group B	Group C
Society 1	$300,000	$500,000	$5
Society 2	$50,000	$40,000	$45,000
Society 3	$70,000	$200,000	$150,00

The classical utilitarian conception of justice, aiming for the greatest aggregate good, would favor Society 1 since the total of $800,005 is a higher total than those of the other two societies. An egalitarian conception, seeking a relatively equal distribution of goods, would favor Society 2 since members of each group would have about equal shares. In contrast, Rawls's maximin strategy would opt for Society 3, as the worst possible outcome for an individual would be to be born into Group A, where members earn an annual $70,000 each. Yet, this worst outcome in Society 3 is better than the worst outcome in Society 2 ($40,000) and far superior to the worst outcome in Society 1 where Group C's members earn only $5 each per year. Rational individuals who have an interest in maximizing their primary goods would try to play it safe and seek the alternative with the best possible worst outcome according to John Rawls's political liberalism. In practice, the difference principle and maximin reasoning would support welfare programs, free health care, free public education, low-income housing, and progressive taxation since presumably these policies would improve the economic conditions for the worst-off in society. Thus, Rawls supports democratic principles and ideals agreed upon by rational citizens who may possess different worldviews but share common human reason and "strive for the best [they] can attain within the scope the world allows" (John Rawls, Political Liberalism: Expanded Edition).

Exercise 7-D: Reading Questions on Rawls's *Theory of Justice*

1. What is the first virtue of social institutions for Rawls? What is his conception of justice?
2. What is the original position and what role does it play in establishing the principles of justice? How does Rawls describe citizens in the original position?
3. What is the purpose of the veil of ignorance? What can a person know and not know under the veil of ignorance?
4. What can persons in the original position know about the state of the world and human nature?
5. What are Rawls's two principles of justice? Related to the second principle, what are the fair opportunity and difference principles? Which of his principles have priority over the others?
6. If the enslavement of a minority group could lead to a much more prosperous nation, would it be morally permissible to allow slavery? Why or why not in Rawls's view?

7. Why would higher salaries for doctors or subsidies to farmers be justified in Rawls's view when not everyone is given the same high salary or given extra monetary support?
8. For an egalitarian, what would a just distribution of goods look like? How would classical utilitarianism answer? What sort of distribution of primary goods would Rawls's theory support?
9. What is Rawls's maximin strategy? Why does Rawls think people employ maximin reasoning?
10. Does Rawls justify progressive taxation where the wealthy are taxed more to provide government assistance to the poor (e.g., welfare, food stamps, public education)? Why or why not?

Aristotle and Virtue Ethics

By Nicholas Ford

Aristotle (384–322 BCE) was an ancient Greek philosopher who developed many of the scientific and philosophical disciplines that shaped much of Medieval scholarship, up to the present day. He spent two decades being taught at Plato's Academy, tutored Alexander the Great, and founded the Lyceum. Many of Aristotle's writings were lost through the ages, and only his lecture notes survive until this day, which were not meant for publication.

Aristotle divided knowledge into three kinds: theoretical (physics, mathematics, and theology) pursued for their own sake, practical (politics and ethics) to guide human behavior, and productive (engineering, architecture, medicine, and the arts) to produce crafts. As part of practical wisdom, ethics is teleological and seeks to obtain a goal, a goal that is intrinsically valuable and sought for its own sake: *eudaimonia*, which is usually translated as happiness or human flourishing. All human endeavors that aim at wealth, health, or political power are pursued because they promote happiness. To obtain *eudaimonia*, one needs to develop virtues or excellence in traits and dispositions.

The virtues can be divided into two types: intellectual and moral. Intellectual virtues are excellences of the mind, such as the ability to understand, reason, and judge well, which are acquired through inheritance and education. Moral virtues are dispositions to behave in a correct manner or to act excellently and unlike intellectual virtues, cannot be taught, but are only acquired through practice and habituation. The moral virtues are principally courage, justice, friendliness, modesty, aspiration, pride, liberality, temperance, and wittiness. A moral ideal acts according to moral virtues automatically and spontaneously without the need to think about what to do.

Moreover, for Aristotle, being a good person is not based on *what* one does but on *how* one ought to be. While action-based ethics such as utilitarianism or Kantian ethics emphasize the rightness or wrongness of a given action performed by an agent (and in Kant's case there is also an emphasis on the agent's intention), Aristotle's ethics is virtue-based. Virtue-based ethics focus on the character of a person and considers what sorts of traits or dispositions a good person should have. Action-based ethics prescribe that one perform the right actions and refrain from wrong actions; virtue-based ethics focus on intrinsic properties and teaches people to improve their character and to develop the correct habits. Becoming virtuous is not always an easy task for moral virtue is not something that one is innately born with but must be acquired and cultivated. It may be a struggle at first for many, and for some people an impossible feat.

Indeed, Aristotle believed that the virtuous life was not meant for everyone, for there are certain prerequisites that must be met. These include being born in the right community with the right type of government, having enough luck, good friends, political influence, honor, and beauty to lead a good life, along with enough wealth to have leisure time to develop the virtues. Accordingly, anyone who works for wages does not have the time or resources to become virtuous. Aristotle's audience was wealthy aristocrats who lived during times of war and were concerned with the traditional values of the upper class, and these prerequisites for virtue would belong to this group. Thus, Aristotle was an elitist in believing that happiness or *eudaimonia* was only within the reach of the upper classes, specifically aristocratic males who possessed the external material goods to achieve happiness.

While Aristotle lists what he considers to be moral virtues, he knew that these labels may be too abstract to guide action. To cultivate moral virtues, Aristotle offers the principle of the Golden Mean. According to this principle, every virtue lies in between two vices, one of excess and one of deficiency. For example, the virtue of courage lies between the vice of recklessness (excess) and the vice of cowardice (deficiency). Similarly, the virtue of friendliness lies between the vice of flattery and the vice of quarrelsomeness. The kind of person we should strive to be, according to Aristotle, is a virtuous person who uses reason to find the virtuous mean between two extremes. A morally good person must, through habit and practice, cultivate moral virtues until they are established as permanent dispositions. When truly virtuous, the morally ideal person spontaneously and easily knows and does the right things. Aristotle's morally good person acts without much effort or thought because virtue has become second nature, a habit ingrained in the person's character.

Two additional qualifications should be made to Aristotle's general principle. First, when applying the Golden Mean, the particular circumstances of the individual must be considered. Just as the amount of food each person needs to eat is particular to their composition, with athletes requiring more than office workers, so too are virtues to be tailored to the individual. There is no universal rule as to how each person should exemplify the virtues but must use their rationality to judge their own personal traits and circumstances. Second, there is a distinction between "If something is a virtue, then it lies between two vices," and "If something lies between two vices, then it is a virtue." According to the second phrasing, stealing a moderate amount from the store would lie between the vice of stealing a little and the vice of stealing a lot, but would not be a virtue itself. Thus, the Golden Mean does not prescribe doing everything in moderation; otherwise, lying, cheating, or stealing in moderation would be deemed virtuous.

In addition to the Golden Mean, a person may learn how to become virtuous by following the example of moral ideals. This implies that a person has some idea of what virtue is, though not perfectly. Moral exemplars are those who have acquired virtues and act virtuously without hesitation or temptation. These role models are individuals who have spent their lives fulfilling their function. According to Aristotle, everything has a particular function—a tree grows and reproduces, a boat transports objects across water, etc.— and the function of humans, in addition to those associated with being animals, is to exercise reason. So, the moral exemplars are those who utilize their reason to determine the virtues through the Golden Mean and apply them to various situations based on particular circumstances. Those who are most apt to act in such ways are those who spend their time deep in contemplation, the philosophers. And it is these philosophers—who fulfill their function—who are the happiest, as contemplation is intrinsically valuable and co-extensive with happiness. Thus, the philosophers are not only the happiest but are also the moral exemplars who should be followed. By emulating these moral exemplars and through repetitive practice, we can become virtuous. Such a process is hard at first, but with habituation, the virtuous action in any situation becomes easy.

Nicomachean Ethics

By Aristotle; trans. D. P. Chase

Book II

Well: human Excellence is of two kinds, **Intellectual and Moral**: now the Intellectual springs originally, and is increased subsequently, from teaching (for the most part that is), and needs therefore experience and time, whereas the Moral comes from custom ...

Men come to be builders, for instance, by building; harp-players, by playing on the harp: exactly so, by doing just actions we come to be just; by doing the actions of self-mastery we come to be perfected in self-mastery; and by doing brave actions brave ... For by acting in the various relations in which we are thrown with our fellow men, we come to be, some just, some unjust: and by acting in dangerous positions and being habituated to feel fear or confidence, we come to be, some brave, others cowards.

Similarly, is it also with respect to the occasions of lust and anger: for some men come to be perfected in self-mastery and mild, others destitute of all self-control and passionate; the one class by behaving in one way under them, the other by behaving in another. Or, in one word, the **habits** are produced from the acts of working like to them: and so, what we have to do is to give a certain character to these particular acts because the habits formed correspond to the differences of these.

... We are right then in saying, that these virtues are formed in a man by his doing the actions; but no one, if he should leave them undone, would be even in the way to become a good man. Yet people in general do not perform these actions, but taking refuge in talk they flatter themselves they are philosophizing, and that they will so be good men: acting in truth very like those sick people who listen to the doctor with great attention but do nothing that he tells them: just as these then cannot be well bodily under such a course of treatment, so neither can those be mentally by such philosophizing ...

Aristotle, Selections from "Book II," *The Nicomachean Ethics of Aristotle*, trans. D. P. Chase, J. M. Dent and Sons Ltd., 1911.

Now what the genus of Virtue is has been said; but we must not merely speak of it thus, that it is a state but say also what kind of a state it is. We must observe then that all excellence makes that whereof it is the excellence both to be itself in a good state and to perform its work well. The excellence of the eye, for instance, makes both the eye good and its work also: for by the excellence of the eye we see well. So too, the excellence of the horse makes a horse good, and good in speed, and in carrying his rider, and standing up against the enemy. If then this is universally the case, the excellence of Man, i.e., Virtue, must be a state whereby Man comes to be good and whereby **he will perform well his proper work** …

In all quantity then, whether continuous or discrete, one may take the greater part, the less, or the exactly equal, and these either with reference to the thing itself, or relatively to us: and the exactly equal is a mean between excess and defect. Now by the mean of the thing, i.e., absolute mean, I denote that which is equidistant from either extreme (which of course is one and the same to all), and by the mean relatively to ourselves, that which is neither too much nor too little for the particular individual. This of course is not one nor the same to all: for instance, suppose ten is too much and two too little, people take six for the absolute mean; because it exceeds the smaller sum by exactly as much as it is itself exceeded by the larger, and this mean is according to arithmetical proportion.

But the mean relatively to ourselves must not be so found; for it does not follow, supposing ten minæ is too large a quantity to eat and two too small, that the trainer will order his man six; because for the person who is to take it this also may be too much or too little: for Milo it would be too little, but for a man just commencing his athletic exercises too much: similarly too of the exercises themselves, as running or wrestling.

So, then it seems everyone possessed of skill avoids excess and defect, but seeks for and chooses the mean, not the absolute but the relative.

Now if all skill thus accomplishes well its work by keeping an eye on the mean, and bringing the works to this point (whence it is common enough to say of such works as are in a good state, "one cannot add to or take ought from them," under the notion of excess or defect destroying goodness but the mean state preserving it), and good artisans, as we say, work with their eye on this, and excellence, like nature, is more exact and better than any art in the world, it must have an aptitude to aim at the mean.

It is moral excellence, *i.e.* Virtue, of course which I mean, because this it is which is concerned with feelings and actions, and in these there can be excess and defect and the mean: it is possible, for instance, to feel the emotions of fear, confidence, lust, anger, compassion, and pleasure and pain generally, too much or too little, and in either case wrongly; but to feel them when we ought, on what occasions, towards whom, why, and as, we should do, is the mean, or in other words the best state, and this is the property of Virtue.

In like manner too with respect to the actions, there may be excess and defect and the mean. Now Virtue is concerned with feelings and actions, in which the excess is wrong, and the defect is blamed but the mean is praised and goes right; and both these circumstances belong to Virtue. Virtue then is in a sense **a mean state**, since it certainly has **an aptitude for aiming at the mean**.

Again, one may go wrong in many different ways (because, as the Pythagoreans expressed it, evil is of the class of the infinite, good of the finite), but right only in one; and so, the former is easy, the latter difficult; easy to miss the mark, but hard to hit it: and for these reasons, therefore, both **the excess and defect belong to Vice**, and **the mean state to Virtue**; for, as the poet has it,

"Men may be bad in many ways, But good in one alone." Virtue then is "a state apt to exercise deliberate choice, being in the relative mean, determined by reason, and as the man of practical wisdom would determine."

It is a **middle state between too faulty ones**, in the way of **excess** on one side and of **defect** on the other: and it is so moreover, because the faulty states on one side fall short of, and those on the other exceed, what is right, both in the case of the feelings and the actions; but Virtue finds, and when found adopts, the mean ...

VII

I ... The Mean state is **Courage**: men may exceed, of course, either in absence of fear or in positive confidence: the former has no name (which is a common case), the latter is called rash: again, the man who has too much fear and too little confidence is called a coward.

III. In respect of giving and taking wealth (a): The mean state is **Liberality**, the excess Prodigality, the defect Stinginess: here each of the extremes involves really an excess and defect contrary to each other: I mean, the prodigal gives out too much and takes in too little, while the stingy man takes in too much and gives out too little. (It must be understood that we are now giving merely an outline and summary, intentionally: and we will, in a later part of the treatise, draw out the distinctions with greater exactness.)

III. In respect of what is pleasant in daily life: He that is as he should be may be called **Friendly**, and his mean state Friendliness: he that exceeds, if it be without any interested motive, somewhat too Complaisant, if with such motive, a Flatterer: he that is deficient, and in all instances, unpleasant, Quarrelsome and Cross ...

IX

Now that Moral Virtue is a mean state, and how it is so, and that it lies between two faulty states, one in the way of excess and another in the way of defect, and that it is so because it has an aptitude to aim at the mean both in feelings and actions, all this has been set forth fully and sufficiently.

And so it is hard to be good: for surely hard it is in each instance to find the mean, just as to find the mean point or center of a circle is not what any man can do, but only he who knows how: just so to be angry, to give money, and be expensive, is what any man can do, and easy: but to do these to the right person, in due proportion, at the right time, with a right object, and in the right manner, this is not as before what any man can do, nor is it easy; and for this cause goodness is rare, and praiseworthy, and noble ...

Still, perhaps, after all it is a matter of difficulty, and especially in the particular instances: it is not easy, for instance, to determine exactly in what manner, with what persons, for what causes, and for what length of time, one ought to feel anger: for we ourselves sometimes praise those who are defective in this feeling, and we call them meek; at another, we term the hot-tempered manly and spirited ... At all events thus much is plain, that the mean state is in all things praiseworthy, and that practically we must deflect sometimes towards excess sometimes towards defect, because this will be the easiest method of hitting on the mean, that is, on what is right.

> ### Exercise 7-E: Reading Questions on Aristotle

1. For Aristotle what is the difference between intellectual and moral virtues? What sorts of intellectual virtues are there and how do people come to acquire them? How do people cultivate moral virtues?
2. What does Aristotle mean by "happiness" (eudaimonia)? What material goods or circumstances are also necessary for someone's happiness? What is the function of a human being? What is the ultimate end toward which all our actions are aimed?
3. What characteristics did Aristotle recognize as virtues? How are these sets of virtues generally characteristic of and valued by certain groups of people?
4. Why is a person who is painfully following his or her conscience not thereby virtuous, according to Aristotle? How would one imagine a saint or moral ideal being virtuous? According to Aristotle, would a moral ideal have to fight off temptation and struggle to be good?
5. If you have the misfortune to be brought up rude, inconsiderate, and quarrelsome, is there any hope for you? According to Aristotle, if there is hope, what means can such a person employ to cultivate the virtue of consideration or friendliness?
6. "Men come to be builders, for instance, by building; harp-players, by playing on the harp." What does Aristotle mean by this quote, and what is its significance to moral virtue?
7. "The excellence of the eye, for instance, makes both the eye good and its work also: for by the excellence of the eye we see well." What is the excellence of man?
8. How is choosing the mean relative to the individual and not to be calculated by some arithmetical proportion? For example, how is picking the right amount of food relative to each person and not absolute?
9. In *Nicomachean Ethics*, how does Aristotle describe the virtue of courage, liberality, and friendliness? What vices of deficiency and excess correspond to each virtue?

Fallacies in Ethical Discourse

Some fallacies are especially prevalent in moral reasoning. We shall introduce 10 defects in arguments commonly found in ethical discourse. While we are calling these types of reasoning "fallacious," there are ethical perspectives that may not agree. For example, ethical relativism is founded on the assumption that there is no objective moral code that universally applies to all people. Thus, ethical relativism would see no problem in what we are calling the "relativistic or subjectivist fallacy." Similarly, ethical egoism would fully support the "double standard" view that some persons—namely, we and those who contribute to my happiness—have a special status. For an ethical egoist, it would be morally permissible to hold people to different standards, giving preference to ourselves over others. Utilitarians likewise would reject the saint's license and the futility illusion as fallacious; for them, consequences determine right from wrong action. With these qualifications, let us introduce the fallacies that many, but not all, ethical theories recognize.

"It's Legal" Fallacy

The "It's Legal" Fallacy fails to make an appropriate distinction between what is legal and what is ethical. Somebody who commits this fallacy assumes that what is moral should be legal, and conversely what is legal must be moral. On the other hand, it is supposed that illegal actions are immoral, and morally wrong actions should be made illegal. Yet, there is no direct correlation between what a government has outlawed and what a moral code deems to be morally wrong. There are behaviors such as adultery that may be perfectly legal but are morally impermissible. Likewise, a draft dodger may break the law when she refuses to fight in what she believes to be an unjust war; however, this does not mean what she is doing is morally wrong.

Example: Of course, it's okay for Pakistani farmers to sell their kidneys. After all, it is legal in Pakistan.

The Saint's License

Some ethical theories such as utilitarianism claim that an action is justified if it is for a good cause. The ends justify the means. Other theories see this sort of thinking as a rationalization to cover up immoral acts. According to this latter group, the saint's license is a fallacy that mistakenly justifies wrong actions for the sake of certain good consequences. Whether or not this sort of thinking is a fallacy is a matter of controversy between consequential versus nonconsequential ethical theories. Was Robin Hood's stealing from the rich to give to the poor morally wrong? Many poor people did benefit from the redistribution of the rich people's wealth. So, one might excuse Robin Hood's act of theft because it was for a good cause. However, if you don't accept that the ends justify the means, this sort of reasoning is fallacious.

Example: We should cover up and ignore the child molesting priests in our diocese because news of these scandals would harm the Church. We should remember that the Catholic Church does much good in the world and offers hope to many believers.

The Futility Illusion: "If I Don't Do It, Somebody Else Will"

This sort of rationalization excuses someone from doing a wrong thing because no matter what one does, the bad consequence of such an action would happen anyway. It is futile to do the right thing when the results will be no better. For example, one might think that recycling is a waste of time because so many others will refuse to recycle. Thus, your recycling will not have much of a positive impact on the environment. However, this thinking is flawed because on the contrary, it does make a small difference, and many others may also join in the effort.

Example: A soldier thinks, "I had better follow my orders to shoot the innocent women and children of this village. If I don't, the other soldiers will kill them anyway, and I'll just end up in the brig."

The Comparative Virtue Excuse: "There Are Worse Things"

The comparative virtue excuse condones a person's bad behavior by comparing it to behavior that is relatively much worse. However, one's actions do not become morally right just because other people's conduct is bad on a greater scale. The fact that someone else's actions are less ethical than your actions has no effect on the ethical nature of your own conduct. You should strive to be the best person you can be rather than aiming to be just better than other people. We are all better, let's hope, than a serial killer, but that does not prove us to be perfectly good moral agents.

Example: I know I took some office supplies from the company for my own personal use, but that's not as bad as the secretary who brought home a brand-new computer belonging to the company. She claims she'll use it to do work at home, but she'll just play video games and log into Facebook.

Golden Mean Fallacy

Also called the Fallacy of Moderation, Middle Ground, this fallacy is committed when it is assumed that the middle position between two extremes must be the correct one. This reasoning is fallacious because being in the middle of two extremes does not prove that your view or action is good. This fallacy arises because sometimes two extreme positions are cases where one extreme is "too much" and the other extreme is "too little." In these cases, the moderate position is the correct one, but not because it lies in the middle; it is because there is some other legitimate reason for it.

Example: My mom lied about being sick for a whole week. My dad lied about being sick for three weeks. I guess it would be fine for me to call in sick for two weeks, even though I am perfectly fine.

Accident

We often follow general rules but do not or cannot list all the exceptions. When we apply general rules as if they have no exceptions, we commit the fallacy of accident. An accident occurs when a general rule has been misapplied to a specific instance that the rule was not meant to cover. This fallacy is sometimes called the fallacy of sweeping generalization.

Example: People should not make promises they cannot keep. I loaned Albert my knife, and he promised to return it when I asked for it back. Now he is refusing to give it back when I need it to slash my neighbor's throat. Albert should give me back my knife as he had promised.

Double Standard

Things or persons should be judged by the same standard when they are equal in relevant respects. One commits the fallacy of double standard when one judges equal groups by a different set of rules or criteria. It is unfair to treat equals differently, giving preferential treatment to one group to the exclusion of the other group. For example, sometimes, parents treat daughters differently from their sons when it comes to curfew and dating. During the civil rights movement, Rosa Parks refused to give up her seat for a white person on the grounds that a double standard was being applied to black versus white passengers.

Example: Female politicians should have more experience on the job to be elected for a top political position because women often have to take care of their children.

Is-Ought Fallacy/Naturalistic Fallacy

The is-ought fallacy occurs when a conclusion about what should be done is inferred from premises about how things are in the world. This fallacy attempts to argue from "is" statements to "ought" statements, from the way things are to how they should be. Like other "fallacies," the is-ought fallacy may not be recognized as faulty reasoning by some ethical theories. In particular, natural law theories would deny its fallaciousness.

One subvariety of the is-ought fallacy is the **naturalistic fallacy**. The fallacy is committed when someone offers a description of "natural" facts as the basis for accepting a moral judgment. Many thinkers would deny that a simple description of facts can ever imply the truth of some moral judgment. It seems the naturalistic fallacy mistakenly concludes that some action X is moral (or immoral) because X is natural (or unnatural). The naturalistic fallacy has been used condemn "unnatural" acts such as in vitro fertilization, genetic cloning, and homosexuality.

Example: A man is generally stronger and more aggressive than a woman. So, men ought to be the leaders of our societies.

Relativist Fallacy

Just as natural law theory would deny the fallaciousness of the naturalistic fallacy, ethical relativism would not recognize the relativist fallacy as a fallacy at all. The relativist fallacy (also known as the subjectivist fallacy) points out the undeniable differences among cultures and tries to infer from those differences that any moral claim someone believes is true.

If this kind of thinking is a fallacy, then it is one that relativists commit on a regular basis. Ethical relativists claim that there is no objective moral truth. There is only what is "true for me," or with respect to different societies, there is only "true for them." A person who commits this fallacy would claim that what might be true for others is not for her. For, the morally right thing to do is relative to a person, culture, place, etc. According to this line of thinking, a claim can be true for one person and yet false for another person at the same time.

Example: Jill: "I read that people often do not report what they earn in tips. So, I believe this is dishonest!" Bill: "That may be true for you, but it is not true for me."

Two Wrongs Make a Right

When you defend your wrong action as being right because someone previously has acted wrongly or would wrong you, you commit the fallacy called two wrongs make a right. This fallacy justifies some action that hurts another person on the grounds that the other person has done (or is likely to do) the same kind of harm. If morality is objective, then this "reasoning" is fallacious because moral rules apply to everyone and are not subject to an individual's preferences or a given society's conventions.

Example: The waitress thinks "It's okay for me to spit on this customer's order because he has been rude to me all night!"

Exercise 7-F: Moral Fallacies

Identify the fallacy committed by each passage. In some cases, more than one fallacy is committed.

1. In China, many young children work in sweatshops for extremely low pay. China's government deems child labor as legal, so it is morally right to force children to work.
2. It's okay to drink and drive, for it's not as bad as driving while snorting cocaine, shooting up heroin, dropping acid, eating mushrooms, and smoking crystal meth all at once.
3. My car stereo was stolen yesterday. Since someone stole from me, it's only fair that I steal a new stereo from someone else's car to replace mine.
4. It is a general truth that no one should lie. Therefore, no one should lie if a murderer at the point of a knife asks you for information you know would lead to a further murder.
5. Of course, I have every right to have an affair with my best friend's wife. After all, back in college, he stole my girlfriend, and I've resented him for that ever since.
6. Sydney plays video games five hours a day, while Michael spends only one hour per day. So, I guess I should play my favorite video games three hours a day.
7. Football players may get bad grades, but the faculty should overlook those grades because they are winning championships, which is good for the whole school.
8. I really don't feel so bad about cheating on my boyfriend of four years. We may have been together for a long time, but I am not breaking any laws when I cheat on him.
9. Jamie: "I brush my teeth daily because a study shows that people should brush their teeth daily to help fight cavities." Lydia: "That may be right for you, but I don't think it is right for me."
10. Why should I recycle when more than half of the world does not? One recycled can isn't going to save the world. We'll still have mounds and mounds of trash in our landfills.
11. I know I helped beat up the 13-year-old boy, but my friend here killed the kid. In all fairness, my friend should get punished and not me.
12. Some people argue that former president Bill Clinton lied to the nation about his affair, but I see it as just a little white lie. It doesn't bother me much; after all, he was a good president!
13. When Danielle was a junior in high school, her curfew was 11:00 p.m., and she was not allowed to have any boys in her room. When Adam, her younger brother, was a *sophomore*, he had the same curfew, and he was always allowed to have girls in his room, even with the door closed. It's okay though because he's a boy, so of course he is more mature.
14. Store Clerk: "It's no big deal for me to sell alcohol to this underage girl because she is going to get drunk tonight anyway—no matter if I sell it to her, or if she goes to a frat party."
15. My mom freaked out when she caught me smoking weed, but it's not even nearly as bad as my brother who, I'm sure she knows, sells weed to our entire neighborhood.
16. It's a natural instinct for humans to act on sexual urges. So, even though I'm only a 15-year-old girl, it's moral for me to have sex with whomever I feel like.
17. That cop had no right to give me a ticket for loitering—even though it's illegal, I should be let go since I was collecting money for charity when I got that ticket!

18. Bob should keep his promises. Bob told me that he would give me a ride across the state border in exchange for the $30 I loaned him. Well now I need a ride because I just killed my wife, and I need to flee the state, but Bob will not come and pick me up. I can't trust him anymore.

19. I don't want to tell the cops that Gary was the one who stole Jake's car, because I don't want to lose Gary's trust as a friend. But I also don't want to just keep my mouth shut, because Jake is my friend too and he deserves to get his car back. I guess a compromise is called for. I'll just give the cops a little innocent tip of where the car *might* be.

20. There is no reason to tell my mom the truth about taking drugs. There are no laws stating I have to tell the truth to my mother. Therefore, it is morally right to not tell my mom the truth.

21. If I don't tell my girlfriend that she looks fat in her new jeans, someone else will. So, I might as well tell her.

22. I figured it was okay to miss just one assignment, given that Jessica has missed four of them.

23. I promised to take Stan to the football game this afternoon, but Stan was an hour late picking me up from the airport last month. So, I think I'll just make him wait for me this time. He'll just have to miss the first quarter of the game. Serves him right!

24. Well since Sydney decided to shoplift that designer Gucci purse she always wanted, it's okay that I steal my favorite band's new CD, which just came out.

25. A few boys go out and steal stuff from cars. One of the boys justifies his involvement by thinking, if he didn't steal from one of the cars, one of his buddies would.

26. Heroin is a natural plant derivative that people use to make themselves feel good. Since heroin is a natural supplement, it is morally okay to use it.

27. When several people in Harvey's department get new computers, he is annoyed because he is not among them. "I'll tell you what," Harvey says to his wife, "if they want to rip me off by not getting a new computer for me, I'll just rip them off for extra office supplies. They've got a lot of stuff at work we could use around here. Turnabout's fair play."

28. I could buy a BMW for $35,000.00, or I can buy a Honda for $20,000.00 and save money. I think the best choice would be to buy the Volkswagen for $27,000.00. It is in the middle of the price range I want to spend, so I think that is what I should buy.

29. We should not dwell on the fact that certain organizations take money for themselves, even though they claim to be nonprofit. They give some help to starving children. So, it is okay.

30. There's no law in Mexico requiring me to be twenty-one to drink alcohol, which allows me to feel morally right about getting wasted at age 18 in Mexico.

31. Sure, she killed that one high school student, but it is not as bad as the person who shot up a high school and killed several more students.

32. A woman, Sue, steals a dress from a store. As Sue leaves, the store owner spots her. Instead of calling the authorities she grabs Sue and begins hitting her. Eventually, the police arrive, and the store owner explains to them that Sue stole from her first, so she hit her to make things even.

33. I might as well eat meat and not become a vegetarian because if I don't eat it, someone else will. One person will make no difference.
34. My friend Alex is a stud because he kisses a lot of girls, but my friend Ashley is easy because she kisses a lot of boys.
35. Why should I help that old lady cross the street? There are no good humanitarian laws in this state that say I have to help her. So, I should not help her.
36. O. J. Simpson murdered his wife and the cops found blood on his clothes, but he shouldn't be convicted of murder. He helps underprivileged kids and has donated money to the poor.
37. Justine has just given Jake her reasons for not texting while driving. Jake, not wanting to accept her conclusion, responds with, "Sure, that's what you think, but not me! I think there's nothing wrong with texting while you drive."
38. Children belong with their biological parents. So, we should return the two young boys to the custody of their parents even though they have complained of neglect and abuse at home.
39. Oops, no paper this morning. Somebody in our apartment building probably stole my newspaper. So, it is okay if I steal one from my neighbor's doormat.
40. The pickpocket stole all the cash from my wallet, but she's not so bad, at least she didn't take any of my credit cards and left my passport behind.

Exercise 7-G: Fallacy Letter

In the following letters/dialogues, identify any moral fallacies committed.

Dear Sam,
   I still can't believe you didn't drink with us while you were visiting me in San Diego. It would have made your stay so much better. Sam, you and I both know there are worse things than drinking alcohol. I could have forced you to smoke marijuana with me, but all I wanted was for you to loosen up a little with a beer or two.
   Now don't get me wrong. I don't want you to go crazy and drink more than you can handle. There's no need to be belligerently intoxicated! I just wanted you in a state where you would have been between sober and wasted.
   Besides, a little drink would have helped you talk to that girl who was looking at you all night. LIQUID CONFIDENCE! Also, that vodka I gave you was made from all-natural potatoes. If eating potatoes is natural, then drinking them surely is as well! We just turned 18 years old, Sam; we are considered adults now. Isn't it only fair that we share the rights that all other adults do? So, on that note, come back to SDSU soon, and let's kick back and enjoy.

Sincerely,
Tim

CHAPTER 8
Other Ethical Theories

> In Chapter 8, we will survey and evaluate more ethical theories, including existentialism and Buddhism. After completing the chapter, readers will be able to
>
> - evaluate Kierkegaard's form of existentialism,
> - analyze Nietzsche's version of existentialism,
> - examine Sartre's existentialism, and
> - understand Zen Master Hakuin's Buddhist philosophy.

Chapter Seven introduced several traditional schools of ethical thought including ethical relativism, consequentialist ethics, and deontological ethics. These ethical theories were developed in and adopted by Western civilization. Chapter 8 will explore a few other ethical perspectives on self-identity and life choices. One philosophical movement known as existentialism emphasizes the need for individuals to create their own meaning in life and assume responsibility. Philosophers such as Kierkegaard, Nietzsche, and Sartre write about living an authentic and meaningful existence grounded on one's free will and unique interpretation.

Another perspective included in this chapter is Zen Buddhism. This philosophy emerges from the Eastern tradition originating in India and spreading to the other Asian countries such as China and Japan. Zen Buddhism's goal is to find an escape from suffering and to cultivate a lifestyle conducive to spiritual enlightenment. Zen Buddhism identifies Four Noble Truths and recommends the practice of the Middle Way and the Eightfold Path to Enlightenment. Buddhist teachings may employ practices such as meditation and koan studies to clear the mind of abstract concepts and foster an awareness of ultimate reality.

Existentialism

In the nineteenth and twentieth centuries, there was a philosophical movement that emerged in Europe that focused on human existence and individual choice. Philosophers such as Nietzsche,

Kierkegaard, Camus, Sartre, and Beauvoir tried to make sense of the human condition. According to Sartre, our human existence is absurd. As we attempt to find meaning and purpose, we find nothing. The world is indifferent, uncaring, and gives us no rational guidance. Even Christian existentialist, Kierkegaard, intimates that there are no fixed objective standards, and we must subjectively interpret the right path to follow, knowing full well that the path we pick may just as likely be wrong as right. Nonetheless, Kierkegaard urged individuals to live authentically by making a "leap of faith," which requires making seemingly irrational choices despite uncertainties and without assurances.

Kierkegaard and Christian Existentialism

Soren Kierkegaard was a Danish philosopher who lived in the nineteenth century. He is considered, by some, to be the father of the philosophical movement called existentialism. Existentialism is a philosophy that asserts that the most important questions about human life concern meaning and choice as experienced by actual individuals. Fundamental themes for existentialism include identity, freedom, authenticity, choice, alienation, and despair. The real problems of human existence involve questions such as "What am I to do? To what can I commit myself? What does my life mean?"

Kierkegaard observes that awareness of one's freedom can cause angst or anguish. Everyone, even a child, has an intimate knowledge of what anguish feels like. A person feels dread or anguish when she looks into the future and considers all the choices she must make. These choices often come with risks. Life may be experienced as dread or anxiety, which can easily turn into a fear of our own freedom—fear of having to make choices. However, to become authentic, the individual must make decisions and take responsibility for them. Then, the truth of one's experience will become one's truth alone. There are no shortcuts; one cannot borrow "someone else's truth" by following another's path. One can gather no deep insights or clues from books or from teachers regarding personal decisions. At most, teachers can point students in the right direction, but teachers cannot spoon-feed them any particular truths.

A person's experience of reality is indirect and differs from the way infants first perceive their surroundings. Kierkegaard observes that infants and animals have immediate contact with their environment. In contrast, the adult human mind processes reality indirectly through concepts and language. Language and thought mediate a person's experiences by abstracting and distancing one from real existence. The things we sense are interpreted by our minds, and we describe them with words and analyze them according to categories. People might try to define the roles they play and come up with labels such as son, waitress, mother, sister, American, youth, student, teacher, etc. These labels are merely general concepts, abstract categories. Yet, real individual human existence is concrete, never abstract. Thus, language fails to fully capture human identity.

Real human existence cannot be simply thought; it must be lived. In Kierkegaard's view, lived existence involves passion, decision, and action. The world and human experiences are uncertain and can never be revealed as a unity but are always presented as fragmented and incomplete. The self is continually being constructed and reconstructed. There are three spheres of existence in which an individual can exist and define himself.

The first sphere is the **aesthetic sphere**. A person operating in the aesthetic sphere pursues pleasure and avoids pain. An aesthete is someone who lives a hedonistic lifestyle. His aim is primarily that of self-gratification whether that be in art, music, literature, or relationships. The Aesthetic Model is someone like Don Juan, a fictional Spanish libertine who lived in the seventeenth century. Don Juan is a womanizer who is attracted to the chase and the pleasures of beautiful women. Don Juan employs the rotation method to keep from boredom. After a conquest, he cannot commit to a relationship, inevitably loses interest in the woman, and leaves her in pursuit of the next challenge. There are no feelings of guilt or remorse, for Don Juan has no moral sense of right or wrong. The aesthete reasons that given only one life to live, he might as well make it enjoyable. For this individual, life is ultimately meaningless and there are no serious commitments or choices.

The aesthete becomes addicted to pleasure and constantly seeks more, needing the next high and even more excitement. After a time, the aesthete grows bored with past pleasures and seeks more intense ones. In the aesthetic sphere, an individual has no true self and must wear different masks to please and attract others. For example, Don Juan might act like a lovestruck, sensitive suitor to win one woman's heart, but a sophisticated, successful entrepreneur to impress yet another desirable prospect. Thus, an aesthete must depend on others to define him; he must pretend to be whatever it is that can best gain him his desired goal—pleasure.

Inevitably, there comes a point when the individual finally grows tired of chasing fleeting pleasures and feels only despair. At this point, the individual can make a negative judgment about his old, sick self. He can choose for himself, a new self. The individual making this move in passion for a new way to exist takes a leap, leaving behind his old self to gain a true, more authentic, self. At this point, the individual may choose to live in a different sphere beyond self-serving hedonism.

Instead, a person who refuses to live in the aesthetic sphere may take on certain commitments. A person might choose to live in the ethical sphere. In the **ethical sphere**, the individual will seek self-perfection and will be committed to other human beings. The ethical individual will follow a moral code and will renounce all that does not serve his cause. Such an individual finds himself by giving himself up to something greater. Socrates is an example of the ethical ideal, for he was a virtuous and courageous man willing to die for principles. According to Kierkegaard, Socrates could not go beyond the ethical sphere because he stayed within the boundaries of reason. Since Socrates predated Jesus Christ, the leap of faith into the religious sphere was not available to Socrates.

Another way to live in the ethical sphere is through marriage. A couple publicly commits themselves to one another. Through marriage, an individual becomes related to other human beings. The individual defines himself in his relation to another human being. Kierkegaard contemplated marriage with a young Danish woman named Regine; however, he broke off his engagement to her for reasons not quite clear. Possibly, he felt at odds with his love for Regine and his commitment to God. Kierkegaard doubted whether his love for God could be compatible with a marriage to Regine.

The final sphere of existence is one that is related to religious life. It is a state that is submerged in paradox. In the **religious sphere,** to gain everything, one must seemingly give up everything. Kierkegaard criticized the Christians of his times for being corrupt, hypocritical, and dispassionate. These followers did not follow the true spirit of Christianity; rather than sacrificing their worldly goods and genuinely caring for others, the Christians in his day were materialistic and were not truly committed to their faith. Kierkegaard disapproved of the rich, indulgent churchgoers who worshipped God in ostentatious cathedrals. In his writings, Kierkegaard sarcastically described the Christian preacher as an insincere representative of Christianity:

> Ah, when a gentlemanly man clad in a silken gown says this in a pleasant, harmonious voice so that the words pleasantly resound in the handsome vaulted church, a man in silk who radiates honor and respect on all who listen to him; ah, when a king in purple and velvet says this, with the Christmas tree in the background on which are hanging all the splendid gifts he intends to distribute, why, then of course there is some meaning in these words! But whatever meaning you may attach to them, so much is sure that it is not Christianity, but the exact opposite, something as diametrically opposed to Christianity as may well be; for remember who it is that invites! ("Preparation for a Christian Life," p. 69)

In contrast, the religious ideal was the biblical figure of Abraham. Abraham was willing to give up everything in what Kierkegaard describes as "a movement of infinite resignation" for the sake of his faith. God had commanded that Abraham sacrifice his only beloved son. Abraham was willing to lose his most precious son, a consequence tantamount to giving up everything. In losing his son, he loses the world and even his old self, but in the "double movement of faith," Abraham is spared from having to kill his son and regains everything that he was willing to part with. Abraham emerges from this ordeal transformed into a new self. Kierkegaard claims that it is a tremendous step to truly dedicate oneself to God, for it requires laying down one's life for one's faith. In his book *Fear and Trembling*, Kierkegaard marvels at how people like Abraham have the strength to accept the Christian call: "But if being a Christian is something so terrifying and awesome, how in all the world can a man get it into his head to wish to accept Christianity? ... Christianity is, and shall ever be, the greatest absurdity, or else the greatest terror."

Central themes of existentialism emerge in the Abraham story. First, Kierkegaard's existentialism places much weight on individual responsibility. Even though it may seem that Abraham is simply following orders from God, Kierkegaard stresses that Abraham must still determine the meaning of the command for himself. Abraham, not God, is responsible for the source of his action. There were a number of ways that Abraham could have interpreted the command; however, he chose to interpret the command as one coming from God and accepted it as a test of faith.

Another existentialist theme is the absurdity of the world in connection to the individual. Just like other existentialists, Kierkegaard believes the world to be absurd and disconnected. Abraham's faith might be construed as a kind of divine madness, for Abraham's faith leads him to an irrational experience that is like a kind of madness. Kierkegaard writes, "Abraham was greater than all, great by reason of his power whose strength is impotence, great by reason of his wisdom whose secret is foolishness, great by reason of his hope whose form is madness."

Kierkegaard claims that an individual emerges from the ethical sphere into the religious sphere by making the leap of faith just like Abraham. Each person is alone before God and must choose in absolute isolation whether or not to commit to a relationship with a God that defies objective analysis. Kierkegaard explains, "If I cannot find out whether or not a certain thing exists, but its existence is critically important for me, then I should simply make a leap of faith that it exists."

For Kierkegaard, one's belief in God is not an objective truth that can be proven true and communicated to others like the evidence-based truths of math, science, or history. These subjects yield hard, cold facts that are existentially indifferent to the individual; the individual has no essential relationship with objective truths. For example, knowing the weight of hydrogen, the distance to the moon, or the Pythagorean Theorem does not passionately and intensely involve one in these truths. The objective thinker reasons and collects data, activities that are intellectual, dispassionate, and scientific. God is not an object of knowledge that can be proven objectively. Believers must choose to have faith, realizing full well that they have no deductive proof or sufficient evidence, aware of the possibility that they may be wrong.

Religion involves subjective truths that are only true for a particular individual and are not communicable. The subjective thinker has a profound personal concern over subjective truths concerning life and death questions, the meaning of one's existence, and one's ultimate destiny. The relationship between the believer and God is more of an experiential rather than a rational one. Kierkegaard states that the believer is involved in a subjective inwardness in which the individual confronts God as an unknown, not something knowable. Each individual is responsible for finding meaning out of the meaninglessness of life in the chaotic world he finds himself. Thus, religion requires an individual to make choices and bear the responsibility for these choices.

In the following excerpt from *Fear and Trembling*, Kierkegaard imagines the biblical story of Abraham. Kierkegaard characterizes Abraham as a "knight of faith" who has complete faith in God. Abraham is willing to sacrifice his son yet trusts that he will somehow regain it all back again. Given the divine command to kill his son, Abraham must struggle with and transcend the ethical law not to kill. Against all reason and despite his own personal anguish, Abraham is resigned to follow God's command. In doing so, he rises to a higher sphere of existence, the religious sphere, which is submerged in absolute paradox.

Fear and Trembling

By Søren Kierkegaard, trans. L. M. Hollander

No, no one shall be forgotten who was great in this world. But each hero was great in his own way, and each one was eminent in proportion to the great things he loved. For he who loved himself became great through himself, and he who loved others became great through his devotion, but he who loved God became greater than all of these. Every one of them shall be

Søren Kierkegaard, *Selections from the Writings of Kierkegaard*, trans. L. M. Hollander, University of Texas at Austin, 1912.

remembered, but each one became great in proportion to his trust. One became great by hoping for the possible; another, by hoping for the eternal; but he who hoped for the impossible, he became greater than all of these. Everyone shall be remembered; but each one was great in proportion to the power with which he strove. For he who strove with the world became great by over-coming himself; but he who strove with God, he became the greatest of them all. Thus, there have been struggles in the world, man against man, one against a thousand; but he who struggled with God, he became greatest of them all. Thus, there was fighting on this earth, and there was he who conquered everything by his strength, and there was he who conquered God by his weakness. There was he who, trusting in himself, gained all; and there was he who, trusting in his strength sacrificed everything; but he who believed in God was greater than all of these. There was he who was great through his strength, and he who was great through his wisdom, and he who was great through his hopes, and he who was great through his love; but Abraham was greater than all of these—great through the strength whose power is weakness, great through the wisdom whose secret is folly, great through the hope whose expression is madness, great through the love which is hatred of oneself ...

Through his faith Abraham received the promise that in his seed were to be blessed all races of mankind. Time passed, there was still the possibility of it, and Abraham had faith ...

... He did not sadly count the days as time passed; he did not look at Sarah with suspicious eyes, whether she was becoming old; he did not stop the sun's course lest Sarah should grow old and his hope with her; he did not lull her with his songs of lamentation. Abraham grew old, and Sarah became a laughing-stock to the people; and yet was he God's chosen, and heir to the promise that in his seed were to be blessed all races of mankind. Were it, then, not better if he had not been God's chosen? For what is it to be God's chosen? Is it to have denied to one in one's youth all the wishes of youth in order to have them fulfilled after great labor in old age?

But Abraham had faith and steadfastly lived in hope. Had Abraham been less firm in his trust, then would he have given up that hope. He would have said to God: "So it is, perchance, not Thy will, after all, that this shall come to pass. I shall surrender my hope. It was my only one, it was my bliss. I am sincere, I conceal no secret grudge for that Thou didst deny it to me." He would not have remained forgotten; his example would have saved many a one; but he would not have become the Father of Faith. For it is great to surrender one's hope, but greater still to abide by it steadfastly after having surrendered it; for it is great to seize hold of the eternal hope, but greater still to abide steadfastly by one's worldly hopes after having surrendered them.

Then came the fulness of time. If Abraham had not had faith, then Sarah would probably have died of sorrow, and Abraham, dulled by his grief, would not have understood the fulfilment, but would have smiled about it as a dream of his youth. But Abraham had faith, and therefore he remained young; for he who always hopes for the best, him life will deceive, and he will grow old; and he who is always prepared for the worst, he will soon age; but he who has faith, he will preserve eternal youth. Praise, therefore, be to this story! For Sarah, though advanced in age, was young enough to wish for the pleasures of a mother, and Abraham, though grey of hair, was young enough to wish to become a father. In a superficial sense it may be considered miraculous that what they wished for came to pass, but in a deeper sense the miracle of faith is to be seen in Abraham's and Sarah's being young enough to wish, and their faith having preserved their wish and therewith their youth. The promise he had received was fulfilled, and he accepted it in faith, and it came to pass according to the promise and his faith ...

But it was not to remain thus; for once more was Abraham to be tempted ... "And God tempted Abraham, saying to him: take now thine only son Isaac, whom thou lovest, and get thee into the land of Moriah; and offer him there for a burnt offering upon one of the mountains which I will tell thee of."

All was lost, then, and more terribly than if a son had never been given him! The Lord had only mocked Abraham, then! Miraculously he had realized the unreasonable hopes of Abraham; and now he wished to take away what he had given ... Is there no pity for the venerable old man, and none for the innocent child? And yet was Abraham God's chosen one, and yet was it the Lord that tempted him. And now all was to be lost! The glorious remembrance of him by a whole race, the promise of Abraham's seed—all that was but a whim, a passing fancy of the Lord, which Abraham was now to destroy forever! ... He was to say farewell to Isaac, to be sure, but in such wise that he himself was to remain behind; death was to part them, but in such wise that Isaac was to die. The old man was not in happiness to lay his hand on Isaac's head when the hour of death came, but, tired of life, to lay violent hands on Isaac. And it was God who tempted him ...

But Abraham had faith ...

"He laid the wood in order, and bound Isaac his son, and laid him on the altar upon the wood. And Abraham stretched forth his hand and took the knife to slay his son." My listener! Many a father there has been who thought that with his child he lost the dearest of all there was in the world for him; yet assuredly no child ever was in that sense a pledge of God as was Isaac to Abraham. Many a father there has been who lost his child; but then it was God, the unchangeable and inscrutable will of the Almighty and His hand which took it. Not thus with Abraham. For him was reserved a more severe trial, and Isaac's fate was put into Abraham's hand together with the knife. And there he stood, the old man, with his only hope! Yet he did not doubt, nor look anxiously to the left or right, nor challenge Heaven with his prayers. He knew it was God the Almighty who now put him to the test; he knew it was the greatest sacrifice which could be demanded of him; but he knew also that no sacrifice was too great which God demanded—and he drew forth his knife.

Who strengthened Abraham's arm, who supported his right arm that it drooped not powerless? For he who contemplates this scene is unnerved. Who strengthened Abraham's soul so that his eyes grew not too dim to see either Isaac or the ram? For he who contemplates this scene will be struck with blindness. And yet, it is rare enough that one is unnerved or is struck with blindness, and still more rare that one narrates worthily what there did take place between father and son. To be sure, we know well enough—it was but a trial!

... But what did Abraham? He arrived neither too early nor too late. He mounted his ass and rode slowly on his way. And all the while he had faith, believing that God would not demand Isaac of him, though ready all the while to sacrifice him, should it be demanded of him. He believed this on the strength of the absurd; for there was no question of human calculation any longer. And the absurdity consisted in God's, who yet made this demand of him, recalling his demand the very next moment. Abraham ascended the mountain and whilst the knife already gleamed in his hand he believed—that God would not demand Isaac of him. He was, to be sure, surprised at the outcome; but by a double movement he had returned at his first state of mind and therefore received Isaac back more gladly than the first time ...

Infinite resignation is the last stage which goes before faith, so that everyone who has not made the movement of infinite resignation cannot have faith; for only through absolute resignation do I become conscious of my eternal worth, and only then can there arise the problem of again grasping hold of this world by virtue of faith.

Exercise 8-A: Reading Questions on Kierkegaard's *Fear and Trembling*

1. Who is Abraham? What sacrifice was Abraham asked to make?
2. Why was this command difficult to understand and to obey for Abraham?
3. For Kierkegaard, was Abraham greater than other heroes? Why or why not?
4. What promise had Abraham received from God, and why was this promise difficult to believe?
5. What is infinite resignation? What can occur after this stage or movement?
6. How is Abraham a knight of faith and representative of the religious ideal?

Nietzsche and Atheistic Existentialism

By Noah Jerge

Friedrich Nietzsche was a nineteenth-century German philosopher and philologist who sought to examine critically the history and basis of the canonical Western moral values. He is often remembered for his sustained and aggressive criticisms of Christianity and is notorious for his declaration that "God is dead." Unlike many philosophers in the Western tradition, however, Nietzsche wrote in a free and highly literary style. He embraced the use of symbolism, expressed ideas through the mouths of characters, and often favored complex yet striking aphorisms to extended discussion. While for many, these aspects make Nietzsche an immensely fascinating (and enjoyable) author to read, they also create the danger of misinterpretation. Thus, readers of Nietzsche will find that careful attention to detail and a willingness to look beyond the everyday meaning of words are necessary to grasp the whole of the content that is expressed. This is particularly well-illustrated in the chapter "On War and Warriors" from his work *Thus Spoke Zarathustra*. Despite its apparent praise of literal war, "On War and Warriors" actually explains a method by which one can live what Nietzsche thought would be a meaningful and successful life.

The first sections of *Thus Spoke Zarathustra*, in which "On War and Warriors" is found, were published in 1883. "On War and Warriors" represents a clear example of one of Nietzsche's carefully presented and highly symbolic arguments. There, Nietzsche presents war as an analogy to life and urges his readers to live a life of constant striving for the achievement and overcoming of one's life goals. However, unlike many other philosophers, Nietzsche, in "On War and Warriors," does not present his argument through enumerated premises. Moreover, he does not even present the words as coming from his own mouth, as he instead represents them as a speech given by his titular character, Zarathustra.

Zarathustra begins his speech by asserting that one should want to know the truth about oneself, and that this truth should be accepted from any source that presents it. "We do not want to be spared by our best enemies, nor by those whom we love thoroughly," he says, for we should desire honesty from all of the people in our lives. He then begins to share his truth with the reader, first recognizing that even great individuals feel hatred and envy, but that these seemingly negative traits can actually inspire personal overcoming. Zarathustra states that "you are not great enough not to know hatred and envy," but that one should "be great enough, then, not to be ashamed of them." If one wishes to grow, then it is necessary to recognize, and affirm, the foundation that one has to work with. If one is ashamed of how one feels, then it is impossible to escape one's current situation. This is because one will seek to deny the only possibility for self-overcoming that is available. Without self-overcoming, the inevitable result would be the inability to progress, for nothing would be left to harness as a source of motivation. Hatred and envy must be used for productive purposes. One should live the life of a warrior.

Zarathustra continues by asserting that warriors should constantly be seeking new battles and new enemies, for only in doing so are they able to persist in their capacity as a warrior. According to Nietzsche, they must "have eyes that always seek an enemy." Warriors are inspired to do battle by the hate that they feel for their enemy, and this hate often emerges spontaneously upon the recognition of an opponent. In addition, an enemy should be personal to the individual who marks him out as such, because each warrior is waging war for the sake of their own thoughts. Hence, any obstruction from another would have a profound impact and elicit the greatest hate, only for oneself. According to Nietzsche, "Your enemy you shall seek, your war you shall wage—for your thoughts."

The aim of this war of ideas is not simply a single triumph, but rather constant and continual victory. A victory, then, is not an end but a means, and the subsequent period of peace is merely a brief respite after an instance of self-overcoming. "You should love peace as a means to new wars—and a short peace more than the long," says Nietzsche, for one should always seek new opportunities to overcome while also spurning any extended time without it as personal stagnation. Living with this warrior ethos, however, is very difficult because it largely precludes one from respite. Fighting a war is not just a hard activity—it is deeply personal and arduous. That is why Nietzsche differentiates it from other occupations by writing that "to you I do not recommend work but struggle," and "let your work be a struggle." Work is a mere occupation. A struggle, though, strikes at one's core.

Warriors are nevertheless followers because their passion chose them and commanded them to wage war for its sake. Obstinance in the face of such a command is "the nobility of slaves," for weak are those who subsume their own selves into the expectations of society. In contrast, the "good warrior" moved by an inward passion wills himself to follow, reverently viewing the command as 'thou shalt' rather than 'I will.'" They allow themselves to be commanded because they recognize that life can only be lived best if they accept Zarathustra's core teaching that "man is something that shall be overcome." With this, Zarathustra concludes, "thus live your life of obedience and war." Nietzsche urges his readers to live as warriors and to view life as a battlefield—an opportunity to strive, achieve success, and strive again.

Thus Spoke Zarathustra

By Friedrich Nietzsche; trans. Thomas Common

Thus Spoke Zarathustra is a book written by Friedrich Nietzsche about the fictitious encounters of his main character Zarathustra. In the course of his travels, Zarathustra teaches people about the struggles and stages of the Overman.

First Part. Zarathustra's Discourses
Zarathustra's Prologue.

1. When Zarathustra was thirty years old, he left his home and the lake of his home and went into the mountains. There he enjoyed his spirit and solitude, and for ten years did not weary of it. But at last, his heart changed …

Thus began Zarathustra's down-going.

2. Zarathustra went down the mountain alone, no one meeting him. When he entered the forest, however, there suddenly stood before him an old man, who had left his holy cot to seek roots. And thus, spake the old man to Zarathustra:

"No stranger to me is this wanderer: many years ago, passed he by. Zarathustra he was called; but he hath altered. …

Altered is Zarathustra; a child hath Zarathustra become; an awakened one is Zarathustra: what wilt thou do in the land of the sleepers? …

Go not to men but stay in the forest! Go rather to the animals! Why not be like me—a bear amongst bears, a bird amongst birds?"

"And what doeth the saint in the forest?" asked Zarathustra.

The saint answered: "I make hymns and sing them; and in making hymns I laugh and weep and mumble: thus, do I praise God. …"

When Zarathustra was alone, however, he said to his heart: "Could it be possible! This old saint in the forest hath not yet heard of it, that GOD IS DEAD!"

3. When Zarathustra arrived at the nearest town which adjoineth the forest, he found many people assembled in the market-place; for it had been announced that a rope-dancer would give a performance. And Zarathustra spake thus unto the people:

Friedrich Nietzsche, *Thus Spake Zarathustra*, trans. Thomas Common, 1909.

I TEACH YOU THE SUPERMAN. Man is something that is to be surpassed. What have ye done to surpass man?

All beings hitherto have created something beyond themselves: and ye want to be the ebb of that great tide, and would rather go back to the beast than surpass man?

What is the ape to man? A laughing-stock, a thing of shame. And just the same shall man be to the Superman: a laughing-stock, a thing of shame.

Ye have made your way from the worm to man, and much within you is still worm. Once were ye apes, and even yet man is more of an ape than any of the apes. ...

Lo, I teach you the Superman!

The Superman is the meaning of the earth. Let your will say: The Superman SHALL BE the meaning of the earth!

I conjure you, my brethren, REMAIN TRUE TO THE EARTH, and believe not those who speak unto you of superearthly hopes! Poisoners are they, whether they know it or not.

Despisers of life are they, decaying ones and poisoned ones themselves, of whom the earth is weary: so away with them! ...

4. Zarathustra, however, looked at the people and wondered. Then he spake thus: Man is a rope stretched between the animal and the Superman—a rope over an abyss. A dangerous crossing, a dangerous wayfaring, a dangerous looking-back, a dangerous trembling and halting.

What is great in man is that he is a bridge and not a goal: what is lovable in man is that he is an OVER-GOING and a DOWN-GOING. ...

5. When Zarathustra had spoken these words, he again looked at the people, and was silent. "There they stand," said he to his heart; "there they laugh: they understand me not; I am not the mouth for these ears. ...

6. Then, however, something happened which made every mouth mute and every eye fixed. In the meantime, of course, the rope-dancer had commenced his performance: he had come out at a little door, and was going along the rope which was stretched between two towers, so that it hung above the market-place and the people. When he was just midway across, the little door opened once more, and a gaudily-dressed fellow like a buffoon sprang out, and went rapidly after the first one. "Go on, halt-foot," cried his frightful voice, "go on, lazy-bones, interloper, sallow-face!—lest I tickle thee with my heel! What dost thou here between the towers? In the tower is the place for thee, thou shouldst be locked up; to one better than thyself thou blockest the way!"—And with every word he came nearer and nearer the first one. When, however, he was but a step behind, there happened the frightful thing which made every mouth mute and every eye fixed—he uttered a yell like a devil, and jumped over the other who was in his way. The latter, however, when he thus saw his rival triumph, lost at the same time his head and his footing on the rope; he threw his pole away, and shot downwards faster than it, like an eddy of arms and legs, into the depth. The market-place and the people were like the sea when the storm cometh on: they all flew apart and in disorder, especially where the body was about to fall.

Zarathustra, however, remained standing, and just beside him fell the body, badly injured and disfigured, but not yet dead. After a while consciousness returned to the shattered man, and he saw Zarathustra kneeling beside him. "What art thou doing there?" said he at last, "I knew long ago that the devil would trip me up. Now he draggeth me to hell: wilt thou prevent him?"

"On mine honour, my friend," answered Zarathustra, "there is nothing of all that whereof thou speakest: there is no devil and no hell. Thy soul will be dead even sooner than thy body: fear, therefore, nothing anymore!"

The man looked up distrustfully. "If thou speakest the truth," said he, "I lose nothing when I lose my life. I am not much more than an animal which hath been taught to dance by blows and scanty fare."

"Not at all," said Zarathustra, "thou hast made danger thy calling; therein there is nothing contemptible. Now thou perishest by thy calling: therefore, will I bury thee with mine own hands."

When Zarathustra had said this the dying one did not reply further; but he moved his hand as if he sought the hand of Zarathustra in gratitude. ...

X. War And Warriors

By our best enemies we do not want to be spared, nor by those either whom we love from the very heart. So let me tell you the truth!

My brethren in war! I love you from the very heart. I am, and was ever, your counterpart. And I am also your best enemy. So let me tell you the truth!

I know the hatred and envy of your hearts. Ye are not great enough not to know of hatred and envy. Then be great enough not to be ashamed of them!

And if ye cannot be saints of knowledge, then, I pray you, be at least its warriors. They are the companions and forerunners of such saintship.

I see many soldiers; could I but see many warriors! "Uniform" one calleth what they wear; may it not be uniform what they therewith hide!

Ye shall be those whose eyes ever seek for an enemy—for YOUR enemy. And with some of you there is hatred at first sight.

Your enemy shall ye seek; your war shall ye wage, and for the sake of your thoughts! And if your thoughts succumb, your uprightness shall still shout triumph thereby!

Ye shall love peace as a means to new wars—and the short peace more than the long.

You I advise not to work, but to fight. You I advise not to peace, but to victory. Let your work be a fight, let your peace be a victory!

One can only be silent and sit peacefully when one hath arrow and bow; otherwise one prateth and quarrelleth. Let your peace be a victory!

Ye say it is the good cause which halloweth even war? I say unto you: it is the good war which halloweth every cause.

War and courage have done more great things than charity. Not your sympathy, but your bravery hath hitherto saved the victims.

"What is good?" ye ask. To be brave is good. Let the little girls say: "To be good is what is pretty, and at the same time touching."

They call you heartless: but your heart is true, and I love the bashfulness of your goodwill. Ye are ashamed of your flow, and others are ashamed of their ebb.

Ye are ugly? Well then, my brethren, take the sublime about you, the mantle of the ugly!

And when your soul becometh great, then doth it become haughty, and in your sublimity there is wickedness. I know you.

In wickedness the haughty man and the weakling meet. But they misunderstand one another. I know you.

Ye shall only have enemies to be hated, but not enemies to be despised. Ye must be proud of your enemies; then, the successes of your enemies are also your successes.

Resistance—that is the distinction of the slave. Let your distinction be obedience. Let your commanding itself be obeying!

To the good warrior soundeth "thou shalt" pleasanter than "I will." And all that is dear unto you, ye shall first have it commanded unto you.

Let your love to life be love to your highest hope; and let your highest hope be the highest thought of life!

Your highest thought, however, ye shall have it commanded unto you by me—and it is this: man is something that is to be surpassed.

So, live your life of obedience and of war! What matter about long life! What warrior wisheth to be spared!

I spare you not, I love you from my very heart, my brethren in war!—

Thus spake Zarathustra.

Friedrich Nietzsche: "The Parable of the Madman"

One of Nietzsche's most famous stories is the Parable of the Madman from his book The Gay Science or Joyful Wisdom. In this story, the madman announces the startling news—God is dead.

The Madman

By Friedrich Nietzsche; trans. Oscar Levy

Have you ever heard of the madman who on a bright morning lighted a lantern and ran to the market-place calling out unceasingly: "I seek God! I seek God!"—As there were many people standing about who did not believe in God, he caused a great deal of amusement. Why! is he lost? said one. Has he strayed away like a child? said another. Or does he keep himself hidden? Is he afraid of us? Has he taken a sea-voyage? Has he emigrated?—the people cried out laughingly, all in a hubbub.

The insane man jumped into their midst and transfixed them with his glances. "Where is God gone?" he called out. "I mean to tell you! We have killed him,—you and I! We are all his murderers! But how have we done it? How were we able to drink up the sea? Who gave us the sponge to wipe away the whole horizon? What did we do when we loosened this earth from its sun? Whither does it now move? Whither do we move? Away from all suns? Do we not dash on

Friedrich Nietzsche, "The Madman," *The Gay Science*, trans. Oscar Levy, 1910.

unceasingly? Back-wards, sideways, forewards, in all directions? Is there still an above and below? Do we not stray, as through infinite nothingness? Does not empty space breathe upon us? Has it not become colder? Does not night come on continually, darker and darker? Shall we not have to light lanterns in the morning? Do we not hear the noise of the grave-diggers who are burying God? Do we not smell the divine putrefaction?—for even Gods putrefy! God is dead! God remains dead! And we have killed him!

How shall we console ourselves, the most murderous of all murderers? The holiest and the mightiest that the world has hitherto possessed, has bled to death under our knife,—who will wipe the blood from us? With what water could we cleanse ourselves? What lustrums, what sacred games shall we have to devise? Is not the magnitude of this deed too great for us? Shall we not ourselves have to become Gods, merely to seem worthy of it? There never was a greater event,—and on account of it, all who are born after us belong to a higher history than any history hitherto!"—Here the madman was silent and looked again at his hearers; they also were silent and looked at him in surprise.

At last he threw his lantern on the ground, so that it broke in pieces and was extinguished. "I come too early," he then said, "I am not yet at the right time. This prodigious event is still on its way, and is travelling,—it has not yet reached men's ears. Lightning and thunder need time, the light of the stars needs time, deeds need time, even after they are done, to be seen and heard. This deed is as yet further from them than the furthest star,—and yet they have done it!"—It is further stated that the madman made his way into different churches on the same day, and there intoned his Requiem aeternam deo. When led out and called to account, he always gave the reply: "What are these churches now, if they are not the tombs and monuments of God?"

Exercise 8-B: Reading Questions on Nietzsche

1. Who is Zarathustra in Nietzsche's writings? How does Nietzsche, through the teachings of Zarathustra, describe mankind in relation to animals and the overman?
2. What occurs when Zarathustra encounters the tightrope walker? How does Zarathustra view the risks of the tightrope walker?
3. In his analogy of war and warriors, how are individuals like warriors? How is one to view feelings such as envy? What attitude should one have toward one's enemies?
4. What occurs in the "Parable of the Madman"? What is the madman carrying and what is he looking for?
5. How did people react to the madman? What is the death of God likened to?
6. What does Nietzsche mean, "God is dead, and we have killed Him"? What impact does this event have on the meaning of human life?

Sartre and Existentialism

By Gabrielle Peñaranda

Jean-Paul Sartre was a French writer, philosopher, and playwright (among other things). He is associated with the metaphysical philosophies espoused in the 19th and 20th centuries called existentialism. The following essay, "Existentialism is a Humanism," originates from a lecture Sartre gave in Paris on October 29, 1945. In this lecture, Sartre defends existentialism from criticisms commonly made against the theory. Additionally, he introduces what is, perhaps, his most famous quote, a phrase that best captures the ontological view of existentialism: Existence precedes essence. Sartre writes:

> If one considers an article of manufacture as, for example, a book or a paper-knife—one sees that it has been made by an artisan who had a conception of it… When we think of God as the creator, we are thinking of him, most of the time, as a supernal artisan… [and] the conception of man in the mind of God is comparable to that of the paperknife in the mind of the artisan: God makes man according to a procedure and a conception, exactly as the artisan manufactures a paper-knife, following a definition and a formula. Thus, each individual man is the realization of a certain conception which dwells in the divine understanding… Man possesses a human nature; that "human nature," which is the conception of human being, is found in every man; which means that each man is a particular example of a universal conception, the conception of Man… Atheistic existentialism, of which I am a representative, declares with greater consistency that if God does not exist there is at least one being whose existence comes before its essence, a being which exists before it can be defined by any conception of it. That being is man or, as Heidegger has it, the human reality. What do we mean by saying that existence precedes essence? We mean that man first of all exists, encounters himself, surges up in the world—and defines himself afterwards.

In this excerpt, Sartre maintains that humans are very different from manufactured items because humans have free will. Let us examine word for word the phrase "Existence precedes essence." By "existence," Sartre means being or presence in the world. To simplify this concept, we can use Sartre's own example of a manmade object, like a paperknife or a book. A book exists, and we can perceive it to exist with our senses. The verb "precedes," means to come before. "Essence" is the thing that Plato would call our nature, that which makes persons who they are. "Essence" can also connote purpose. Moreover, a book is designed for the purpose of being read. For a book or other manmade object, its essence precedes its existence. The maker must first have an idea, a plan, or blueprint before the thing is created or comes into existence.

In contrast, humans exist first and later determine their own individual identity or purpose. Sartre, an atheist, claims that humans were not made by an omnipotent God who had a master plan for his creatures. Humans were not designed to conform to a certain image, to follow some predetermined path, or to carry out a particular purpose that God had in mind.

Jean-Paul Sartre, Selections from "Existentialism Is a Humanism," *Existentialism from Dostoyevsky to Sartre*, ed. Walter Kaufman, trans. Philip Mairet. Copyright © 1989 by Meridian Books.

Thus, for humans, existence precedes essence. We humans come to exist in this world, must create our own identity, and determine the meaning of our lives. Sartre emphasizes:

> If man as the existentialist sees him is not definable, it is because to begin with he is nothing. He will not be anything until later, and then he will be what he makes of himself. Thus, there is no human nature, because there is no God to have a conception of it. Man simply is. Not that he is simply what he conceives himself to be, but he is what he wills, and as he conceives himself after already existing—as he wills to be after that leap towards existence. Man is nothing else but that which he makes of himself. That is the first principle of existentialism.

The decisions we make define us, and not just individually but in a more universal sense. Sartre says that in choosing for ourselves, we also choose for others. Our freedom entails a great deal of responsibility since in defining ourselves we define all humanity. Sartre claims that with freedom comes responsibility, and with responsibility anguish. The knowledge that we are essentially alone (no God to watch over us and guide us) along with the myriad of choices that face us can leave us in a state of anguish, abandonment, and despair.

Exercise 8-C: Reading Questions on Sartre's "Existentialism is a Humanism"

1. What kind of existentialism does Sartre offer? What does he think about God's existence as it relates to man's freedom?
2. For Sartre, what does it mean to say, "existence precedes essence"?
3. On what basis does Sartre hold there is no human nature (essence)? Explain this with reference to the artisan and the paper knife.
4. In another quote from the same essay, Sartre writes, "In choosing for himself, he chooses for all men." What do you think Sartre means by this?
5. What does Sartre identify as the causes that can leave people in a state of anguish?

Eastern Philosophy—Buddhism

Buddhism and the Four Noble Truths

By Terrence Chu

In 563 BC, Siddhartha Gautama, later to be known as the Buddha, was born the son of an aristocratic family in the city of Lumbini, in what today is southern Nepal at the foothills of the Himalayan mountains. When he was young, Siddhartha was prophesied to become a powerful ruler if he was kept isolated from the outer world; otherwise, he was destined to become a great holy man. Desiring that their son become a political leader, Siddhartha's parents kept him within the confines of the palace, secluded from anything that might influence him to turn to religion. As a young prince, Siddhartha was pampered with material comforts, boundless wealth, and pleasures of all sorts.

However, Siddhartha grew restless and found opportunities to escape the palace. In his travels into the city, he encountered "four passing sights," which affected him profoundly: an old man, a sick man, a corpse, and an ascetic. The first sight was of a destitute and homeless old beggar. Siddhartha had never encountered old age. In the effort to shield him from the ugliness of life and the ravages of age, his parents had always surrounded him with young attractive servants. Another sight that disturbed Siddhartha was a diseased and handicapped person. A third sight that saddened him greatly was the sight of a dead man and weeping mourners. Used to luxury and comforts, Siddhartha was shocked at the pain and suffering that inevitably befalls all humans. The prospect of sickness, age, and death elicited feelings of compassion in Siddhartha. These experiences opened his eyes to the reality of old age, sickness, and death. Siddhartha could not shake the haunting images and his anxiety grew.

On another one of his travels, Siddhartha met a wandering monk, absorbed in ascetic practices. The monk's ascetic practices involved long hours of prayer and fasting, living on plain food, wearing simple clothes, and sometimes undergoing painful treatment of the body. Ascetics turn away from pleasure and severely limit all sensual appetites in order to achieve salvation or peace of mind. This monk's spiritual quest was the fourth sight, leaving Siddhartha with the hope that there may be a way to attain peace in this troubled world.

Thus, in search of meaning and peace, Siddhartha at the age of 29 abandoned his princely life, renounced his riches, and wandered through the forests of northern India seeking peace and a meaning to life. Siddhartha lived as a homeless monk with only a simple robe and a beggar's bowl. He sought one master or guru after another but could not find from them answers to his timeless questions. Eventually, Siddhartha decided to settle and form a little community of ascetics in a grove of trees on the outskirts of a village in India. For about six years, he practiced extreme asceticism, often denying his body comforts, rest, and food. He learned the eight states of meditation, followed Vedic traditions, but still did not find any answers. Siddhartha discovered that this rigorous and torturous lifestyle proved fruitless; it brought him no closer to spiritual fulfillment, but instead, he nearly died of starvation.

Afterward, Siddhartha concluded that there must be a better way and came up with the "Middle Path," which teaches one to avoid both the extremes of hedonism and asceticism; neither overindulging nor denying the body lead to spiritual growth. By following the Middle Path, Siddhartha finally reached supreme enlightenment or nirvana (nibbana). At the age of 35, Siddhartha sat by a fig tree also called the Bodhi tree and he determined not to rise up until he was enlightened. He meditated for 49 days under the Bodhi tree with little or no food to drink. During those 49 days, Siddhartha underwent temptations of desires and experienced doubts about his beliefs. Finally, the awakening came. Siddhartha was transformed and reached nirvana. Henceforth, he was known by the title of "Buddha," meaning the enlightened one. For the rest of his life, the Buddha endeavored to guide people out of their ignorance into enlightenment. In his teachings, Buddha's primary goal was to teach people how to eliminate "duhkha" or suffering from their lives.

Buddha realized that the problem was not suffering, but the illusion in the minds of individuals. Individuals construct and believe in the idea of the *Atman*, the notion of an "I" or "ego." However, Buddha points out that the "sufferer" exists only in the mind of the individual. In reality, there is no Atman; there is no self. When people let go of their illusions of the self, they can eliminate "the sufferer," and hence lessen their suffering in the world. This message is encapsulated in Buddha's basic teachings known as the "Four Noble Truths":

1. Suffering (duhkha) exists. Life is suffering.
2. The origin of suffering is desire. Desire causes suffering and is the root of ignorance.
3. The cessation of suffering comes about when one extinguishes desire. The end of desire brings the end of suffering.
4. The path leading to cessation of suffering is the Eightfold Path. The end of desire and the way to nirvana is through the Eightfold Path.

According to the first Noble Truth, *duhkha* or suffering is found throughout the world, in birth, death, illness, dissatisfaction, and being apart from the things which produce satisfaction. Buddha teaches that there is in reality no self, and as long as people cling to the illusory notion of self, they are subject to dukkha or suffering. The first necessary step to reaching enlightenment is to become aware of this impermanence and a non-self.

The second Noble Truth identifies the origin of suffering. What causes suffering? Buddha explains that it is *tanha*, "this craving (thirst) which produces re-becoming." Tanha causes the cycle of rebirth of the self along with the craving for all things that identify with the self. It is a craving for pleasures, desires, existence, non-existence, and identity. Buddha realized that the craving is what causes suffering because craving is never ending and will never lead to satisfaction, and thus the cycle of suffering will continue. Now that Buddha is aware of the cause, he then acknowledges that this cause "should be eradicated."

After identifying suffering and the origin of suffering, Buddha introduces the third Noble Truth regarding the cessation of suffering. To end suffering, we must end craving. When craving ceases, one stops feeding that source of suffering, "relinquishing it ... and detaching oneself from it." This allows us to be free from its control, and since we no longer crave, we no longer are controlled, and we no longer suffer. This third Noble Truth acknowledges the cause-and-effect connection between craving and suffering. This leads Buddha to the fourth Noble Truth, the final truth needed to reach nirvana.

The fourth Noble Truth prescribes the way to reach nirvana, the path leading to the cessation of suffering. This is called the Eightfold Path consisting of, "namely: right understanding, right thought, right speech, right action, right livelihood, right effort, right mindfulness and right concentration." According to Buddhism, by following the Eightfold Path, any person may, like Siddhartha, achieve "buddhahood," i.e., a state of enlightenment that brings the final end to suffering. The Four Noble Truths enable people to understand the how, what, and why of suffering, to end the cycle of rebirth, and to reach nirvana. Buddha's own process of awakening revealed to him the truth of reality—that we are all interconnected and there is no self.

The Eightfold Path

The Eightfold Path consists of eight aspects that must be practiced by the individual to achieve enlightenment. It is the path to nirvana. Each aspect is practiced and supported simultaneously through each of the preceding aspects. Hence, the Eightfold Path is normally depicted on the Dharma Wheel to symbolize the nonlinear progression of the path itself.

The eight aspects are commonly divided into three groups. The first group is known as Wisdom and consists of right understanding and right thought. To begin our journey, we must have **right understanding** or right view of how the world works. We must deconstruct dualistic ways of thinking supported by social constructs. We must accept that suffering exists, and desires are the cause of suffering. Once we have right understanding, we can proceed to have **right thought**, or the acceptance of detachment. We accept that we must detach from our desires to end suffering. Once we have deconstructed our thinking of reality, we are able to obtain the wisdom needed to move forward on the path to enlightenment.

The second group is known as Ethical Conduct and consists of right speech, right action, and right livelihood. Here ethical conduct is synonymous with expressions of compassion. To conduct oneself ethically is to conduct oneself compassionately. We must practice **right speech**, or speech that is truthful and compassionate. We should refrain from lying and avoid speech that would incite violence on others. We must practice **right action**, or right behavior, by acting compassionately. We should avoid any misconduct such as stealing, cheating, or any actions that would harm others. We must also practice **right livelihood** and live ethically. This means we should choose a job or career that does not violate ethical conduct or harm society.

The final group is known as Mental Discipline and consists of right effort, right mindfulness, and right concentration. We have gained wisdom and practiced conducting ourselves ethically in society. We are now ready to practice inner cultivation. **Right effort** is the will to practice the previous aspects and the endeavor in the continual practice of speaking, thinking, and acting compassionately. We can then move on to **right mindfulness**, or awareness. Here we are mindful of our minds, bodies, and emotional states. Finally, we practice the last aspect of the Eightfold Path, **right concentration**, or meditation. Through the practice of the previous seven aspects, we can skillfully meditate and concentrate to achieve a peaceful, joyful, and compassionate mind.

Meditation

Meditation is a core practice among Buddhists that is required to attain enlightenment. The purpose of meditation is to allow us to become more aware of our minds and our bodies. Awareness allows us to see the mind and body as constantly changing. We are then able to let go of the illusion of a permanent self, which has long been reinforced by suffering and desires. Meditation allows us to remove the self-ego and thus come to an understanding of non-self and true reality as simply interconnected impermanence.

The practice of meditation can have many forms. In one common pose, a person sits on the ground, legs crossed, and hands on the knees with fingertips touching and pointing upward. However, less important is the physical position than the internal experience. Therefore, it is best to find a location and comfortable position where you can focus on meditating at ease. Closing one's eyes helps remove distractions from one's view. One can maintain awareness of the mind by focusing on one's breath or tingling sensation in the body. If the mind wanders, simply acknowledge it and refocus the mind back to one's breath or inner body. With practice, one will be able to master skillful meditation.

One benefit of meditation is the calming of the mind. Our minds are constantly running with thoughts, worries about the future, and memories of the past, all of which lead to a spectrum of emotions. Even when we sleep, our unconscious minds are still turned on and dreaming. Meditation allows us to temporarily shut off or slow down our minds so they can recharge. This allows our minds to become more peaceful and serene. It creates in us a mood of calmness that can help lower levels of stress and anxiety and encourages clarity and peace.

Another benefit of meditation is the development of mindfulness. While the first benefit of meditation calms the mind, this second benefit allows us to become more aware of our thoughts and the emotions that arise from them. Once we've cleared the clutter, we can more easily identify which thoughts bring about positive emotions and which thoughts bring about negative emotions. The purpose of meditation is not to remove negative emotions but to be aware of them and acknowledge them. If we are more aware of negative thoughts, we can be more in control of how we react when they arise. Similarly, if we are more aware of what thoughts bring about positive emotions, we can focus on developing our minds in a way that will promote feelings of joy and love. Meditation does not rid us of our emotions; instead, it allows us to become more aware of them and thus develops a mindful nature.

Finally, through calming the mind and developing mindfulness we become more compassionate. If our minds are in a state of calm, joy, and inner peace, they most likely will make us happier individuals. If we are in a state of happiness, we are more inclined to let down our guard and become more empathetic and loving of others. Our actions would be guided by pure joy and compassion for one another and the world. Feelings of compassion help break down dualistic views commonly found in society and replace them with a view of oneness and collective harmony.

Hakuin: "The Sound of One Hand"

What is the Sound of the Single Hand? When you clap together both hands a sharp sound is heard; when you raise the one hand there is neither sound nor smell. ... This is something that can by no means be heard with the ear. If conceptions and discriminations are not mixed within it and it is quite apart from seeing, hearing, perceiving, and knowing, and if, while walking, standing, sitting, and reclining, you proceed straightforwardly without interruption in the study of this koan, you will suddenly pluck out the karmic root of birth and death and break down the cave of ignorance. Thus you will attain to a peace in which the phoenix has left the golden net and the crane has been set free of the basket. At this time the basis of mind, consciousness, and emotion is suddenly shattered; the realm of illusion with its endless sinking in the cycle of birth and death is overturned.

Song of Zazen

Zen Master Hakuin; trans. Daisetz Teitaro Suzuki

All beings are primarily Buddhas.
It is like water and ice:
There is no ice apart from water;
There are no Buddhas apart from beings.
Not knowing how close the truth is to them,

Beings seek for it afar—what a pity!
They are like those who, being in the midst of water,
Cry out for water, feeling thirst.

They are like the son of the rich man,
Who, wandering away from his father,
Goes astray amongst the poor. ...

When they wander from darkness to darkness,
How can they ever be free from birth-and-death? ...

... when you turn your eyes within yourselves
And have a glimpse into your self-nature!
You find that the self-nature is no-nature ...

For you, then, open the gate leading to the oneness of cause and effect.
Before you, then, lies a straight road of non-duality and non-trinity.

When you understand that form is the form of the formless,
Your coming-and-going takes place nowhere else but where you are.
When you understand that thought is the thought of the thought-less.
Your singing-and-dancing is no other than the voice of the Dharma. ...
And your person—the body of the Buddha.

Zen Master Hakuin, Selection from "Song of Zazen," *Essays in Zen Buddhism*, First Series, trans. Daisetz Teitaro Suzuki. Copyright © 1994 by Grove Books.

Exercise 8-D: Reading Questions on Buddhism

1. Who is Siddhartha Gautama? What four passing sights did he encounter?
2. What are the Four Noble Truths? What is the Eightfold Path?
3. What is a koan? What is the sound of one hand clapping a koan?
4. How does the *Song of Zazen* describe beings and the nature of the self?
5. How does meditation affect a person's mind and happiness?

CHAPTER 9
Writing Philosophy

> In Chapter 9, we will discuss the basic components of philosophical writing, as well as techniques and principles for writing clear and precise arguments. After completing the chapter, readers will be able to
>
> - identify principles for effective argumentative writing,
> - analyze the writing process,
> - evaluate objections and learn how to reply, and
> - identify more fallacies in writing and argumentation.

Keep word choice simple and precise. When writing, especially for philosophy papers, it is very important to be concise and clear. An excessive literary style or flowery writing is discouraged; instead, focus on clearly stating and defending your ideas. Use straightforward language rather than long words and complex sentence structures. Unless you are a relatively polished writer, keep sentences short. Doing so will help you to express one idea at a time, to increase precision, and avoid wordiness. While maintaining an academic writing style, it is imperative to communicate ideas clearly, and often this is achieved by straightforward and concise sentences.

Write academically. Academic writing is generally formal in style and professional in tone as opposed to more conversational vernacular. Avoid popular expressions or clichés such as "to make a long story short" or "in a nutshell." Also, do not use casual everyday words, such as "a lot," "kind of," "okay," "really," "pretty much," "cool." For example, instead of saying, "Robin Hood's action is okay," write "Robin Hood's action is morally right, permissible, acceptable, or justified." It is more informative to write, "During Ed's summer vacation in Hawaii, he went surfing in Maui, snorkeling at Hanauma Bay, and spelunking through the Kula Kai caverns. Never before had he experienced such breathtaking sunsets, pristine beaches, and colorful wildlife." The level of precision and quality of writing is much higher than simply saying, "Ed's summer vacation was pretty cool, and he really enjoyed it a lot!" Also, to keep a certain level of formality, avoid contractions or shortened forms such as "it's" or "should've."

Maintain gender-neutral language. Historically, the English language has preferred gendered nouns, such as mailman, policeman, and mankind, and the masculine pronouns "he" and "him." More gender-inclusive writing does not assume the gender of the reader. One way to promote more gender-neutral writing is to replace the masculine pronoun with the feminine pronoun. Another solution is to replace "he" with "he or she," but this option may contribute to wordiness. Alternating the use of male and female pronouns might be a better option. For the sake of consistency and to offset the overuse of the pronoun "he," some writers simply switch over to the female pronoun. It is best to choose a pronoun and stick to it.

Proofread paper. Proofread carefully to avoid misspellings, punctuation errors, ambiguous modifiers, etc. You should write in complete, grammatically correct sentences, avoiding run-ons and sentence fragments. Furthermore, it is better to directly state claims rather than hint at them. Using rhetorical questions is also not the most effective form of communication. A reader can better grasp the writer's points when the writer states them directly. The following exercise will focus on common grammatical and spelling errors. When you are not certain about the spelling of a word, you should take the time to look it up.

Exercise 9-A: Sentence Revisions

Rewrite the following sentences to improve clarity, precision, grammar, and spelling. Also, be sure to maintain gender-neutral language and an academic style.

1. Bubbling in the pot, the cook said the soup was ready.
2. Roberto found his dog, he was tired, hungry and overjoyed.
3. Veronica did not go to school, she missed the bus.
4. My seven year old son asked weather its lunch time.
5. You're nurse gave you easy to follow directions.
6. Rio de Janeiro was the sight of the 2016 summer Olympics.
7. The soldiers of the invading army was near by.
8. A writer that guides their readers use transitions.
9. Running for fear, the dog ran after James cat.
10. The actions of the strong willed leader has large scale affects.
11. A child should read the classics to peak their interests in literature.
12. The flock of ducks flying over the snowcapped mountains.
13. Lucille could of drove to school but walked their instead.
14. The carpenter fixed the chair, the plumber replaced the sink.
15. Shopping at the mall, a pair of black women's shoes were purchased by Tina.
16. Its better not to fear death, you can not prevent it.
17. My sister who you all ready met is taller than me.
18. If Pete exercises daily he will be ready for the triathlon in Spring.
19. Separated at birth the reunion of the identical twins.
20. Less people visit my family and I during the holidays.

Writing an Expository Essay

Writing in philosophy will generally consist of two types: expository and argumentative essays. In this section, we will focus on expository writing. The word "expository" originates from the Latin verb *exponere* meaning to put forth, expose, or exhibit. Accordingly, for an expository piece, the writer's job may require that she analyze articles, explain a process, examine evidence, compare things, or report news.

Expository writing is explanatory in nature; the writer must explain something without giving an opinion or critique of it. On the other hand, argumentative essays must not only explain, but they must also evaluate something such as another person's argument or theory. While expository writing does not evaluate another person's argument, it may require the writer to interpret other people's text or understand other viewpoints. Listed below are types of expository writing followed by a sample expository writing prompt:

- Summary of theory or article—Explain Sartre's view on existentialism as revealed in his essay, "Existentialism is a Humanism."
- Comparison of two things—Compare and contrast Plato's and Nietzsche's use of allegory.
- Causal explanations between events—Analyze the effect that online dating websites have on marriage diversity.
- Definitional essay on a complicated term—Explain what "inductive reasoning" is.
- Manual or how-to guide to teach a process—Show beginning writers how to compose an expository essay.
- Solution to a problem or question—Discuss the problem of obesity among children in the United States and offer possible solutions to it.
- Narrative of events—Describe what occurred in the World Trade Center during the terrorist attack on September 11.

Expository writing is informative or instructive. The writer should assume that the reader has little background knowledge about the subject and should aim at giving the reader detailed information about the subject. Expository writing seeks to explain views, processes, or experiences. As we will learn in the next section, argumentative essays may also explain or summarize, but it requires the additional task of proving a thesis and refuting objections.

Writing an Argumentative Essay

1. Support with Reasons

A philosophy paper, in the form of an argumentative essay, is usually not primarily a summary or explanation. An argumentative essay aims at developing ideas and defending a position by giving reasons and replying to objections. It is perfectly fine to use the pronoun "I" so long as you do not merely offer opinions or assume that anything is "obvious." Every claim made, especially if it is questionable or open to debate, should be supported. Support the conclusion with relevant reasons and adequate data. A good essay is as complete as space permits. Every argument is well-developed; every disputable claim comes with some defense.

2. Stick to the Issue

An argumentative essay will focus on a specific issue and take a position on that issue. This position should be clearly stated by the thesis at the beginning of the essay. Thus, the thesis statement is the conclusion that the writer has drawn about the issue under discussion, and the rest of the essay aims at developing the issue and defending the writer's position. It is generally more effective to use a single argument and make it as compelling as you can rather than introducing multiple weaker arguments or digressing to less relevant points. Make sure that all the claims in the essay directly connect to the issue or clarify significant concepts.

3. Omit Unnecessary Claims

Do not try to impress readers with your wide knowledge of everything related to the topic. Instead, focus on the details that are essential to the argument. If a sentence doesn't directly support the thesis or explain the complexities of the argument, it probably should be left out of the paper. A sentence should not be left in the essay just because it sounds good or is well written; everything in the paper should aim at addressing the main argument. In a sense, the structure of a philosophy paper is very much like a mathematical or logical proof. Do not add anything that doesn't somehow help to support your position, and all the points in the paper should aim toward the same goal of proving the thesis statement.

4. Write a Concise Introduction

Although introductions often begin with general points, many beginning writers digress too much. Some writers begin with overly general remarks about how important the issue is, how troubled thinkers have been for centuries, how opinions on the topic vary, ad nauseam. In doing this, the writer may waste her limited and valuable space on points already known to the reader. Do not pad the introduction with wordy "filler" or "fluff." Instead, it is better to get directly to the purpose of the essay. In the introduction, the writer should make clear what the main thesis is, how it will be supported, and what obstacles or objections must be overcome. Usually, in the introductory paragraph, the writer sets out the structure so that the reader knows what to expect and the order in which ideas will be presented.

5. Define Key Terms

Any serious attempt to argue a position requires not only a clear statement of the thesis but the definition of key terms. Previously, we explored the many ways a word may be defined. We can explain what the word connotes by offering an etymological or synonymous definition. Furthermore, analytic definitions are especially helpful for identifying the kind of thing it is, i.e., the genus, and for specifying the ways it differs from other things of the same kind. Giving examples is another way to explicate a term by picking out individual members or subgroups through the use of enumerative definitions or definitions by subclass. Defining key terms and offering relevant, original examples help the reader understand the complexities of the issue. We should take care not to use ambiguous language or assume that the reader will know what we mean. We have explored the confusion caused by amphibolies, equivocations, grouping ambiguities, and other rhetorical devices, and so to avoid them, we should take care to be precise and consistent in the use of terms.

6. Guide the Reader

Good writers do not make the reader struggle to understand the argument. Abrupt jumps between ideas, sudden shifts in direction, and huge gaps in logic can confuse the reader. Effective essays avoid red herrings and non sequiturs. Instead, arrange ideas in a logical sequence, and guide the reader through your train of thought. It is a good idea to include transitions that reveal how one idea links to another. Possible transitions include "therefore," "because," "however," "on the other hand," "for example," "in contrast," "likewise," "similarly," "subsequently," "first," "finally," "as a result," "more importantly," etc. The reader should not have to do the work and should be able to move easily from sentence to sentence and from paragraph to paragraph without becoming lost.

7. Anticipate Objections

Anticipate and discuss what opponents might say. Doing this will make the essay appear balanced and will create the impression that you are reasonable and thoughtful. Discussing opposing viewpoints will also show that you have considered all the options and are open-minded. The reader will then be more likely to believe what you have to say. Before or after giving a positive case for your position, present and defend against the objections that critics might raise. Some writers prefer to give their positive arguments first and then follow with objections to their position. Others begin with the counterarguments and then attempt to prove how their own arguments are stronger.

8. Adopt a Charitable Tone

When opposing another person's views, adopt a tone that is generous and sympathetic. It is best to refrain from condescending remarks, personal attacks, and verbal abuse. These tactics may work in political debates, but not for scholarly papers. Although you may feel that it defeats the purpose of the essay, present the strongest counterarguments against your position rather than make up unconvincing ones that are easier to refute. Also, try to give an accurate representation of rival viewpoints in the most charitable light. Doing so will demonstrate your understanding of the complexities of the issues, as well as your open-mindedness and your willingness to entertain serious objections. Later in the paper, you can argue that, despite the merits of the opponent's counterarguments, your reasons offer stronger empirical support or have greater moral weight.

9. Do Not Commit Fallacies

You may also defeat counterarguments by showing how they rest on fallacious reasoning. Your own arguments, however, should be clear of fallacies. The purpose of an argumentative essay is to convince people of your view, not by tricking them, but by providing strong justification. The best way to convince a perfect audience of critical thinkers is to present a strong, nonfallacious argument. A good argumentative essay should not commit fallacies. The writer should carefully read over her arguments and consider whether she has committed any hasty generalizations, weak analogies, false causes, appeals to emotion, non sequiturs, ad hominems, false dilemmas, etc. An effective essay provides arguments that are well supported by empirical evidence and logical reasoning.

10. Quote and Explain Significance

Sometimes it is a good idea to quote a particular author in your writing. If the source is an expert authority, the quote lends credibility to your claims. In some cases, the language of the author contains a unique phrase or has historical significance that would otherwise be lost. However, the paper should not be merely a string of quotes with an occasional idea from you. Some writers may err in excessively using quotes to make the points for them. Quotes should not replace your own explanations or commentary. When quoting a source, you should provide the context of the quote and offer the meaning and significance of it. It is also important to integrate quotes effectively in the body of the essay and to cite your sources.

11. Cite Sources

In academic writing, we may take credit for the writing that we produce but not for other people's ideas. If we use other people's ideas, whether they be in books, journals, or websites, we must cite our sources and give others the credit they deserve. Failing to cite sources and taking credit for other people's work is a form of plagiarism, a serious academic offense. Citing sources not only acknowledges another researcher's ideas and writing, but it allows readers to track down the source. Sources can be cited through footnotes, endnotes or the bibliography, and there are a number of citation styles to choose from (e.g., MLA, APA). You should check with the instructor about the citation style he or she prefers.

12. Revise Draft

After completing a draft, reread the essay for coherence, focus, and errors in spelling and grammar. It is a good idea to revise an essay repeatedly. After finishing the first draft, set it aside and return to it later with fresh eyes. If someone is available, it may help to get someone else's opinion. The opportunity for revising drafts, of course, assumes that you had started the writing process early enough to allow time for edits and changes.

The Writing Process—How to Begin?

By Tom Gustafson

Answering the question is a crucial starting point for writing a paper. The question is posed in the prompt. Sometimes, the prompt may have other directions in addition to the question, and the question may be implied. However, all prompts ask a question. Begin the process of writing by first understanding the question. Questions posed in prompts are seldom black and white, or simple. Rather, the question must be understood before it is answered. This means that you must give the question more than just a cursory glance.

Often, answering the question requires answering several of its constituent questions, and sometimes in a particular logical order. You should begin by parsing the question. "To parse" is to split apart. So, we first must split apart the question proper into multiple smaller ones. The question asks the writer something. However, the question usually brings with it certain assumptions. It is the writer's job to understand and to address these assumptions. It is best to begin answering the question in the prewriting phase. Perhaps you can use a separate sheet of paper or document to parse out the larger question into smaller questions. What are the simpler component questions that must be answered as part of the more complex overarching question of the prompt? During this process, make a note of any assumptions made in the question and ensure the answer is in line with them.

By following these prewriting guidelines, you will be sure to have answered the question posed in the prompt to a greater or lesser degree. After this prewriting phase, you should begin to write. Do not attempt to write the paper in one go. For rarely does this produce a polished essay and well-reasoned arguments. Instead, use your answers to the questions as building blocks for the thesis statement, then develop topic sentences to support them. The thesis is a concise statement of the paper's central argument. For example,

> Electric cars are actually bad for the environment because of the mining practices involved in obtaining rare elements for their batteries, the short lifespan of the batteries, and the space used batteries will take up in landfills.

This statement contains both the main claim and the subclaims of the paper. If the paper is an argumentative essay, the main goal is to convince readers of the conclusion of your argument. The main claim of the thesis should express the conclusion, while the subclaims states the premises or the main reasons for the conclusion. Thus, for the thesis above:

Main Claim (Conclusion): Electric cars are actually bad for the environment.
Subclaims (Premises):

A: battery mining practices
B: battery lifespan
C: battery waste

Each subclaim can be expressed as a topic sentence and start off a supporting paragraph within the body of the essay. A topic sentence is basically a declarative statement at the beginning of a new paragraph that tells the reader what is to follow while supporting the thesis itself. Subclaims A, B, and C can be expressed as the following topic sentences:

A. The harsh mining practices used to extract rare minerals from the earth do extensive damage to the environment in developing countries.
B. The batteries used in electric cars have a relatively short lifespan.
C. These faulty batteries cannot just disappear; instead, they will pile up in landfills, creating an environmental disaster.

The topic sentence performs two functions. First, it implicitly tells the reader what is to follow in the paragraph by referencing point A, mining practices. Second, it builds on the thesis statement's mere mention of point A by being more specific, noting that mining is harsh and does extensive damage to developing countries. Once the thesis and topic sentences are written, proceed to fill in your body paragraphs by supporting those topic sentences. After you have a thesis, topic sentences, and fleshed-out body paragraphs, then it is time to write the introduction and conclusion.

Once all the constituent parts of the paper have been drafted, you can begin the revision and editing process. This approach leaves polishing and revisions to the last step since it is most important to have answered the question. You can always refine and develop the finer points of a paper, but an off-topic paper cannot be salvaged and must be thrown out.

Exercise 9-B: Thesis or Main Claim

In response to a specific issue, three subclaims are presented. Write a thesis statement or main claim that encompasses all three subclaims. The thesis statement or main claim may consist of one or more sentences.

1. Is it true that life 100 years ago was easier?

- Subclaim A: Technology has progressed offering modern society time-saving conveniences and enhanced mobility.
- Subclaim B: Medical advances have eradicated once-fatal diseases and have improved the quality of life for the sick.
- Subclaim C: There is a growing social tolerance for individuals belonging to different racial, religious, and personal backgrounds.

2. Should juveniles be treated as adults?

- Subclaim A: Juveniles have not developed a wisdom or level of maturity that can only be gained through life experiences.
- Subclaim B: During the stage of puberty, the human brain experiences hormonal changes that can affect moods and behaviors.

- Subclaim C: Youths are highly impressionable and can easily succumb to peer pressure and societal influences.

3. Does constant social media connection make people feel lonelier and more stressed?
    - Subclaim A: Many popular social media websites encourage users to create personas that are often false or superficial images of themselves, thereby alienating their real self from their online one.
    - Subclaim B: Users of social media tend to post exciting or noteworthy aspects of their lives, causing others s to view their own lives as dull or insignificant in comparison.
    - Subclaim C: Communication through social media promotes anonymity and distance amongst users rather than close and personal engagement with others.

4. Should recreational marijuana be legal or not?
    - Subclaim A: Marijuana does not lead to serious health problems when consumed responsibly and can help with anxiety and pain relief.
    - Subclaim B: Police and prison resources can be better utilized toward violent crimes.
    - Subclaim C: Legalization can increase state and federal revenue from taxes on marijuana sales.

5. Economically, is space travel worth the cost?
    - Subclaim A: Space travel inspires scientific curiosity and motivates humans to expand their domain of knowledge.
    - Subclaim B: Discoveries made through space travel contribute to advancement in other fields such as in defense systems, GPS, smart phones, solar panels, and cancer therapy.
    - Subclaim C: Satellite data can be used to predict natural disasters, to study climate change, to measure pollution, and to discover other life forms or essential minerals in space.

Exercise 9-C: Main Claim and Subclaims

For each controversial issue, imagine you are writing an argumentative essay. Choose a position and then write a main claim (conclusion/thesis) and three subclaims (premises/topic sentences).

1. Should universities require knowledge of at least one foreign language?
2. Are fully automated cars beneficial to society?
3. Should adults have the right to own guns to defend themselves?
4. Should prostitution be legal or not?
5. Can we call superheroes misleading role models?
6. Should people live together before they marry?
7. Do nursery rhymes have secret ulterior meanings?
8. Do people depend on computers and other gadgets too much?
9. Is buying a lottery ticket a good idea?

10. Is it irresponsible to have many children (five or more)?
11. Should siblings of different gender be treated the same way by parents?
12. Do all kinds of sports bring benefits to people's health?
13. Do long-term relationships make people happier?
14. Should elementary students wear school uniforms?
15. Should exotic animals be kept in captivity?
16. Should daylight saving be abolished or maintained in the U.S.?
17. Should children trick-or-treat for candy on Halloween?
18. Is it a bad idea to use your DNA for genealogy?
19. Is it better to have class in person or fully online?
20. Should students be required to take general education courses unrelated to their major?

Objections—How to Respond?

Cowritten by Sean Tracy

In an argumentative essay, it is important to bring up objections. Objections may also be called counterarguments or criticisms, while an objection to an objection is sometimes called a rebuttal. As noted earlier, discussing rival viewpoints will make you appear as if you have done the research and have considered different alternatives. People respect the reasonable, objective thinker who is seeking the truth rather than just trying to win the debate. Appearing open-minded to ideas, you are then more likely to persuade others of your own views.

All too often, we only consider our own side of the story and do not concern ourselves with the possible problems our arguments might have. By anticipating possible criticisms, we then give ourselves the chance to fix the problems ourselves before our opponents have a chance to point them out. Confronting strong counterarguments is challenging and involves a great deal of work, but your arguments will become stronger and more compelling because of it.

Good places to look for criticisms of your view are in course readings, primary sources (Kant or Mill), secondary sources (John Rawls on Kant, or Colin Heydt on Mill), other scholarly (peer-reviewed) journals, credible news outlets, etc. These sources are filled with conflicting opinions from thoughtful and inquisitive minds, just the sort of perspectives that can challenge your viewpoint, and thereby strengthen your argument.

Before responding to objections, first, introduce what exactly critics might say. Following the principle of charity, try to explain the objections in the strongest possible light and not purposefully try to weaken them just to make the task of refutation easier. When discussing opposing views, it is best not to resort to name-calling, sarcasm, or personal attacks. It is also important to make sure the reader understands that the objections put forth are distinct from your own arguments. Make it clear that you are presenting a rival view, one that you do not personally endorse. This can be accomplished by transitions:

It could be objected that ...
In contrast to my own views, others may claim ...
Opposing arguments may point out ...
One objection against my position is the one raised by X. X claims that ...
Before offering my positive arguments, I will present the opposing view of X.
My position on this issue is not shared by everyone ... including X. X contends that ...
Now that I have given several arguments for ..., let us consider some objections. X argues ...

After presenting possible objections or counterarguments, then give your reply. Generally, you should save your own response until after you have given a strong and charitable representation of the opposing argument. Let critics or opponents have a chance to lay out the justification for their position first. When discussing the counterargument, there is no need to interject your own opinion right away or insist at once that the opponent is mistaken; be patient and bide your time. There will be opportunity enough perhaps in the next paragraph to respond and evaluate opposing views.

There are three possible ways to respond to an objection: **refute, concede, or compromise**. When there is a conflict of opinion and two sides debate an issue, either one side wins, or there is some middle ground or truce that is reached. First, let us begin with the strategy of refutation. In successfully refuting an objection, you come out the winner of the debate by showing that the opposing argument is bad.

How to Refute?

There are a number of strategies for refuting counterarguments because there are so many ways in which an argument can potentially go wrong. The two main strategies for proving that a counterargument is bad are to demonstrate that (1) it rests on false premises or (2) depends on faulty logic. If you can show that one or more of the opponent's premises are false or questionable, then his/her counterargument would be uncogent or unsound. To prove that an opponent's premises are false, sometimes you will need to provide counterevidence from qualified sources. Of course, opponents will present their own evidence supported by their own sources. If this is the case, then it will boil down to who has the best evidence and the most credible sources. So as not to run the risk of proof surrogates, be sure to select a number of different independent sources that are informed and impartial. By providing counterevidence from more than one informed source, you can demonstrate that some of the opponent's premises are false.

A second way to defend a view from an objection is to identify a flaw in the opponent's logic. Perhaps, the opponent's premises, even if they are true, do not really support the conclusion; that is, there is not a strong or valid inferential link between the premises and the conclusion. Faulty logic may also be due to fallacies committed by the opposing side. If we recall some fallacies discussed in previous chapters, we can come up with a short checklist of possible problems of which the opposing side may be guilty:

- Emotional appeals—Do they resort to appeals to pity, outrage, scare tactics, guilt trips, apple polishing, or wishful thinking?

- Appeal to the people—Do they arouse the feelings of the multitude, use peer pressure, or appeal to tradition, vanity, elitism, nationalism, popular trends, etc.?
- False cause—Do they oversimplify the potential causes? Do they infer causation from coincidence or mere correlation?
- Weak analogy—Do they draw comparisons between things without relevant similarities?
- Hasty generalization—Do they draw conclusions from small or nonrepresentative samples? Do they make general claims that can be disproven by counterexample?
- Begging the question—Does one of the premises restate or presume the truth of the conclusion they are supposed to prove? Do they commit circular reasoning?
- Equivocation—Do they use ambiguous terms in multiple ways throughout the argument?
- False dilemma—Do they advocate for one option because they have overlooked alternatives or reduced the number of possible choices?
- Straw man—Do they distort or misrepresent your argument? Is their criticism based on a fundamental misunderstanding of your position?
- Formal fallacy—Do they commit a denial of the antecedent or affirmation of the consequent?

What if You Concede?

Sometimes, as you examine opposing arguments, you may find the criticisms are valid. The opposing side is correct, and no fault, try as you might, can be found in the counterarguments. If this is the case, then you must concede to your opponent's objection and rework your thesis. Yet, all is not lost; it can be just a temporary setback. What is lost is the initial view that you once held, but what is gained in its stead can be a new perspective on the issue. Being intellectually honest requires that we abandon our beliefs when we can no longer justify them.

Even if you were halfway through the paper, you can still salvage much of your work. You can modify the thesis to reflect a new stance and rearrange the arguments. Some of the counterarguments now become the ones that lend support to your new thesis. Those arguments that had formerly supported the old view can then be reworked as the new objections to your modified thesis. This time around, you will be able to refute the objections.

How to Compromise?

For some controversial matters, it may appear that both sides offer compelling arguments. If this is the case, open-minded and objective writers may point out the merits of the opponent's arguments before identifying the weaknesses. If you find the opposing arguments are good, but not so good as to completely alter your stance, explain why the reader should prefer your position. There is no catch-all solution for showing how your argument is stronger; however, we can offer you a few possible strategies that might help:

Make an Exception

First, consider whether you can make your stance the general rule and relegate the opponent's point as a legitimate exception. For example, we may argue that, as a general rule, parents should be informed if their teenage daughter wants to have an abortion. An objection may be raised that abusive parents would harm their daughter if they were told of her pregnancy. As a compromise, we can concede that the objection is a good one for which we would willingly make an exception. In this way, you can still maintain the original thesis with the added qualification that parental notification is subject to a few safeguards.

Prefer Your Value

Another strategy is to convince the audience that your value is to be preferred. You may concede that the opponent's value is a worthy one, but it does not have priority over other values in cases of conflict. Imagine the conflict between a patient's right to autonomy versus the principle of beneficence. The patient does not want a life-saving blood transfusion, but the doctor believes that the patient will die without it. Suppose we want to argue that the patient should not be given the transfusion for the sake of autonomy. The opponent argues that the principle of beneficence justifies the life-saving medical procedure because the doctor has a duty to promote the patient's well-being. In this case, we don't have to deny the value of the patient's well-being, we just have to show that autonomy outweighs beneficence.

Broader Scope

A third strategy for dealing with a strong objection is to agree with it but point out that it is too narrow in scope; it ignores other important moral considerations. One notable philosopher, Don Marquis, argues that it is wrong to have an abortion because it would deprive a being (the fetus) of a valuable future. Thus, Marquis concludes that abortion is, in most cases, morally wrong. If we hold a utilitarian perspective, we can concede that preserving valuable futures is good. Yet, we can observe that Marquis's focus is limited in scope, for he is only considering the fetus's valuable future and ignoring the valuable future of the pregnant woman and possibly the valuable futures of other family members. We can argue that our pro-choice argument is the stronger one because our focus is broader in scope. We have taken into consideration the futures of everyone concerned, not just that of the fetus.

> **Exercise 9-D: Reply to Objections**

After writing the main claim and subclaims for the questions in Exercise 9-B, identify a strong objection someone might raise against your position. Explain and provide justification for this objection. Then give your response to the objection.

Fallacious Counterarguments

A counterargument is a special type of argument that sets forth reasons against another's argument. To successfully argue against an opposing point of view, someone should focus on whether the other person's premises are true and provide support for the conclusion. There are, however, fallacious attempts to oppose another person's argument. One type of fallacious counterargument is called an **ad hominem fallacy**, a Latin term that translates to "against the person." In an ad hominem fallacy or argument against the person, the person making an argument is attacked, while the substance of the argument is largely ignored.

One form of this fallacy is the **personal attack** ad hominem or ad hominem **abusive**. An ad hominem abusive brings up negative traits about a person in order to sway others from siding with the person's position. Regardless of whether these allegations are true, the vices, failings, or features of a person often do not invalidate that person's argument. It may well be that the person you are arguing with is a tall, bald, bowlegged, freckled, fat, sloppy, cross-eyed, grouchy old man, but these attributes have no bearing on the strength of his arguments. An ad hominem abusive is a fallacious counterargument because it attacks a person's character and fails to refute the person's argument.

The ad hominem **circumstantial** likewise sidesteps the actual argument of the opponent and focuses instead on the circumstances of the person. Circumstances such as group membership or affiliations are purported to create a bias and thus damage the credibility of the speaker. For example, "We all know Morris will support full medical benefits for substitute teachers because he is after all a substitute teacher. Therefore, we can dismiss his arguments." However, just because a person stands to gain from a favorable outcome does not mean that the person's arguments are automatically weak or invalid. Perhaps Morris can offer strong reasons to support medical benefits for people in his profession.

A more specialized personal attack goes by the name of the **inconsistency** ad hominem or ad hominem **tu quoque** ("you also"). This fallacious counterargument rejects a person's view due to behavior they deem inconsistent. The person is being attacked for hypocritical actions and is charged with not practicing what he/she preaches. Example: "My sister says I should eat healthy, but I see her eating her daily donut this morning!" While people may be hypocrites for not following their own advice, they may nevertheless have good reasons for holding the views that they do.

Another type of ad hominem argument is **poisoning the well**. This personal attack occurs before the targeted person even presents her argument. The one committing this fallacy preemptively tries to discredit or ridicule the other side. The term originates from the ancient practice of poisoning the water in a well before the invading enemy has a chance to drink from it. This fallacy begins by saying irrelevant and negative things about a person and then suggesting that what the person is about to say is false and should be rejected. Personal attacks before a person has had a chance to speak is like committing an ad hominem abusive in advance. Example: "Todd will try to convince you not to go on a date with me, but can you really take the word of someone who just dumped his last two girlfriends?" Thus, before Todd even has a chance to present his case, the speaker has attempted to cast doubt on what Todd will say. After poisoning the well, the audience may become biased or distrustful of the person under attack.

The fallacy of **straw man** starts by distorting or exaggerating someone's argument and then proceeds to knock that argument down. In effect, the person who commits a straw man does not tackle the real argument but one that is much weaker and can more easily be refuted. Example: "People who oppose Jane Brown for mayor think that women are unfit to be leaders. This is certainly outdated, sexist thinking!" To identify a straw man, show that the opposition's argument has been misrepresented and a much stronger, more accurate, version of the opposing argument still stands.

More Fallacies in Writing

In this section, we will introduce three more fallacies that are frequently encountered in essays and which we should be careful to watch out for in our own writing.

Red Herring

In an argument, we begin with the premises and follow a train of thought that leads to a conclusion. We might think of a successful argument like a successful hunt. The premises of an argument provide the scent trail we are following with dogged determination, and its conclusion is the fox, our prize. Good hunting dogs will stay on the trail of the fox and not be distracted. When training their hunting dogs, hunters often tested them by placing a red herring in their path. Those dogs that were not diverted by the scent of the fish passed the test and proved themselves to be keen hunting dogs. Similarly, others who want to distract us from the issue at hand may introduce irrelevant information to lure us away from the argument.

> Professor: I see that you have come late to class again, are missing a shoe, and have crumbs all over your shirt. Have you completed your homework for today, Penelope?
> Penelope: Well, Professor, did you happen to catch the game last night? It was a nail-biter all the way to the end!

Non Sequitur

This fallacy happens when the arguer draws a conclusion that has nothing to do with the premises given, or at least, is a very unreasonable far-fetched conclusion to draw based on the premises given. Non sequiturs are closely related to red herrings, as neither addresses the issue at hand. However, a red herring is committed intentionally for the purpose of evading and diverting attention away from the issue, especially when you are losing the argument. A non sequitur is simply a jump in ideas or bad inference often without the nefarious intent on the part of the writer to distract someone from the subject at hand. A non sequitur in Latin means that ideas are "not sequenced" or do not follow, for there is a gap in logic and no strong inferential link to connect the conclusion to the premises. A few examples of non sequitur:

> *Suppose a group of teenagers is sitting around a campfire on a cold night.* "Every time I sneeze the light flickers. That means I must be a wizard!"

Suppose a young girl, Mabel, proposes the following argument to her brother Wally at dinner. "You know, every time Mr. Tibbles takes a bath, he gets really wet. Because he gets really wet, he gets really cold too. And when he gets cold, he sometimes comes into my room. When he comes to my room, he sheds a lot of fur, and I always have to clean it up when he sheds in my room. So, you should give me your piece of the cheesecake."

Mere Assertion

Some claims are based on well-established facts and are widely accepted by the public at face value. Uncontroversial claims do not ordinarily require additional proof and may be stated without the need for justification. However, other claims are matters of dispute and cannot just be taken for granted. Questionable or unestablished opinions require reasons for believing in them. The fallacy of mere assertion occurs when someone makes disputable claims without providing evidence or justification. However, simply because you say something is true, does not make it true. Making an assertion only communicates that you believe something, but you have not given an argument for why others should believe in it, too. The following examples give instances where someone is making a controversial claim that requires additional support or justification.

Suppose a debater is arguing that her values are to be preferred over her opponent's. "Liberty is more valuable than life. For without liberty, life would not be worth living."

Imagine an elementary school student complaining about homework. "Teachers give me hours of homework to do after school. This is just not fair!"

Exercise 9-E: Fallacious Counterarguments

Classify these arguments as either a fallacious counterargument (ad hominem abusive, ad hominem circumstantial, ad hominem tu quoque, poisoning the well, straw man), red herring, non sequitur, or mere assertion. If more than one fallacy seems to apply, prefer the more specific ad hominem or straw man fallacy as your answer over the last three fallacies, which are more generic.

1. Sure, he opposes rent control; he owns two apartment buildings, doesn't he? Because he has something to gain, his argument against rent control must be no good.
2. You can save money, over the course of a month or two, if you buy in bulk. It's cheaper to buy huge packages of food as long as you can finish it. They sell potatoes in bulk for only a few dollars. Therefore, you can enjoy perfectly baked potatoes, crispy on the outside and pillowy in the middle, in just one hour.
3. Mr. Rankin has just given his argument against affirmative action for women. It seems what he is saying is that women should stay out of the workplace altogether. Just keep them barefoot and pregnant. That's what Rankin wants. Well, I think we are all smart enough to reject that argument.

4. I'm not surprised that you're arguing for the legalization of marijuana for recreational use. You're one of the most inane and insensitive people I've ever met. No wonder you have so few friends on campus.

5. Jimmy is running against me for student council president. Now, he is going to say how great a leader he will be, but can you really trust a guy who plays the trombone in the marching band?

6. Sure, it was irresponsible of me to gamble away our rent money. But you have to admit we had fun in Las Vegas. It's one of the trips we will always remember, just like our fabulous honeymoon in Hawaii five years ago. We had a blast kiteboarding and windsurfing, and you were a natural learning how to dance the hula. It was so much fun; we'll travel there again soon.

7. Ms. Thomas has argued for increased expenditures on public schools. But, of course, she argues that way. She has five children in elementary school, and she doesn't have enough money to pay for private education. I wouldn't trust her arguments for a minute.

8. My opponent argues that women do not have the right to choose abortion. That means he denies that women have the right to control their own bodies, and he thus endorses a kind of sexual discrimination. Well, we've worked too long and too hard to ensure equality between the sexes to revert back to that kind of unjust treatment of women.

9. Barbara Burns has argued that we should beef up our high school math and science courses. But Barbara is no one to talk. When she was in high school herself, she avoided those courses like the plague.

10. The Cheshire Cat (*Alice in Wonderland*): "A dog's not mad … you see a dog growls when it's angry and wags its tail when it's pleased. Now I growl when I'm pleased and wag my tail when I'm angry. Therefore, I'm mad."

11. So, your stockbroker has tried to persuade you to buy 1,000 shares of Macro Data. Well, I wouldn't trust his arguments. He just wants to earn that fat commission on the sale.

12. Ms. Morris has argued that money from the defense program should be shifted to public works spending (roads, sewers, etc.) and to education. Now what she is saying really comes down to this: you can improve the education system merely by throwing money at it, and America can leave itself defenseless to invasion by insane dictators. This is absurd. Defense spending should stay where it is.

13. A girl came up to me in a bar and said she wanted to be my apple pie. I wish I'd said something cool, but I was stunned. —Jason Biggs

14. Child: My dad's argument that I should stop stealing candy from the corner store is no good. He told me himself just a week ago that he, too, stole candy when he was a kid.

15. The next applicant we will be interviewing graduated from Yale and has an impressive résumé, but she seems fake to me, and she looks like she would be high maintenance. I wouldn't seriously consider hiring her.

16. It is true that we will not have a company Christmas party this year. This probably disappoints many of you. Yet, it has been a very good year for our business. We appreciate our talented staff delivering high-quality products and excellent customer service.

Our ratings reflect high customer satisfaction, and our sales have almost doubled in the last few months.
17. Mr. Hall has just given us reasons why we should place more emphasis on family values. But he has no business talking. A week ago, he was charged with domestic violence for beating his wife.
18. Professor Newman claims that governments should encourage birth control among their citizens in order to avoid global overpopulation. By this claim, the professor must think that a government has the right to punish parents for having large families and can force mothers to have abortions.
19. If it's your job to eat a frog, it's best to do it first thing in the morning. And if it's your job to eat two frogs, it's best to eat the biggest one first. —Mark Twain
20. Before the next witness comes to the stand, did you know he hasn't paid child support for years? Probably because he hasn't been able to keep a job for more than a few months.
21. I was rushing to class and a police officer stopped me for driving 20 miles over the speed limit. I know I should not have been driving so fast, Dad, and the ticket will cost $300. But you'll be glad to hear I made it to class on time and learned all about the importance of the ecosystem. All living things are interdependent and cannot survive without a healthy ecosystem.
22. You know very well I don't care what Mason argues regarding health care or, for that matter, anything else. That guy is the most obnoxious creep I've ever run into. He walks around in his underwear and drinks beer all day.
23. Gentlemen, the dean has accused our department of irresponsibly managing our budget. But I happen to know that the dean has overspent his own budget this year in every category. It follows that the dean's accusations are unwarranted.
24. A psychology professor from Cambridge says that genes are only one contributing factor to longevity. Even more important are exercise and a healthy diet. Exercise and healthy meals can lift your spirit and energy levels, making you feel better. My grandpa is turning 99 tomorrow! Hence, he must have married the right woman.
25. Ms. Knight has just argued that we abolish capital punishment in our state since it costs too much. This is just another one of those arguments in favor of the poor, misguided criminal, who has gone astray. Using her logic, all these killers need is a little love and affection. Well, I can tell you that this tactic has been tried before, and it has failed.
26. Yes, I realize access to affordable health care is a major worry for senior citizens. As a senator of this state, I am looking into expanding health care for all, just like I have with affordable housing. For years, I have helped to provide supportive services for vulnerable low-income families who are most at risk of homelessness.
27. Mr. Simmons has not given a single dime or volunteered his time to help school kids. Now, he is going to come and tell you that we should increase funding to support our local schools. Let me just remind you, that actions speak louder than words!
28. The auto industry lobbyists have been arguing that tax reform is unnecessary. But just remember this: It is the auto industry that stands to benefit the most if there is no change in the current tax laws.

29. Here's the application from Mary for the position of sports editor. Yeah, I know, what does a girl know about baseball and football? Let's give it a glance. It won't take but a minute to decide.

30. A world-renowned architect advises a family to follow sound design principles when planning their new home. The architect states, "For the sake of privacy, bedrooms should be situated upstairs. For maximum morning sunlight, they should face eastward. And to encourage sibling closeness, bedrooms should be shared but offer designated separate spaces for each child." The father listens and concludes, "Ah, I see, that settles it then! Pack your bags. We're going camping!"

Writing a Compare-and-Contrast Essay

Another type of writing assignment often involved in longer research papers is a compare-and-contrast essay. When you compare two different things, you focus on the ways in which they are alike, resemble each other, or agree with one another. On the other hand, contrasting two things involves picking out the ways they are different, dissimilar, or disagree with one another. The two things that you may be comparing and contrasting can range from a wide number of objects such as places, times, artists, authors, theories, policies, novels, sports, animals, gadgets, occupations, etc. An insightful compare-and-contrast essay will not just point out the obvious similarities and differences but endeavor to reveal subtle or unexpected traits that the two things have in common as well as to distinguish the nuanced or surprising differences between the two.

As you begin your thought process, it might be helpful to list the similarities and the differences with the help of a Venn diagram. A Venn diagram is a logical tool consisting of overlapping circles, with each circle representing one of the two things. You can list the common properties within the intersection of the two circles and the differences in the sides of the circles that do not overlap. Suppose we are comparing and contrasting butterflies and moths. We might draw a Venn diagram as a visual aid, organizing the similar and different traits like this:

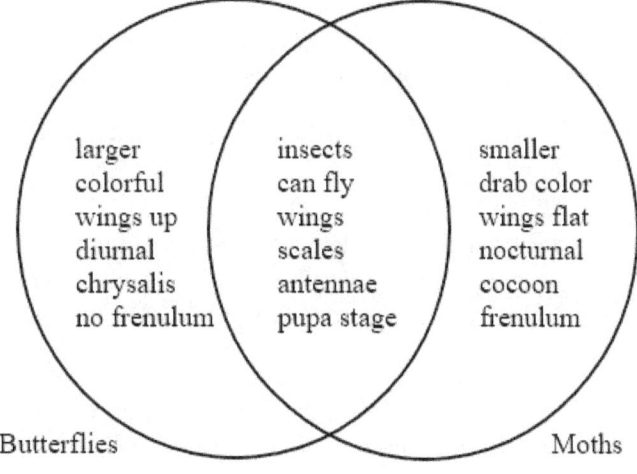

IMG 9.1

Exercise 9-F: Venn Diagrams

Draw Venn diagrams to compare and contrast the following pairs of items. In the intersection, list several traits that the pairs have in common. Write the trait differences in the nonoverlapping sections of the circles.

1. Punk rock versus rap music
2. Wonder woman versus Batman
3. Tokyo versus Athens
4. Michael Jordan versus Michael Phelps
5. Spring versus autumn
6. Vampires versus zombies
7. Muhammad Ali versus Bruce Lee
8. Facebook versus Instagram
9. George Washington versus Abraham Lincoln
10. David (Michelangelo) versus The Birth of Venus (Botticelli)
11. Descartes's rationalism versus Hume's skepticism
12. Paley's Teleological Argument versus Anselm's Ontological Argument
13. Pascal's Wager versus Hume's Problem of Evil
14. Mill's utilitarianism versus Kant's duty ethics
15. Aristotle's virtue ethics versus feminist ethics of care

After you brainstorm the main similarities and differences, you are then ready to write a provisional thesis, which you later may revise as more ideas and details arise. There are a number of ways you might formulate your thesis statement. Let us suppose our task is to compare the moral theories of two authors. For brevity and given our familiarity with the use of letters in symbolization, let us refer to one author as X and the other author as Y. Also, we will use a, b, c, p, q, r, s, etc., to stand for subjects, claims, or actions. Possible thesis statements may then have the following structure:

> **Thesis Sample 1:** While X and Y agree about a, b, and c, they have opposing views about p, q, and r.
> **Thesis Sample 2:** Although X rejects p and q, Y assumes p and q are true about the world. Nonetheless, they both ultimately conclude a, b, and c.
> **Thesis Sample 3:** Both X and Y view society as a, b, and c. However, X emphasizes the individual's need to p and q. On the other hand, Y argues that one ought to do r and s.

While the introductory paragraph communicates the thesis of your paper, the body of the paper will provide support for the thesis. Since there are a number of similarities and differences between the two things, it is crucial to organize your essay carefully and consistently so the reader can easily follow your train of thought. Be sure to guide the reader by including transitions and topic sentences at the beginning of each paragraph.

Transition words that convey similarity: like, likewise, similarly, akin, in the same way, also, in common, analogous, allied, equally, identical, indistinguishable, just as, in like manner, again, agree, concur, share, resemble, coincide, support, approve, commend, favor, accept, match

Transition words that convey difference: unlike, however, nevertheless, even though, conversely, although, yet, but, whereas, despite, while, on the other hand, in contrast, on the contrary, disagree, differ, vary, oppose, reject, diverge, conflict with, contend, vary with respect to, contradict, clash with

When structuring the body of the essay, there are several ways to organize your paragraphs. For example, when comparing two authors, you could discuss each author separately with respect to several subjects; you could introduce one subject at a time revealing each author's view on the subject; you could explain similarities between the two authors followed by the differences between them:

- One author at a time: What author X thinks about subjects a, b, c, p, and q. Then follow with what author Y thinks about subjects a, b, c, p, and q. Emphasize (in the second half of the paper) that Y agrees with X about a, b, and c, but disagrees with X about p and q.
- One subject at a time: What X and Y think about subject a; what X and Y think about subject b; what X and Y think about subject p, etc. As you discuss each subject, explain to what extent X and Y agree or disagree.
- Similarities and differences: What X and Y agree with (similarities) and then what X and Y disagree with (differences). This is like the "one subject at a time" organization, but you divide the subjects into two groups: similarities and differences. You may also begin with the differences first and then proceed to the similarities.

Exercise 9-G: Thesis for Compare-and-Contrast Essay

For the pairs of items in Exercise 9-E, write a thesis statement similar to one of the three sample thesis statements. Be sure to include transition words that convey similarities or differences.

Bibliography

Anagnostopoulos, Georgios. *A Companion to Aristotle*. Chichester, UK: Wiley-Blackwell, 2009.

Boss, Judith A. *Analyzing Moral Issues*. California: Mayfield Publishing Company, 1999.

Cahn, Steven M. *Classics of Western Philosophy*. 8th ed. Indianapolis, IN: Hackett Publishing Company, Inc., 2013.

Descartes, René. *Meditations on First Philosophy*. Raleigh, NC: Alex Catalogue, 1996.

Epstein, Richard L., and Michael Rooney. *Critical Thinking*. 4th ed. New Mexico: Advanced Reasoning Forum, 2012.

Flew, Antony. *An Introduction to Western Philosophy*: Ideas and Argument from Plato to Popper. Rev. ed. New York, NY: Thames and Hudson, 1989.

Hurley, Patrick J. *A Concise Introduction to Logic*. 2nd ed. Belmont, CA: Wadsworth Pub. Co., 1985.

Kalish, Donald, and Richard Montague. *Logic: Techniques of Formal Reasoning*. New York: Harcourt, Brace & World, 1964.

Moore, Brooke, and Richard Parker. *Critical Thinking*. 7th ed. New York: McGraw-Hill Companies, 2001.

Morrow, David, and Anthony Weston. *A Workbook for Arguments*. 2nd ed. Indianapolis, IN: Hackett Publishing Company, 2016.

Papineau, David. *Western Philosophy : An Illustrated Guide*. London: Oxford University Press, 2004.

Pojman, Louis P, and Lewis Vaughn. *Philosophy The Quest for Truth*. 8th ed. New York: Oxford University Press, 2012.

Rachels, James. *The Elements of Moral Philosophy*. 4th ed. New York: McGraw-Hill Companies, 2003.

Rawls, John. *A Theory of Justice*. Rev. ed. Cambridge, MA: The Belknap Press of Harvard University Press, 1999.

Russell, Bertrand. *A History of Western Philosophy*. New York: Simon and Schuster, 1972.

Smith, John H. *Dialogues Between Faith and Reason: The Death and Return of God in Modern German Thought*. Ithaca, NY: Cornell University Press, 2011.

Solomon, Robert C. *Introducing Philosophy*. 6th ed. San Diego, CA: Harcourt Brace, and Company, 1997.

Suzuki, Daisetz Teitaro. *The Essentials of Zen Buddhism: Selected from the Writings of Daisetz T. Suzuki*. Edited, and with an Introduction, by Bernard Phillips. 1st ed. New York: E.P. Dutton & Co., Inc., 1962.

Teller, Paul. *A Modern Formal Logic Primer: Sentence Logic, Volume 1*. Hoboken, NJ: Prentice Hall, 1989.

www.ingramcontent.com/pod-product-compliance
Lightning Source LLC
Chambersburg PA
CBHW080410300426
44113CB00015B/2470